New Progress

to First Certificate

Teacher's Book

D1500808

Leo Jones

CAMBRIDGE
UNIVERSITY PRESS

CAMBRIDGE UNIVERSITY PRESS

Cambridge, New York, Melbourne, Madrid, Cape Town, Singapore, São Paulo, Delhi

Cambridge University Press
The Edinburgh Building, Cambridge CB2 8RU, UK

www.cambridge.org
Information on this title: www.cambridge.org/9780521499866

First published 1996
10th printing 2007

Printed in the United Kingdom at the University Press, Cambridge

A catalogue record for this publication is available from the British Library

ISBN 978-0-521-49986-6 Teacher's Book
ISBN 978-0-521-49985-9 Student's Book
ISBN 978-0-521-49988-0 Self-study Student's Book
ISBN 978-0-521-49987-3 Class Cassette Set
ISBN 978-0-521-77426-0 Workbook
ISBN 978-0-521-77425-3 Workbook with answers
ISBN 978-0-521-77424-6 Workbook Cassette
ISBN 978-0-521-79764-1 Workbook Self-study Pack

Contents

Thanks

Many people contributed their hard work, fresh ideas and sound advice to this book:

Niki Browne edited the book with sensitivity and thoroughness.
Liz Sharman supervised and guided the project from start to finish.
Hilary Fletcher was responsible for picture research and permission.
Sophie Dukan was responsible for text permission.
Oxprint Design designed the book.

James Richardson produced the recordings at Studio AVP, the engineer was Andy Taylor. More than 30 actors (too many to name individually) took part in the studio recordings.

Derek Mainwaring and Linda Thalman in France, Annette Blanche Ceccaveavelli and Hilary Isaacs in Italy, Zofia Bernacka-Wos and Joanna Burzynska in Poland and Derek Leverton and Jesús Marin in Spain gave us detailed comments on the previous edition of *Progress to First Certificate*. Almost 100 teachers from all over the world (too many to name) also gave us feedback on the previous edition through a questionnaire.

Annie Broadhead, Henrietta Burke, Anne Gutch, Jane Hann, Nick Kenny, Sean Power, Liz Tataraki and Clare West commented on sample and draft units.

To all the above: thank you very much!

From the second edition

No book of this kind can be produced by one person alone and in this case countless people have generously contributed their ideas and advice.

In particular, I'd just like to say how grateful I am to the following friends, colleagues and teachers:
Jeanne McCarten for guiding the New Edition through from start to finish and for her encouragement, perfectionism and good ideas; Jill Mountain and Kit Woods for their detailed comments on the first edition and for subsequently reading, evaluating and suggesting improvements to the first draft of this New Edition; Alison Silver for her editing expertise and sensible suggestions; Peter Taylor and Studio AVP for their professional skills in producing the recorded material; Peter Ducker for his meticulous work on the illustrations and design; Sue Gosling for her help and advice.

And thanks to the following teachers whose detailed comments on the first edition and helpful ideas led to many valuable changes in the New Edition:
Susan Barber, Lake School of English in Oxford; John Bradbury, FIAC Escola d'idiomes moderns in Sabadell, Catalonia, Spain; Susan Garvin, British Institute of Florence, Italy; Roger Johnson and Nick Kenny, British Council in Milan, Italy; Fern Judet, Swan School in Oxford; Lynne White, Godmer House School of English in Oxford.

And thanks to the following teachers who kindly wrote about their experiences of using the first edition, some of whom gave us their students' feedback:
H.G. Bernhardt, Tony Buckby and colleagues, J. Carvell, Emily Grammenou, Michael Hadgimichalis, Pearl Herrmann, Jill Jeavons, Katherine Karangianni, Marie Anne Küpper-Compes, Bryan Newman, Cathy Parker and colleagues, Véronique Rouanet, Claire Springett, Andrew Tymn, Robin Visel and J.T. Ward.

Finally, thanks to the numerous other teachers in many different countries (and their students) who have given us useful informal feedback on the first edition.

Thank you, everyone!

From the first edition

I'd like to express my thanks to Sue Gosling and Christine Cairns for all their encouragement and help during the planning, writing and rewriting of this book. Many thanks are also due to all the teachers who used the pilot edition and made so many useful and perceptive comments. Thanks are due in particular to staff at the following schools and institutes: the British Centre in Venice, the British Institute in Paris, the British School in Florence, the Newnham Language Centre in Cambridge, the Studio School of English in Cambridge and the Université II in Lyons.

Acknowledgements

The sample answer sheets on pages 155–158 are reproduced by kind permission of the University of Cambridge Local Examinations Syndicate. For details of sources of illustrations and other copyright material, please see the Student's Book.

Introduction

New Progress to First Certificate

New Progress to First Certificate is a completely new edition and very different from the second edition. Most of the reading and listening texts, activities and exercises are completely new, but the features that teachers and students have appreciated and which led to so many successful exam results have been retained.

The revisions and changes are based on detailed comments and reports from teachers who had been using the second edition successfully for many years. The format of each unit in *New Progress to First Certificate* provides a more balanced lesson structure and increased flexibility. *New Progress to First Certificate* is easy to use and helps students to make progress throughout their First Certificate course to the point where they can realise their potential in the exam and achieve the best possible grades.

The revised FCE examination, introduced in December 1996, ushered in many changes to the exam syllabus. The level of the exam remains the same, and each paper focuses on the same skills: Reading, Writing, Use of English, Listening and Speaking. But the tasks in each paper of the exam have changed significantly and so *New Progress to First Certificate* takes account of all these changes.

New Progress to First Certificate includes:
- twenty units, covering all of the topics that are specified in the revised FCE examination specifications
- four double-page spreads in every unit, each providing material for a 90-minute lesson
- vocabulary development exercises with plenty of opportunities for students to use the new words in discussion tasks and communication activities
- exercises on word study and word formation
- new and up-to-date reading texts, with pre- and post-reading tasks and discussion questions
- thorough training in writing skills with completely new exercises on the specific skills required for the exam
- Grammar Review with thorough coverage of problem areas together with exam-style exercises
- a Grammar Reference section at the end of the book with examples and explanations
- new listening comprehension exercises based on the type of tasks used in the exam
- speaking exercises to prepare students for the Speaking paper, including Communication Activities
- special sections on exam techniques, covering every paper in the revised exam
- advice, hints and tips on exam techniques
- exercises on verbs and idioms, phrasal verbs and prepositions

New Progress to First Certificate retains the most popular and effective features of the second edition: students **progress** from exercises which develop the necessary language skills to the kind of exercises and tasks used in the exam.

Besides the 'normal' Student's Book, there is also a Self-study Student's Book (with answers) – this special edition is designed for students who are working partly or entirely on their own. It includes the full text of the Student's Book as well as:

– model answers to all the exercises
– transcripts of all the listening exercises.

The Self-study Student's Book is recommended for adult students and more mature teenage students. Using this version will enable students to do any of the exercises and check their answers on their own, leaving more time in class for the activities that depend on discussion and conversation.

Preparing for the FCE exam

To some extent, every examination requires candidates to 'jump through hoops' and perform tasks which they might never have to do in real life. When we read a text or listen to a broadcast or watch TV we don't expect to have to answer comprehension questions afterwards! When we talk to other people we don't usually compare photographs! Some of us don't have to write very much at all, but if we do, we don't usually spend our leisure time writing compositions! Yet students have to master special exam skills and techniques if they want to do well in the exam. However, we should never lose sight of a longer term aim: students should be improving their English in ways that will not only lead to success in the exam but also provide them with worthwhile practical skills they can use when communicating with people in English in the real world – and when reading, writing or listening to English for pleasure, in their studies or in their work.

In an examination preparation course there must be a balance between helping students to be successful in the exam and helping them to improve their ability to communicate with people in English in real-life situations. An examination certificate is of little practical value if the proud holders can't actually use their English in communication! That is why there are many opportunities in *New Progress to First Certificate* for students to speak together, share ideas and communicate with each other in class, not just become proficient at answering exam questions.

Eventually, as the exam gets closer, no doubt you will decide to use practice tests or past exam papers with your students – as suggested towards the end of the book. However, doing tests too early can be counter-productive, confusing and demoralising. Real exam papers contain some questions that are very hard (which only the very best candidates are likely to get right) and your students may get so many answers wrong that they feel scared or inadequate.

When you do decide to do a practice test, make sure that your students don't waste time worrying about questions they can't answer – and reassure them that they still have lots of time to go before the real exam, and more time to improve their skills before then. In the exam they don't need to get all the answers right to pass – the pass mark is 50 to 60 per cent, not 100 per cent!

If you haven't taught a First Certificate class before, you should familiarise yourself with the format of the exam by looking at one or more of the following:

– *Specifications and Sample Papers for the Revised FCE Examination* and/or *First Certificate Examination Handbook* obtainable from:

> UCLES
> Marketing Department
> Syndicate Buildings
> 1 Hills Road
> Cambridge
> CB1 2EU
> England
> Fax (44) 1223 460278

– The practice tests in *Cambridge Practice Tests for First Certificate* (published by Cambridge University Press, 1996 or later) and the accompanying Teacher's Books.
– The latest Examination Regulations, obtainable from your Local Examinations Secretary, which also includes a list of the books for prescribed reading.

How long does the course take?

Each unit in the Student's Book contains enough material for about four 90-minute lessons making a total of about 120 hours – plus about two hours' homework. If you decide to devote a lot of time to the discussion activities, you may well need more time. A slow class would need longer than this, and every class is likely to have its own strengths and weaknesses which will lead you to spend more or less time on particular sections in a unit. Moreover, some topics may interest your students more than others and consequently there is likely to be more discussion on these than the ones that are of less interest to them.

If your students are using the Self-study Student's Book, and can spend more than two hours on their homework, you will be able to devote more time to the discussion activities.

New Progress to First Certificate is a complete course, including sections on grammar, word study, prepositions and verbs and idioms. Each unit contains up to nine sections, each of which consists of several steps. The material is designed to be used selectively: some exercises or whole sections can be left out if the class is unlikely to have difficulty with them (or if they are likely to find them **too** difficult). Some exercises or sections can be set for homework and checked quickly in class. Ideally, steps which require time for thought and which can be done by individual students on their own (for example, preparing reading passages, doing some of the gap-filling exercises and all the time-consuming writing tasks) should be done for homework, so that more time is available in class for discussion and Communication Activities.

Working in pairs or groups

Many of the exercises in *New Progress to First Certificate* are designed to be done by students working together in pairs or in small groups of three or four. They are **not** designed to be done quickly 'round the class' with each student answering one question.

There are several advantages to this approach:

- Students get an opportunity to communicate their ideas to each other while they are discussing each exercise.
- Students are more likely to remember answers they have discovered or worked out by themselves than answers other students give – or answers the teacher announces to the class.
- Students working in groups are more active than if they are working as a class: they talk more and do more thinking too. If a class of, say, 20 were doing a ten-question exercise 'round the class', half of them wouldn't answer a single question.
- If an exercise is done 'round the class', the lazier students can simply answer 'I don't know' when their turn comes and go to sleep the rest of the time. The weaker students can be lulled into a false sense of security by writing down all the correct answers and kidding themselves that they have 'done' the exercise. The exercises in *New Progress to First Certificate* are designed to help students to **learn**, not merely to test their own knowledge, and the idea isn't for students to say to themselves 'Another 66 pages to go and then we've finished!'

The drawback of doing exercises in pairs or groups is that it does take time. However, as many of the exercises can be done as homework, time can be saved by setting some exercises to be done at home. Then, back in class next time, students can begin the session by comparing their answers in pairs or groups, and discussing as a class any problems they encountered.

How does each type of section work?

VOCABULARY

Each unit contains a vocabulary exercise near the beginning covering vocabulary connected with the topic of the unit.

Before each vocabulary exercise there are warm-up discussion questions, to allow students to talk about the new topic briefly. These questions are open-ended and, in a talkative class, could lead to a lengthy discussion – sometimes you may have to interrupt the discussion to allow enough time for the vocabulary exercise to be done.

There is a progression in the vocabulary exercises from:

Questions where the first letter of the missing word is given but the rest is m............ .

to:

Questions like this where the whole word is ....

to:

Multiple-choice questions where there is a choice of four possible . . .
   replies   sentences   answers   alternatives

The missing words are mostly placed near the end of their sentences to allow students to revise the exercise more easily. This can be done by asking them to cover up the right-hand side of the page with a piece of card or thick paper and to try to remember the words they have hidden.

Your students are sure to want to find out more words to use in discussion about the topics that interest them most, so time must always be allowed for your students to ask questions on vocabulary. Further vocabulary is introduced in the other sections in each unit and many of the words used in the vocabulary exercise come up again.

After the vocabulary exercise there are further discussion questions or a Communication Activity to encourage students to use some of the new words they have encountered in the exercises.

Remembering and storing vocabulary

Highlighting vocabulary in their Student's Book turns each person's book into an instant revision aid. Every time they look back at sections they have already done, the vocabulary they want to remember 'jumps out from the page', reminding them of the vocabulary items and showing the words in contexts. Just leafing back through previous units in a free moment (on the bus or standing in a queue, for example) will help them to revise vocabulary really easily.

What students should **not** do is highlight whole paragraphs of text (as if they were memorising passages from a textbook for an exam). The selective approach of highlighting just a few chosen words on each page is much more effective.

Besides highlighting new words, students should be encouraged to store vocabulary in other ways: a loose-leaf personal organiser or Filofax is particularly useful for this. This is best done by topics, with each new topic starting on a new page. Fresh pages can be inserted whenever necessary and the pages and topics can be rearranged easily.

Here's one suitable method of organising a vocabulary notebook – translations might also be included:

TRANSPORT

seat belt
Don't forget to fasten your seat belt.

spare wheel
If you get a flat tyre you'll have to fit the spare wheel.

boot
Put your luggage in the boot. (USA: trunk)

WORD STUDY

Word formation is tested in Part 5 of the Use of English Paper in the FCE exam.

Most units contain a section on word formation or vocabulary development. Some exercises in these sections are recorded on the cassettes (shown with [cassette icon] in the Student's Book and the Teacher's Book), and full instructions are given together with a script in the Teacher's Book (and in the Self-study Student's Book).

These sections are designed to help students to consolidate what they already know about the important aspects of word formation and vocabulary, enabling them to correct any errors they make and to widen their knowledge.

1.3	Using a dictionary
2.2	Abbreviations and numbers
3.5	Using prefixes – 1
4.4	Using prefixes – 2
5.7	Using prefixes – 3
7.7	Spelling and pronunciation – 1: Vowels
8.6	Spelling and pronunciation – 2: Diphthongs
9.4	Spelling and pronunciation – 3: Consonants
10.5	Compound words – 1
11.4	Compound words – 2
12.6	Using suffixes – 1: Adjectives
13.5	Using suffixes – 2: Actions and people
14.7	Using suffixes – 3: Abstract nouns
15.6	Opposites
17.5	Stressing the right syllable
19.6	Synonyms

GRAMMAR REVIEW

In the Use of English Paper of the FCE exam there are five parts:

Part 1 Multiple-choice cloze with an emphasis on vocabulary
Part 2 Open cloze with an emphasis on grammar and vocabulary
Part 3 Key word transformations with an emphasis on grammar and vocabulary
Part 4 Error correction with an emphasis on grammar
Part 5 Word formation

The exercises in the Grammar Review sections reflect Parts 2, 3 and 4, but there are also different exercises which focus on particular aspects of grammar.

The Grammar Review section in each unit is designed to revise the main problem areas of English grammar that FCE candidates find tricky. Each set of exercises has an accompanying Grammar Reference section at the end of the book with further examples and explanations of the basic rules. Students may refer to the Grammar Reference sections before or after doing the Grammar Review exercises, and they are particularly useful for pre-exam revision.

1.4 Present tenses
2.4 Questions and question tags
3.2 The past – 1
4.6 The past – 2
5.5 Articles and quantifiers – 1
6.4 Articles and quantifiers – 2
7.6 Modal verbs – 1
8.3 Modal verbs – 2
9.5 *If . . .* sentences – 1
10.3 *-ing* and *to . . .* – 1
11.2 *If . . .* sentences – 2
12.3 *-ing* and *to . . .* – 2
13.4 Joining sentences – 1: Relative clauses
14.3 Joining sentences – 2: Conjunctions
15.2 Using the passive
16.5 The past – 3: Reported speech
17.2 Comparing and contrasting
18.3 The future
19.2 Adverbs and word order

Students should realise that the Grammar Review sections provide **revision** of points that they have probably covered in previous courses. The summaries given in the Grammar Reference pages are necessarily brief and simplified and do not cover elementary points or more advanced points. If students require more detailed rules or guidelines, they should refer to a reference grammar book. Students should be encouraged to ask questions if they are unsure about any points in the grammar sections.

PREPOSITIONS

These sections cover the important uses of prepositions in prepositional phrases and after certain verbs, nouns and adjectives. As these are often just 'things you have to know and remember' rather than aspects of interesting communication, many of these sections consist of straightforward gap-filling exercises. They can be done at any stage of the unit (i.e. 1.6 doesn't necessarily have to be done between 1.5 and 1.7), or set for homework and checked in class.

The points covered in these sections are:

1.6 Remembering prepositions
2.6 Position and direction
5.4 Compound prepositions
8.7 *At . . .*
9.3 *By . . .*
10.6 *On . . .* and *out of . . .*
11.5 *In . . .*
12.5 Words + prepositions – 1
13.6 Words + prepositions – 2
14.5 Words + prepositions – 3

VERBS AND IDIOMS

These sections deal with phrasal verbs and the collocations in which certain common verbs are used. Like the preposition exercises, these can be fitted in when there is a little spare time during the unit, or set for homework and checked in class later. As these things are basically just 'things you have to know and learn', the exercises are not communicative.

These sections deal with the following verbs and phrasal verbs:

3.6 Looking and seeing
4.5 *Make* and *do*
6.3 I don't get it!
7.4 *Have* and *give*
15.7 Coming and going
16.7 *Put*
17.6 *Bring, call* and *cut*
18.6 *Fall* and *hold*
19.7 *Leave, let, pull* and *run*

READING

In the Reading paper of the FCE exam there are four parts, each with different tasks:

Part 1   A text divided into sections: students have to choose a suitable summary or heading for each section from a jumbled list of possible summaries or headings.
Part 2   A text with multiple-choice questions
Part 3   A text from which paragraphs or sentences have been removed: students have to choose from a jumbled list of answers which paragraphs or sentences fit in which places in the text.
Part 4   One long text or several shorter texts: students have to find the answers to a list of questions by locating the information in the text(s).

Each unit in *New Progress to First Certificate* contains one or two reading texts with tasks and questions.

Before the reading comprehension questions there is a pre-reading task, for example preliminary discussion questions or questions about the theme that students may be able to answer from their own previous knowledge. This task helps students to approach the text with more interest and curiosity than if they merely had to read the text and answer the questions.

Before they attempt the comprehension task for each text get the class to decide:

• what the text is about
• who wrote it and for whom
• where they think it's taken from.

Then they should skim the text (read it through very rapidly to get an idea of what it's about and what the main points are). Finally, they should read it through more carefully and answer the questions.

It is essential for students to realise that they don't have to be able to understand every single word to answer the questions in class – or in the exam. They should concentrate on what the writers are trying to say and the information they are communicating. Unfamiliar words in a reading text may be distracting but students should not assume that they are all important and 'worth learning'.

There is a progression from exercises which help students to develop their reading skills to exercises which reflect the format of the exam and its task types exactly. For example, in early units there are straightforward true/false questions instead of demanding multiple-choice questions.

Reading exercises and task types:

1.5	Etiquette	Text with seven sentences removed
2.7	Department stores	Finding specific information in two texts
3.4	From someone who loves you	True/false questions
4.2	Fitness or fun?	Finding specific information in a text
4.8	It's tough at the top	True/false questions
5.2	The weather	Matching a list of topics to information in the text
5.3	The greenhouse effect	Text with six sentences removed

Some reading sections include vocabulary development exercises, to draw students' attention to the vocabulary in the text.

After the reading comprehension questions there are further discussion questions to encourage students to use some of the new words they have encountered in the text and share their reactions to its content with each other.

LISTENING

In the Listening paper of the FCE exam there are four parts, each with different tasks:

Part 1 Eight short monologues or conversations: students have to answer a multiple-choice question about each one.

Part 2 One longer monologue or conversation: students have to note down a word or a short phrase in the spaces provided, or fill in a grid.

Part 3 Five short monologues or conversations: students have to choose answers from a jumbled list of six possible answers.

Part 4 One longer monologue or conversation: students have to answer true/false, yes/no, *Who said what?* or multiple-choice questions about it.

Each unit in *New Progress to First Certificate* contains recorded listening texts with tasks and questions.

There is a progression from exercises which help students to develop their listening skills to exercises which reflect the format of the exam and its task types exactly. The tasks and questions become progressively more difficult. The speed and complexity of the recordings themselves does not change: they are all spoken at a normal speed.

Before the listening comprehension tasks there is often a pre-listening task, for example, preliminary discussion questions or some questions about the theme that students may be able to answer from their own previous knowledge. This task helps students to approach the recording with more interest than if they merely had to listen to the cassette and answer the questions.

Try to 'set the scene' for students before they hear the recording by explaining where the speakers are and what their relationship is (colleagues, good friends, etc.). In class (as in the exam) students will be trying to understand disembodied voices coming out of a loudspeaker and this is much more difficult than being in the same room as a real person who is speaking.

Most classes will need to hear each recording at least twice to extract all the required information. In some cases, where a class is weak at listening, you may need to pause the tape frequently and re-play certain sections to help them to understand more easily. However, it is essential for students to realise that they don't have to be able to understand every single word to answer the questions in class – and in the exam. They should concentrate on what the speakers are trying to say and the information they are communicating, **not** the actual words they are using.

Listening exercises and task types:

After the listening comprehension task there are further discussion questions to encourage students to share their reactions to its content with each other and discuss the implications of what they have heard. In some cases there is a complete Communication Activity, related to the theme of the listening text.

Voices video

If you would like your students to listen to authentic British speakers and **see** the speakers at the same time, you might like to use *Voices* (published by Cambridge University Press) with them. This video contains seven documentary sequences on topics that are closely related to the topics in *New Progress to First Certificate*:

Voices sequence	*New Progress to First Certificate*
Language and national identity – Language learning in Wales	Unit 1 Communication
A wedding	Unit 3 Friends and relations
Dartmoor – A National Park	Unit 5 The world around us
Get in shape! – A morning at a leisure centre	Unit 8 Looking after yourself and/or Unit 4 Time off
St Ives – Holidaymakers, artists and surfers	Unit 9 Having a great time! and/or Unit 18 Yes, but is it art?
Enjoy your meal!	Unit 10 Food for thought
A family airline	Unit 14 All in a day's work!

Voices is accompanied by a Student's Book, containing a variety of tasks and exercises, and a Teacher's Book with answers, teaching notes and transcripts. The material in *Voices* complements but does not duplicate the material in *New Progress to First Certificate*.

WRITING

In the Writing paper of the FCE exam there are two parts, each requiring students to write 120–180 words.

Part 1   Question 1, writing a transactional letter, is compulsory. Students have to compile information from one or more short texts or visual prompts and then write a letter according to the instructions given.

Part 2   Students must choose one of Questions 2–5 to answer: these could be an article, an informal letter or non-transactional letter, a discursive composition or essay, a descriptive or narrative composition or short story, or a choice of two compositions about a prescribed background reading text. In each question the imagined reader and purpose of the writing is specified.

In *New Progress to First Certificate* there is a progression in the composition exercises from tasks where students are free to write as much or as little as they like, using a dictionary and taking as long as they like, to tasks where compositions of 120–180 words have to be written against the clock without a dictionary, as required in the exam.

The Writing sections focus on the types of composition that students are expected to write in Paper 2 and on specific aspects of effective writing:

1.8   What are your strengths and weaknesses?
2.3   Spelling and punctuation
2.8   Describing a place
3.7   Writing a story
4.9   Paragraphs
5.8   Making notes
6.7   Personal letters
7.5   Compiling information and writing a transactional letter
7.8   Starting and ending well
8.2   Writing a report
8.8   Compiling information and writing a transactional letter
9.6   Writing a description for a brochure
10.7   Writing a letter of instruction to a friend
11.8   Writing an article: Advantages and disadvantages
12.7   Short sentences? Or long ones?
13.7   Writing against the clock – Exam techniques
      (Writing about a set book – see Communication Activity *19*)
14.8   Including relevant information
15.8   Describing a process

In every unit, emphasis is placed on the need for good planning, making notes and checking work through for mistakes before handing it in – aspects of composition writing that are crucial for success in the exam. Students are encouraged to develop their writing skills through short writing tasks, by comparing different versions of compositions and, of course, by writing their own full-length compositions and having them assessed and marked by you.

When marking students' written work, don't forget how discouraging it is to receive back a paper covered in red marks! It's better for students to locate and correct their own mistakes, rather than have corrections written out for them. This is particularly important when you believe that a student has made a careless mistake or a slip of the pen.

Often, once mistakes are pointed out to students, they can correct them themselves. A marking scheme like the following is recommended – but whatever scheme you use, make sure your students are conversant with the system you're using. The symbols shown here would appear on the side of the page in the margin – make sure your students do leave a margin, therefore!

X   = 'Somewhere in this line there is a mistake of some kind that you should find and correct.'

XX   = 'Somewhere in this line there are two mistakes that you should find and correct.'

An incorrect word or phrase underlined = 'This particular word or phrase is not correct and you should correct it.'

G   = 'Somewhere in this line there is a Grammatical mistake that you should find and correct.'

V   = 'Somewhere in this line there is a Vocabulary mistake that you should find and correct.'

Sp   = 'Somewhere in this line there is a Spelling mistake that you should find and correct.'

P   = 'Somewhere in this line there is a Punctuation mistake that you should find and correct.'

WO   = 'Some of the words in this sentence are in the wrong Word Order; please rearrange them.'

?   = 'I don't quite understand what you mean.'

And equally important:

✔   = 'Good, you have expressed this idea well!' or 'This is an interesting or amusing point.'

✔✔   = 'Very good, you have expressed this idea very well!' or 'Very interesting or amusing point!'

Remember that all learners need encouragement and praise. Just as you might sometimes ignore mistakes when students are speaking, perhaps occasionally some mistakes should be overlooked in their written work.

Make sure you allow everyone time to read each other's written work: this is particularly important if composition writing is to be considered as more than 'just a routine exercise'. Any piece of writing should be an attempt to communicate ideas to a reader. If students know that their partners, as well as you, are going to read their work, they are more likely to try to make it interesting, informative and entertaining! If you, their teacher, are the **only** reader, the process of writing is much less motivating. Students can learn a lot from reading each other's ideas – and from each other's comments on their own work. In the exam, what is most important is the success of each composition as a piece of communication, not simply its lack of grammatical errors.

It is important to realise that in the exam itself, candidates are not expected to write 'great prose'. Indeed, no special credit is given for bright ideas, specialist knowledge or entertaining stories – the more imaginative candidates are not rewarded at the expense of the less imaginative ones. Although in the exam each composition is regarded 'as a piece of communication', better marks do tend to go to candidates whose compositions:

– are grammatically accurate
– use vocabulary appropriately
– are free from spelling mistakes
– fulfil the brief
– judge the intended reader and set the correct tone
– are coherent and cohesive.

Students also need to know that a good composition should not contain irrelevant information and, in the exam, they **must** answer the question asked – not the question they would like to have been asked! Candidates who distort, ignore or misunderstand the question do get penalised for this.

In preparing students for the exam, they should be encouraged to communicate their ideas to you and each other in writing, just as they do in discussions and other oral activities. Otherwise, the exercise of writing compositions becomes sterile and pointless.

In some cases model versions of written tasks are given among the Communication Activities at the back of the Student's Book (shown as 'answers' in the list on pages 17–18). In the Teacher's Book (and also in the Self-study Student's Book) there are model versions for several composition tasks. If you think your students will benefit from seeing any of these, the model versions may be photocopied from the Teacher's Book.

(See page 111 for the official marking scheme used in the FCE exam.)

Background reading

Each year FCE candidates can choose to read one (or more) of five optional 'Background reading texts'. They can write about one of these set books in Part 2 of the Writing paper. Most of the set books are simplified or abridged editions.

New Progress to First Certificate doesn't contain questions on particular books because these change every year. However, in Unit 13 there are opportunities for discussion and writing about a set book. Choosing one of the set books not only gives students an extra topic to choose from in Paper 2, but also gives them a chance to improve their reading skills and enrich their vocabulary. Quite a wide range of tastes is catered for in the list of books, so there's probably at least one that your students would find enjoyable.

If your students are reading a set book, you'll need to discuss it in class regularly, as they read it chapter-by-chapter.

Reading a set book and answering a question about it is optional, and students don't have to answer the question about it unless they want to, even if they have read one of the books.

SPEAKING AND COMMUNICATION ACTIVITIES

In the Speaking paper of the FCE exam students work in pairs with two examiners: one acts as the interlocutor, engaging the candidates in conversation, while the other listens and assesses without speaking. There are four parts, each with different tasks:

Part 1 Short exchanges between each candidate and the interlocutor, focusing on giving personal information and socialising

Part 2 Each candidate speaks for about a minute about two colour photographs and comments briefly on the other candidate's photos. The two candidates exchange information and express attitudes and opinions.

Part 3 The candidates talk to each other in a discussion prompted by photographs or drawings, involving problem solving, decision making, planning, prioritising or speculating.

Part 4 The interlocutor encourages the candidates to discuss matters related to the theme of Part 3.

In *New Progress to First Certificate* the Communication Activities and the discussions that follow most of the reading passages and listening exercises are designed to prepare students for what they will have to do in the Speaking paper. These speaking tasks follow on naturally from the reading or listening text.

Every unit contains plenty of opportunities for students to use their English in realistic communicative situations, but in most units there is a section that is **specifically** directed towards practising the techniques required in the Speaking paper, and improving fluency and pronunciation:

1.7C	Giving your opinions
2.5D	Agreeing and disagreeing
3.3B	Telling stories
4.3	Interrupting politely
5.6	Talking for a minute and 'disguising' hesitation
6.1E	Asking questions and follow-up questions
6.6B	Explaining routes
7.2B & C	Talking about preferences
8.4B	Giving advice
8.8	Talking about photographs and discussing ideas
9.1D	Asking questions and talking about photographs
10.4B	Asking for and giving explanations
14.2	Paper 5: Speaking – mock exam
15.5	Explaining how things work
16.6	Pauses and stress
17.5	Stressing the right syllable
18.5	Joining up words
20.5	Paper 5: Speaking

Many of the speaking activities are based on an information gap, where each member of a pair or group looks at different information in the Communication Activities at the back of the Student's Book. This information is presented on different pages, so that it's difficult for students to 'cheat' by looking at each other's information. This kind of information gap exercise develops into a lively, realistic interaction.

Communication Activities (unit by unit)

Some of these contain model answers or extra information, which students shouldn't see until **after** they have completed an exercise.

Unit	Communication Activities	Content
1	*none*	
2	1 + 29	Names/addresses and numbers to dictate
	54	Punctuation (model answer)
	13 + 40	Photos of people dressed in different styles
	4 + 32	Advertisements
	7 + 35	Explaining positions
3	24 + 31	Picture stories
	33	Phrasal verbs (answers)
	53	Improved version of story
	41	Improved version of story
4	*none*	
5	6 + 34	Global warming
	10 + 38	Photos of people and animals
6	43 + 51	Road safety advice
	9 + 36	Asking for and giving directions
7	57	Letter to owner of flat (model letter)
8	58	Guidelines for writing a report
	16 + 42	Different sports
9	5	Correct spellings (answers)
	14 + 22	Words to dictate
	59	Extract from Discover Scotland leaflet
10	11 + 44 + 52	Menu explanations
	55 + 60	Recipes for refreshing drinks
	61	Guidelines for giving feedback
11	*none*	
12	*none*	
13	19	Advice and topics for set books (extra information)

14	25 + 26 + 27 + 28	Mock speaking exam – Part 1
	47 + 48 + 49 + 50	Mock speaking exam – Part 2
15	15 + 23	How a microwave works (and extra information)
	39 + 45	How a computer mouse works (and extra information)
16	3 + 8 + 12	News reports to be retold in your own words
	56	Shoplifting statistics (extra information)
	46	News items with stressed syllables and pauses marked (answers)
	17 + 20	News items to read aloud
17	*none*	
18	18 + 21	Works of art to compare
19	37 + 62	Group of people to describe
20	2 + 30	Photos from the different times in history

EXAM TECHNIQUES AND TIPS

Many units contain special sections on exam techniques. These sections help students to feel more confident about each paper in the exam, and introduce them to special skills they need to do their best when working under exam conditions.

5.6	Paper 5: Talking for a minute
8.8	Paper 5: Talking about photographs and discussing ideas
9.7	Paper 3: Use of English – Fill the gaps (Parts 1 and 2)
11.7	Paper 3: Use of English – Correcting errors (Part 4)
12.4	Paper 3: Use of English – Rewriting sentences (Part 3)
13.7	Paper 2: Writing – Writing against the clock
14.2	Paper 5: Speaking
14.7C	Paper 3: Use of English – Word formation (Part 5)
15.3	Paper 4: Listening (Parts 1 and 2)
16.4	Paper 4: Listening (Parts 3 and 4)
16.8	Paper 1: Reading
17.8	Paper 2: Writing
18.8	Paper 2: Writing – We all make mistakes (self-correction and proof-reading)
19.3	Paper 3: Use of English – Tricky questions
20.1	Paper 1: Reading
20.2	Paper 2: Writing
20.3	Paper 3: Use of English
20.4	Paper 4: Listening
20.5	Paper 5: Speaking

Throughout the Student's Book, usually in the margin, there are lots of short Exam Tips, giving useful advice and hints on preparing for the exam and coping with exam conditions.

Symbols in the Student's Book

Communication Activity (or extra information or model answer) at the back of the book

Recorded material. A very low-pitched tone is recorded between each section. If your cassette player has CUE and REVIEW controls, you can fast forward or rewind the cassette while hearing the voices very fast – the tone will be audible as a short beep.

Students should use a fluorescent highlighter to highlight certain words. A pencil may be used instead to underline or put (rings) round the words, but a highlighter is more effective.

The FCE exam

The UCLES (University of Cambridge Local Examinations Syndicate) FCE (First Certificate in English) exam is held in June and in December each year. The exam assesses general proficiency in English through the testing of the candidates' abilities in reading, writing, speaking and listening and their knowledge of vocabulary and grammar.

PAPER 1: READING   *1 hour 15 minutes*

Part	Task Type	Focus	Number of Questions	Task Format
1	Multiple matching	Understanding the gist, the main points, detail, the structure of the text, specific information, or deducing the meaning	6–7	A text preceded by multiple matching questions. Candidates have to match an item from one list with an item in another list, or match items to elements within the text itself.
2	Multiple choice	as Part 1	7–8	A text followed by four-option multiple choice questions.
3	Gapped text	Understanding the gist, main points, detail and text structure	6–7	A text from which paragraphs or sentences have been removed followed by the removed items in jumbled order. Candidates have to decide where in the text the items were removed from.
4	Multiple matching or multiple choice	as Part 1	13–15	as Part 1

- One part may contain one text, or two or more shorter texts.
- The texts may come from any of these sources: advertisements, correspondence, fiction, brochures, guide books, manuals, messages, newspaper articles, magazine articles or reports.
- In all, candidates have to read 1,900–2,300 words (about 350–700 words per text).
- Candidates indicate their answers by shading the correct lozenges on the special answer sheet (see page 155). The total number of marks is 40 (20% of the total).

PAPER 2: WRITING   *1 hour 30 minutes*

Part	Task Type and Focus	Number of Tasks and Length	Task Format
1	Question 1 Writing a transactional letter	1 compulsory task 120–180 words	The candidate is guided by 1–3 short texts and sometimes visual prompts as well as by the rubric (instructions).
2	Questions 2–4 Writing one of the following: – an article – an informal or non-transactional letter – a discursive composition – a descriptive or narrative composition or short story	4 tasks from which candidates choose 1 120–180 words	The task or composition is explained in the rubric.
	Question 5 Writing one of the above on a prescribed background reading text	2 options	The task is explained in the rubric.

- Part 1 (Question 1) is compulsory.
- For Part 2, Candidates choose ONE question from Questions 2–5.
- Candidates may be asked to write any of the following task types: letters, articles, reports, compositions or essays – all written for a given purpose and target reader.
- Candidates write in a special answer booklet which is read and marked by an examiner. The total number of marks is 40 (20% of the total).
- The examiners have followed standardised induction, training and co-ordination procedures and use criterion-referenced assessment scales (see page 111). The scales assess such language features as: range of vocabulary and structure; accuracy of vocabulary, structures, spelling and punctuation; appropriacy; organisation and cohesion; task achievement.

PAPER 3: USE OF ENGLISH *1 hour 15 minutes*

Part	Task Type	Focus	Number of Questions	Task Format
1	Multiple choice cloze	Emphasis on vocabulary	15	A 'modified cloze' text with 15 gaps, followed by 15 four-option multiple choice questions.
2	Open cloze	Grammar and vocabulary	15	A 'modified cloze' text with 15 gaps.
3	Key word transformations	Grammar and vocabulary	10	Sentences with gaps. The gaps must be filled using the given word and other words which are necessary, but without changing the meaning of the sentence.
4	Error correction	Emphasis on grammar	15	A text containing errors. Some lines are correct, some lines contain an extra unnecessary word which must be identified.
5	Word formation	Vocabulary	10	A text with 10 gaps. Each gap must be filled with a word formed from the 'stem' word which is given beside the text.

- Candidates write their answers on the special answer sheet (see pages 156–157).
  The total number of marks is 65, which is 'scaled down' to 40 (20% of the total).

PAPER 4: LISTENING *40 minutes approximately*

Part	Task Type	Focus	Number of Questions	Task Format
1	Multiple choice	Understanding gist, main points, function, location, roles and relationships, mood, attitude, intention, feeling or opinion	8	A series of short unrelated extracts (about 30 seconds each) from monologues or interacting speakers. The multiple choice questions have three options.
2	Note taking or blank filling	Understanding gist, main points, detail or specific information, or deducing meaning	10	A monologue or interacting speakers (about 3 minutes).
3	Multiple matching	as Part 1	5	A series of short related extracts (about 30 seconds each) from monologues or interacting speakers. In the multiple matching questions candidates have to select the correct items from a list.
4	Selection from 2 or 3 possible answers	as Part 2	7	A monologue or interacting speakers (about 3 minutes). Candidates have to select between 2 or 3 possible answers: true/false, yes/no, three-option multiple choice, which speaker said what, etc.

- Each text is heard twice.
- The recordings contain a variety of accents.
- The monologues may include the following text types: answerphone messages, commentaries, documentaries, instructions, lectures, news, public announcements, advertisements, reports, speeches, talks, stories or anecdotes.
- The interacting speakers may be taking part in: chats, conversations, discussions, interviews, quizzes, radio drama or transactions.
- Candidates indicate their answers by shading the correct lozenges or by writing the correct word or words on the special answer sheet (see page 158). The total number of marks is 30, which is 'scaled up' to 40 (20% of the total).

PAPER 5: SPEAKING *14 minutes approximately*

Part	Task Type	Focus	Length	Task Format
1	Short exchanges between each candidate and the interlocutor	Giving personal information and socialising	3 minutes	The candidates give personal information about themselves.
3	Long turn from each candidate with brief response from the other candidate	Exchanging personal and factual information, expressing attitudes and opinions, using discourse functions related to managing a long turn	4 minutes	The candidates are in turn given two colour photographs. They each talk about their photographs for about a minute. They are also asked to comment briefly on each other's photographs.
3	Candidates talk with each other	Exchanging information, expressing attitudes and opinions	3 minutes	The candidates are given visual prompts (photographs, line drawings, diagrams, etc.) which generate a discussion while they take part in tasks such as planning, problem solving, decision making, prioritising, speculating, etc.
4	Candidates talk with each other and with the interlocutor	Exchanging and justifying opinions	4 minutes	The interlocutor encourages the candidates to discuss other aspects of the topic of Part 3.

- Parts 2–4 are based on the same general theme.

- There are usually two candidates together with two examiners. One examiner acts mainly as interlocutor and manages the interaction by asking questions or giving the candidates cues. The other acts as assessor and does not join in the conversation.

- The examiners have followed standardised induction, training and co-ordination procedures and use criterion-referenced assessment scales. The scales assess such language features as: use of grammar; use of vocabulary; pronunciation; interactive communication and task achievement.

- This paper contributes 20% of the total marks.

RESULTS

Candidates are given semi-profiled results on their result slips. These show them in which particular papers their performance was very good or very weak. Pass certificates are issued to candidates who gain grades A, B or C. Certificates are not issued to candidates with failing grades: D, E or U (unclassified).

Communication

The *Voices* video sequence *Language and national identity – Language learning in Wales* deals with other aspects of this topic.

The teaching notes for this unit are more comprehensive than later units as they include recommended procedures for the various types of exercise and details of some of the principles underlying them.

1.1 Ways of communicating   VOCABULARY AND SPEAKING

 Arrange the class into pairs or groups of three if you prefer. The questions are intended as a warm-up but they also give students a chance to use the vocabulary they already know to talk about the pictures. Here are some ideas that might come up in the discussion. Useful vocabulary is in italics:

1 In the first photo the woman *seems* to be holding a *phrase* book and she's trying to *make herself understood*, but the man doesn't seem to know what she's *getting at*. He looks very *puzzled*. She might say, 'Can you tell me how to get to the station?' He might say, 'I'm sorry but I don't understand.' I had a similar experience myself once when . . .

2 The man looks very pleased, perhaps because he's been *successful* in something. Maybe he's passed his driving test. His gesture means 'All OK', and instead of making the gesture he might say, 'Everything's fine!' When I took my driving test . . .

3 The two women are having their photograph taken. The *rabbit's ears* gesture doesn't mean anything, it's just a way of making the photo look more *informal* and shows they're *having a good time*. Instead of making the gesture one of them, or the photographer, might say 'Everyone say "cheese"'. The last time I had my photo taken . . .

Allow time at the end for students to ask questions on vocabulary they were searching for. It doesn't really matter if these questions aren't directly relevant to the topic.

B This exercise can be done in pairs, or by students working alone and later comparing answers in pairs before checking their answers as a whole class. The linguistic terms in this exercise are needed for talking **about** English – and for understanding the instructions in forthcoming exercises in this book, and in the GRAMMAR REFERENCE sections at the end.

> **ANSWERS**
>
> **2** abstract   **3** adjectives   adverbs   **4** pronouns   **5** prepositions   **6** conjunctions
> **7** parts   **8** phrasal   **9** capital letter   **10** italics   **11** syllables   **12** prefixes   suffixes
> **13** phonetic   **14** accents

C 1 The answers are a matter of opinion, of course, but recent research has shown that the words you say come a long way down the list when forming a first impression of someone.

2 & 3 Again, these are a matter of opinion. Here are some suggestions (your students may have much better ideas):

> **SUGGESTED ANSWERS**
>
> ✔ sincere   attractive   intelligent   sensible   artistic   pleasant
> ✗ arrogant   unfriendly   rude   self-satisfied   bad-tempered   timid   sensitive

If there's time, it might be useful to explore some opposites of the adjectives the class have come up with. For example: *sensible/silly, sincere/insincere*, etc.

D Remembering vocabulary is one of the most important things your students will have to do during this course. As different people find different methods of storing vocabulary helpful, it may be unwise to lay down one particular method. This is why remembering vocabulary is a discussion topic in this section. There are no 'correct answers' – but you may have your own special recommendations for your students, knowing them as you do.

Here is just one way a page in a Filofax might be organised.

> *PEOPLE*
>
> bad-tempered /bæd tempəd/
> — A bad tempered person easily gets angry, or loses his temper.
> sensible /sensɪbl/
> — A sensible person isn't silly – she has a lot of sense.
> sensitive /sensɪtɪv/
> — A sensitive person can get upset easily.

1.2 Signs LISTENING

A This is a warm-up, but to settle any disputes the meanings of the traffic signs are:

1 Give priority to vehicles from the opposite direction **2** No bicycles allowed
3 No motor vehicles allowed **4** This way to the zoo **5** Mini-roundabout: give way to traffic from the immediate right **6** Road gets narrower on both sides **7** Elderly people
8 Traffic merging with equal priority from the right **9** Quayside or river bank

B 📼 Before playing the recording, maybe ask the students what they know about gypsies. (**WARNING:** It is probably better not to ask this question if your students are likely to have bad feelings about gypsies.)

To do the task, everyone needs to know what the difference is between a horizontal, vertical and slanting line. Draw them on the board if necessary. It will probably be necessary to play the recording twice (or even three times) for the students to get all the information. Between playings, they should compare notes in pairs. (This is not an exam-style listening task.)

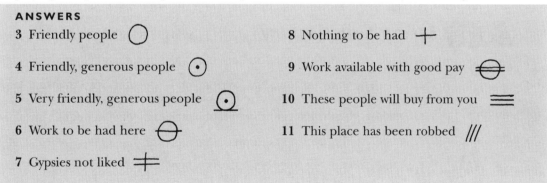

ANSWERS

3 Friendly people ◯

4 Friendly, generous people ⊙

5 Very friendly, generous people ⦿

6 Work to be had here ⊖

7 Gypsies not liked ⧧

8 Nothing to be had ✚

9 Work available with good pay ⊖

10 These people will buy from you ≡

11 This place has been robbed ///

TRANSCRIPT *3 minutes 40 seconds*

GUIDE: . . . and the gypsies also had a whole system of communications of...of...way of communicating with each other as well. When they went from house to house around the country they left behind chalk marks on the wall...um...and these were messages for any other gypsies who came along later. Now, these signs were useful because, for one thing, many gypsies were illiterate in those days but also the signs couldn't be understood by the country people, they were only intelligible to the gypsies themselves.

Now, I'll show you some of the signs, I'll draw them on this board. Now, if there was a dog at the house, then they used this sign, see: a triangle. If it was a fierce dog, then they put a horizontal line through the triangle like this. If the people in the house were friendly, then they'd draw a circle like so.

Now, what do you think this meant? This is a circle with a dot in the middle. Now, I wonder what that meant?

MAN: Angry? Angry neighbours?

GUIDE: No, no, no. It meant 'friendly and generous people'. Now what about this? This is a circle with a dot in the middle and a line underneath and this means very friendly and very generous people. Now, this one, this is a circle with a horizontal line through it and this meant 'work to be had here'.

Now if a house was known to be unfriendly, they would leave a sign like this, this is a vertical line with two horizontal lines and that meant 'gypsies not liked', so they could steer clear of that one.

Now, I wonder what you think about this one? This is a very common one: it's a cross made with one vertical line and one horizontal line. What...what do you think that might have meant?

WOMAN: No idea.

GUIDE: Any ideas? It meant 'nothing to be had' at this house, so again they could...er...they could go on by and not waste their time knocking on the door. Um...here's another one. This is a circle with two horizontal lines and...er...probably fairly uncommon in those days, this one meant 'work available and good pay'. So they'd obviously stop there. Er...now, three horizontal lines – any ideas what that might be? No? Now, this was a very hopeful sign for a gypsy because this meant 'these people will buy from you' so it would be well worth your time stopping by here. Now, here's the last one: three slanting lines, like this. Anyone care to guess? This was a very important one for the gypsies. Three slanting lines means 'don't stop here because this place has been robbed'.

C It's unlikely that you actually use an identical marking system to the one shown here. But it might be worth adopting parts of it. If your students are reasonably sensible and mature, maybe discuss which of the symbols they would find most useful if you did use the same system.

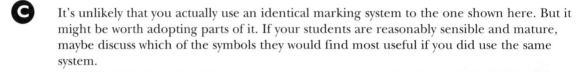

SUGGESTED ANSWERS

✓ good   ✓✓ very good   ✗ one mistake   ✗✗ two mistakes   P Punctuation mistake
Sp Spelling mistake   WO mistake in Word Order   G Grammatical mistake
V Vocabulary mistake   ! I'm surprised!   ? What do you mean?

To help students to avoid repeating spelling mistakes, you could suggest that they write out the misspelt word again correctly, twice and/or have a special section in their vocabulary notebook for 'words I often spell wrong'. When they've stopped spelling them wrong, the words can be crossed out or ticked off.

NOTE
1.3 B can't be done without dictionaries. See the note at the start of 1.3.

1.3 **Using a dictionary**   WORD STUDY

NOTE
Part B can't be done without dictionaries. You'll probably need to take a small selection of dictionaries to class for this lesson – students in each group can share the same dictionary. If your students already have their own dictionaries (English-to-English ones), remind them to bring them along.

A Again, this discussion is intended to encourage students to work out their own strategies, rather than telling them what to think. Here are some points they might come up with in the discussion:

• more examples to see   definitions in other words
  different dictionaries have different strengths and weaknesses in their coverage
  not every dictionary is equally up-to-date or includes every specialised word
• quick to use   translations of every word
• more examples of words in sentences   usually more up-to-date

B This can be done by students working alone (if they each have a dictionary), but is probably best done in small groups, sharing a dictionary. All the answers can be found on the same or adjacent pages in any dictionary.

The purpose of the activity is to encourage students to 'explore' the dictionary, rather than just find definitions or work out translations in their heads. A good dictionary is a wonderful source of information and ideas!

For the answers to any questions you're unsure of you'll need to consult a dictionary. We recommend (in alphabetical order) the following dictionaries:

BBC English Dictionary
Cambridge International Dictionary of English
Collins COBUILD Essential English Dictionary
Longman Active Study Dictionary of English
Longman Dictionary of Contemporary English
Longman Dictionary of English Language and Culture
Oxford Advanced Learner's Dictionary
Oxford Advanced Learner's Encyclopedic Dictionary
Oxford Wordpower Dictionary

Considerations of cost and portability may influence purchase decisions besides the relative excellence of the coverage of the dictionaries!

C **1** This text comes from the foreword of the *Cambridge International Dictionary of English*. Not many people read a foreword or introduction, least of all in a dictionary. But the foreword gives essential information about the way a book is organised and the rationale behind it.

EXTRA ACTIVITY
Has everyone (anyone?) read the introduction on page 7 of the Student's Book? If not, ask them to do so now or to do so at home after the lesson. Ask them to note down two or three points which they think were most important or relevant.

2 Highlighting words is a technique that will be used over and over in this book. As time goes by, students should learn to make **decisions** about which words to highlight – not every word they don't know, but the ones they want to remember. (See page 8.) Students should go back to the dictionaries to look the highlighted words up, working alone, in pairs or in small groups.

3 Students can work in small groups instead of pairs if you prefer. There is no 'correct' arrangement of the features. Finish by reassembling the class. Ask for reports from some pairs and deal with any questions arising.

1.4 Present tenses GRAMMAR REVIEW

Before starting, make sure everyone appreciates that the GRAMMAR REVIEW exercises are **revision** exercises intended to enable students to check what they already know – and discover any gaps in their knowledge.

A You might want everyone to look at the GRAMMAR REFERENCE section on Present tenses on pages 182–183 before the lesson to save time. But as this is their first encounter with it, you may prefer them to do it in class (perhaps in pairs) and answer any queries now. In future, remind everyone to look at the GRAMMAR REFERENCE section **before** you come to the exercises in the GRAMMAR REVIEW sections (the next one is 2.4).

In general, the GRAMMAR REFERENCE sections are intended to be preparation for the exercises, to be consulted if in doubt during the exercises, and to be used for revision after doing the exercises. What they aren't intended to be is a substitute for a complete grammar reference book, which uses many more pages to cover the same ground more thoroughly. The GRAMMAR REFERENCE sections provide **rules of thumb** not a comprehensive study of grammar.

B Discuss any points that have caused disagreement or puzzlement within the pairs. If necessary, call on students with the right matches to justify them to students who have wrong matches.

SUGGESTED ANSWERS	
2 What does she do?	She's a student.
3 How long has she been writing?	For about an hour.
4 How much has she written?	About 200 words.
5 When are you having lunch?	Later than usual today.
6 When do you have lunch?	Usually at one thirty.
7 Where are you going for lunch?	Probably the cafeteria today.
8 Where do you go for lunch?	To the cafeteria most days.
9 Does he speak Japanese or Chinese?	Both, I think.
10 Is he speaking Japanese or Chinese?	It sounds like Chinese to me.

C This type of exercise encourages students to proof-read their own written work and find mistakes they have (carelessly) made.

ANSWERS (Some variations are possible.)

2 *A dictionary isn't costing very much to buy.*   doesn't cost

3 *She is living in London since she has been a child.*   has been   was

4 *What time are you expecting her to arrive?*   ✔ (*or* do you expect)

5 *I am still waiting for her to answer my letter.*   ✔

6 *Are you understanding me if I am speaking*   Do/Can you understand   speak
   very fast like this?

7 *My sister's always annoying me.*   ✔

8 *I'm remembering his face but I'm forgetting*   remember   forget/have forgotten
   his name.

D This is similar to an exercise students will have to do in Part 3 of the Use of English paper. In the exam students must use between two and five words.

ANSWERS (Some variations are possible.)

2 I *(can) never remember* how to spell the word 'pronunciation'.

3 It *doesn't matter* if you don't understand every word.

4 I *have/'ve been learning English since* I was ten years old.

5 How *long has it been* raining?

6 He *is/'s always interrupting* and it's very annoying!

7 She *teaches people (how)* to drive.

8 Oh dear, *it's still raining!*

E This section ends with free, open-ended practice. To start with, if necessary, brainstorm some activities that might be asked about and write them on the board. For example: *breakfast, letters, phone calls, sport, study* and *television.*

1.5   Good manners   READING

A This is an exam-style reading task and it is quite difficult! It's necessary to read the passage quite carefully, looking for clues, but it is **not** necessary to understand every word (or even every sentence).

ANSWERS

2 E   3 G   4 F   5 C   6 B   7 D

B **1–5**   Follow the instructions in the Student's Book. Here we raise the issue of **deciding** which words to highlight according to whether they are worth remembering or not. Some students may need your advice at this stage – for example, words like *appendage* and *clammy* may not be worth remembering, whilst *appreciated* and *compels* may be.

C **1** Encourage everyone to find evidence for their answer to the first question. Don't worry if the students don't appreciate the humorous tone of the passage.

The author is American (he refers to *highways* and a *thousand-dollar bill*). *Exchanging cordialities* means saying a few friendly things to people you meet, such as commenting on the weather.

2 Form groups by combining pairs. At the end ask the groups to report on their discussion and deal with any questions on vocabulary that arise. It might be instructive for you to provide an interpretation of the relative politeness of the things shown in Britain or another country you know which your students are less familiar with.

1.6 Remembering prepositions

PREPOSITIONS

The problem with prepositions is remembering them – especially when there seems to be no logical reason why one is used rather than another.

A The exercise should be done by students alone, before they compare answers in pairs. Note that in some cases more than one answer is possible.

> **ANSWERS**
> **3** of/for **4** for **5** for (*or no preposition*) **6** on/about **7** by **8** of **9** in
> **10** for/to **11** by **12** in **13** on **14** by/on **15** with **16** with **17** at/for
> **18** by to **19** in **20** from/of **21** of **22** at **23** about (*or no preposition*) **24** for

B This won't take long to do, so it's worth doing it in class rather than setting it for homework. Afterwards ask how many they've spotted.

The total number of prepositions is 46. These are ringed below and include *like, as, up to* and *than*. The infinitive forms with *to* . . . (*to subtract*, etc.) are underlined below – but these are not, strictly speaking, prepositions.

Etiquette

It is no secret that human beings have been replaced (by) baskets (at) toll-booth stations throughout the country. I, (for) one, am not (at) all sentimental (about) the substitution since (in) the first place, human money-collecting (on) highways is undignified and probably boring, and (in) the second place, baskets are much better suited (to) the job (than) human hands. Baskets are bigger and never clammy. A basket cannot make change, but that is only a temporary deficiency. (With) very little effort, baskets can be programmed <u>to subtract</u> 25 cents (from) anything (up to) a thousand-dollar bill. There would then remain only one problem (for) the basket. It cannot answer such questions (as) 'What exit do I take if I'm going (to) New Hyde Park?' or, [1] .... Theoretically, a basket can be programmed <u>to answer</u> these and any other reasonable questions, although it is unlikely, even (in) theory, that a basket could ever respond intelligently (to) such a remark as [2] .... Nevertheless, that problem can be solved (by) keeping one human being supplied abundantly (with) towels (in) some sort (of) emergency booth.

infinitive

infinitive

This solves all (of) the problems (from) the basket's point (of) view. But there still remain several (for) the motorists, almost all (of) which concern their sensibilities. Each basket has an appendage that has been programmed <u>to flash</u> 'Thank you' (after) the motorist has performed her civic duty. Common courtesy, (of) course, compels the motorist <u>to respond.</u> (In) these circumstances, however, one feels quite silly saying [3] .... unless one has some sort (of) assurance that one's courtesy has been understood and perhaps appreciated. I know many motorists who refuse <u>to say</u> anything (to) the basket *only* because they assume the basket is indifferent (to) their responses. This is perfectly understandable, but it could be corrected if the basket were programmed <u>to respond</u> (to) a human's 'You're welcome' (by) flashing something like [4] ....

There still remains the problem (of) what one is <u>to do</u> or say when the coin has missed the basket. After you've retrieved the coin and thrown it (in) the basket's appendage still says [5] .... but unquestionably the remark now has a sarcastic ring, which only adds (to) one's sheepishness. (In) such cases, the sensitive motorist will invariably say something (like) [6] .... (to) which the appendage could not, (in) all courtesy, reply, 'Well it *was* awfully nice (of) you.' That simply would not do. Perhaps the basket can be programmed <u>to reply,</u> [7] ....

adverb

Such a reply would make the motorist feel that her efforts are appreciated and she could proceed (down) the highway (with) that exhilarated air that comes (to) those who have exchanged cordialities (with) somebody or something.

1.7 Giving your opinions LISTENING

A 1 🔲 This exercise is similar to an exam-style listening task. It is definitely **not** necessary to catch every word to be able to answer the questions.

Play the recording again if the students find the first task difficult. Play it again before they discuss the answer to the second task.

ANSWERS

1 Julie   **2** no one   **3** Sally   **4** Tom   **5** Anthony   **6** Bill

2 Tom sounded quite unpleasant. His tone of voice made him sound arrogant – and not using any of the phrases underlined in the tapescript to introduce his opinions contributed to this impression.

B 🔲 Play the recording again, pausing it as necessary for students to note down the phrases (which are underlined in the transcript below).

Brainstorm some other ways of introducing opinions. For example:

In my opinion . . .
I believe that . . .
I feel that . . .
I must say that . . .

TRANSCRIPT AND ANSWERS   *2 minutes 40 seconds*
(The phrases used to introduce opinions are underlined.)

ANTHONY: Well, <u>it seems to me</u> that some languages are easier to learn than others. I mean, what about if you had to learn Japanese? <u>I don't really think that</u> as an English speaker I could learn to speak Japanese as easily as I could learn...er...say Italian. I mean for a start I'd have to learn a completely new writing system, and there'd be hardly any words which are the same in English and Japanese. Do you see what I mean, Sally?

SALLY: Yes, but at least Japanese is a living language – ha...I mean millions of people speak it in Japan. So <u>I think it's true to say that</u> learning it would be useful and relevant. But Latin or Ancient Greek are languages that nobody speaks. <u>I mean, don't you agree that</u> learning a dead language is a bit of a waste of time? Some students find them interesting, but <u>I don't really believe that</u> there's any practical value at all in learning classical languages, do you, Bill?

BILL: Not really. But <u>you know what I think? I think that</u> if you learn a foreign language in your own country, it's quite difficult to appreciate the relevance of *any* language. I think this is particularly true if you're learning a language at school, where...er...studying languages sometimes doesn't seem relevant – any more than history or literature seem relevant. And don't you agree that...if your only contact with the language is in the classroom and you only speak and hear it there, you may forget all about it between lessons? So each new lesson begins...um...with time spent trying to remember what you did in the last lesson, doesn't it, Julie?

JULIE: Yes, but I think it's true to say that the reality for most people is that they have to learn foreign languages in classes in their own country. It takes a very long time to learn a language. I...I don't really think that many people can just travel to the country where the language is spoken and live there. <u>The point is that</u> most people have to continue their studies, or earn a living, they...they can't afford to take time off living in another country for as long as it takes for them to learn the language, can they, Tom?

TOM: No, but with a foreign language you never stop learning. You never reach a point where you can say: 'At the end of this course I'll know English and I can stop learning it.' It's a process that goes on and on – you can reach a certain level, or you can pass an exam or even get a university degree. But you still remain a learner all your life.

C The 15 topics listed are the ones that are going to come up in the next 15 units in this book. Students should only pick the topics they have an opinion on, and they can deal with the topics in any order they like.

This may be your first sample of your students' written work, but even if it isn't, treat this exercise as a 'new beginning'.

A This should be set as homework, but spend a few minutes discussing what is required in class and answer any queries your students may have.

B & C Encouraging students to read each other's work is a procedure we'll be promoting throughout this course. Having a genuine reader rather than a critic (you) to read one's work makes the task much more realistic.

If possible, use the marking scheme suggested in 1.2.

If possible, photocopy this written work for future reference. It can be very encouraging for students to see how much their work has improved about half-way through the course, when motivation is dropping off.

Ask everyone to tell you what parts of this unit they found:

• most difficult and least difficult,
• most useful and least useful,
• most interesting and least interesting.

This will help you to plan how to organise the time you will spend on each type of section later.

Draw everyone's attention to the 'advice box' at the end of the section. These boxes provide study tips and, later on, exam tips.

2 At your service!

2.1 Can I help you?   VOCABULARY AND LISTENING

The actual vocabulary exercise comes late in this section, but encourage students to be on the look-out for useful vocabulary in Parts A and B.

A 1 This is a warm-up discussion. If your students are from different places, they should perhaps talk about the place where they're studying.

2 If your students aren't used to playing roles, they may need some help before they do this. Begin by brainstorming some of the questions the visitor might ask. Then do a short demonstration of the beginning of the conversation, choosing two confident students to play the two parts, or playing one of the parts yourself.

  If things seem to be going badly, stop everyone and find out what the problems are. Then tell them to switch roles and start again.

3 Combine the pairs. Encourage everyone to make notes on vocabulary questions that arise so that they can raise them at the end of the discussion.

B   There are four conversations. Pause the recording between each one to give the students time to write in their answers. It will probably be necessary to play the recording two or three times for everyone to get every piece of information.

SUGGESTED ANSWERS

	Where are they?	What does the customer want?	What will the customer say next?
1	in a bank	to change $120 into pounds	'£90 in ten-pound notes and the rest in coins, please.'
2	in a pharmacy/ chemist's	something for her daughter's illness (sore throat or lost voice, perhaps)	'I'll take the tablets/lozenges, I think.'
3	in a bookshop or newsagent's	a street map	'I'll have the ABC, I think.'
4	in a post office	to send a small packet abroad	'Oh, well I suppose I'll have to send it letter rate then, even though it does cost more.'

TRANSCRIPTS   *2 minutes 50 seconds*

1 CUSTOMER: . . . OK, I've got two at fifty dollars and one at twenty dollars.
  CASHIER: So that's 150 dollars altogether.
  CUSTOMER: Er...no, that's 120.
  CASHIER: Oh...right...um...could you sign them there please?
  CUSTOMER: Here? Yep, OK, there you are.
  CASHIER: Thank you. Can I see your passport please?
  CUSTOMER: Ah...yeah, sure here it is.
  CASHIER: OK...Right, so that's 94 pounds 45. How do you want the money?

2 CUSTOMER: . . . um...have you got anything suitable?
  CHEMIST: Yeah, sure. But you don't sound as if you need anything.
  CUSTOMER: Oh no, they're not for me. They're for my daughter.
  CHEMIST: Oh I see. Well...um...these are pretty good. Or you could give her some of this.
    She should take one spoonful three times a day.
  CUSTOMER: Mhm. Is there any limit to how many of those she can take?
  CHEMIST: Er...yes, she should only take eight of them in one day.
  CUSTOMER: Which do you recommend?
  CHEMIST: Well, they're both pretty effective. It depends which is more convenient really.
    Which would you like?

3 CUSTOMER: . . . so what's the difference between them?
ASSISTANT: Well, the ABC covers a larger area a...and it's got the main tourist attractions marked.
CUSTOMER: Mm. And the A to Z?
ASSISTANT: Well, it does cover the whole town, um...but not the surrounding area. Er...what it does have is all the bus routes marked on it, see, there?
CUSTOMER: Ah yes...but it hasn't got an index of street names, has it?
ASSISTANT: Ah, w...i...it has, it has, look look, it's printed on the back.
CUSTOMER: And are they the s...exactly the same price?
ASSISTANT: Aha, almost: the ABC is three ninety-five and the A to Z is three ninety-nine.
CUSTOMER: Ah.
ASSISTANT: Which one would you like?

4 CUSTOMER: . . . Mm, yes, I think so, would that be the cheapest?
COUNTER CLERK: Yes. Um...can you put it on the scales please?
CUSTOMER: OK.
COUNTER CLERK: That'll be four pounds twenty...Oh dear.
CUSTOMER: What's the matter?
COUNTER CLERK: Well, did you wrap this yourself?
CUSTOMER: Yes.
COUNTER CLERK: Well, I can't accept it as a 'small packet'.
CUSTOMER: Why not?
COUNTER CLERK: Well, to go as a 'small packet' it has to be easily openable. You've put sticky tape all over it. Look, do you want to take it away and repack it or do you want to send it at letter rate? If you do that, letter rate would be...six pounds sixty-five.
CUSTOMER: Mhm.

C This can be done in class in pairs, alone, or as homework.

ANSWERS
1 cash   cheque/check (*US spelling*)   2 assistant   counter/cash desk
3 help   looking   4 receipt   5 guarantee   6 trying   size   fit   7 match   suit
8 label   9 queue   10 bargain   sale/sales

D If you think this exercise will be difficult for your students, brainstorm a list of different kinds of shops on the board before starting the exercise. Point out the lack of department stores in the area, thus forcing students to find small specialist shops!

Note that the words *shop* and *store* tend to be interchangeable nowadays in British English, and that *store* is the more common word in American English.

SUGGESTED ANSWERS
2 butcher's – hardware store or ironmonger's or kitchen shop
3 electrical store – music shop or record shop
4 baker's – grocer's
5 *for both*: stationery shop or stationer's or newsagent's or newspaper shop or kiosk
6 *for both*: chemist's or pharmacy
7 souvenir shop or newspaper shop or kiosk – post office or the same shop you bought the card in!

E These activities focus on describing clothes, accessories and shoes (not faces and hair styles). Allow time for questions about different garments which the class may raise.

2.2   Abbreviations and numbers   WORD STUDY

Although this section looks short, it may take longer than you anticipate.

A This is just a tiny selection of thousands of abbreviations and acronyms that are in common use, as a glance at any newspaper will show.

The use of full stops in abbreviations in English is often optional – GMT is also sometimes written G.M.T., for example. If the abbreviation consists only of capital letters, the full stops are not necessary and often omitted in modern English. If the abbreviation is a short form of a longer word, the full stop is usually necessary. For example, dept. (department).

Point out that the best way to learn abbreviations is by noticing them when you come across them. In most cases, students will have to understand these abbreviations, but not use them – of the ones listed in the exercise only c/o, GMT and RSVP are normally used in their abbreviated form, the others can all be written in their full form if you prefer.

ANSWERS

c/o	care of	No.	Number
e.g.	for example	N, S, E & W	North, South, East and West
etc.	and so on/*et cetera*	PTO	Please turn over
FCE	First Certificate in English	Rd.	Road
GMT	Greenwich Mean Time	RSVP	Please reply (to this invitation)
incl.	including/inclusive	St.	Street
info.	information	VAT	Value Added Tax
intro.	introduction	VIP	Very important person
max.	maximum	vocab.	vocabulary
min.	minimum	Xmas	Christmas
misc.	miscellaneous	1st, 2nd & 3rd	first, second and third

B Speaking the numbers aloud could be done in pairs or groups of three, with students taking turns to say the numbers in the list. We wouldn't usually write numbers out in full except on cheques, but this is a good way of focusing on spelling and, paradoxically, exactly how they're said aloud.

ANSWERS (Spelling is important!)

a hundred and forty-four
a hundred and thirteen
two hundred and twenty-seven
eight hundred and fifty thousand
five point seven five
one thousand nine hundred and ninety-two

seven-eighths
one and a quarter plus two and two-thirds
  equals three point nine one six seven
four and three-quarters minus two and a
  half equals two point two five

C Perhaps begin by pointing out that, to the ear, there is not much difference between 14 and 40 or 17 and 70, for example.

Play the recording to the class. You will need to pause it frequently. Pause for a short time after each sentence while everyone is writing and pause for a longer time between each part of the exercise while everyone compares notes. At the end, play the whole tape again for everyone to double-check what they have written.

TRANSCRIPT AND ANSWERS *3 minutes*

My phone number is 5180477.
The number is 617930.
Call me on 0171 2258915.
The fax number is 044 1202 892671.
You can contact me on this number: 01473 993313.
Leave a message at this number: 879615.

The total population of the city is 5,180,477.
Twenty years ago there were only 617,930.
The number of inhabitants of the town is 40,515.
Ten years ago there were only 14,550.
Can you make a note of this number: 17,170,660.
The value of pi is three point one four two – 3.142.

The time's three forty-five pm – 3.45 pm.
It's ten to eleven – 10.50.
It's twenty-five to eight – 7.35.
It's just after a quarter past seven – 7.15.

The total price is forty-five pounds ninety-nine – £45.99.
You'll have to pay twelve dollars and fifteen cents – $12.15.
The cost is £140 plus VAT – £140 + VAT.
You still owe me ninety p – 90p (pence).

D As this is the first Communication Activity that the class have encountered, make it clear that the purpose of the activity is to encourage communication – students should **not** look at each other's information during these activities!

To prevent anyone cheating by peeping at the wrong information, divide the class into pairs and get them to decide who will be Student A and who will be Student B. Then tell all the Student As to look at Activity *1* on page 186 and all the Student Bs to look at Activity *29* on page 196.

If you have an odd number of students in the class, one 'pair' should work as a group of three, with two students working together and sharing their information. This can normally be done in all the pairwork activities.

Each student has a list of names, addresses and phone numbers which they must dictate to their partner – the partner has to write down all the information. Some of these names and numbers are easy, others are more difficult.

To start everyone off and show them what they'll have to do, demonstrate by dictating the first address in Activity *1* to the class, in this way:

'Ms Fiona Farquharson – that's capital M, small S, F I O N A F A R Q U H A R S O N: Ms Fiona Farquharson – 13 Gloucester Road – that's G L O U C E S T E R: 13 Gloucester Road – Kensington, London SW1 4PQ. Telephone number: 0171 819 3232 – all right?'

While the activity is going on, be prepared to answer any questions that the pairs may ask you. Point out that it doesn't matter if you can't pronounce some of the names – as long as you can spell them out to your partner and he or she can understand what you mean, you have succeeded in communicating. And communicating is what this activity is all about.

At the end, each partner looks at the other's information to check that it has been written down correctly.

To take this exercise further and make it more personal, the pairs can continue the activity by dictating their own names and addresses and the addresses and phone numbers of some of their friends or relations, real or imaginary.

2.3 Spelling and punctuation　　WRITING

 A This can be done by students alone or in pairs. Finding every one of the mistakes might take longer than you expect.

> **ANSWERS**
>
> 2 *My brother is <u>ninteen</u> years old.*　　nineteen
> 3 *One day he's <u>hopping</u> to go to <u>Amerika</u>.*　　hoping　America
> 4 *It was a <u>realy</u> <u>wonderfull</u> meal!*　　really　wonderful
> 5 *I <u>recieved</u> <u>you</u> letter this morning.*　　received　your
> 6 *He <u>want</u> to improve his <u>knoledge</u> of <u>english</u>.*　　wants　knowledge　English
> 7 *Concorde <u>flys</u> across the Atlantic in four <u>ours</u>.*　　flies　hours
> 8 *Some people find <u>speling</u> <u>especialy</u> <u>dificult</u>.*　　spelling　especially　difficult

B 1 Perhaps point out that there are different ways of referring to some of the punctuation marks.

> **ANSWERS**
>
> exclamation mark　question mark　full stop / period　comma　semi-colon　colon
> apostrophe　single quotes / single quotation marks　double quotes / double quotation marks
> hyphen　dash　brackets / parentheses

2 This activity can be done in pairs or alone.

> **CORRECTED VERSION** (Some variations are possible.)
>
> Harrods (or Harrod's) is London's most famous department store. You can buy almost anything there and it's one of the landmarks of London. People come to eat at its restaurants and look round its 214 departments, but not everyone comes to buy. Many of the people who go there just enjoy looking at the enormous range of goods on display – and at the other customers.

3 & 4 Make sure the pairs add their own punctuation before they look at the corrected version of the paragraph in Activity *54*.

NOTE

Before doing the exercises in 2.4, remind the class to read the GRAMMAR REFERENCE section on Questions and question tags on pages 183–184 at home beforehand.

2.4 Questions and question tags   GRAMMAR REVIEW

(A) 1 This is a warm-up exercise, but it may bring to light some basic problems which need dealing with. There are no 'correct answers'.

2 Looking at each other's sentences and spotting the mistakes (if any) is something that encourages some students to be more careful (and less inaccurate) in the first place.

(B) 1 The main problem with polite, indirect questions is the word order.

> **ANSWERS** (Some variations are possible.)
>
> 2 When *were you born*?   Could you tell me *when you were born*?
> 3 Where *were you born*?   Can you also tell me *where you were born*?
> 4 Where *do you live*?   I'd like to know *where you live*.
> 5 What *is your phone number*?   Would you mind telling me *your phone number*?
> 6 Who *is the British prime minister*?   Do you know *who the British prime minister is*?
> 7 How many *people live in the UK*?   Do you happen to know *how many people live in the UK*?

2 👥 Student A looks at Activity *13*, Student B (and C in a group of three) at *40*. Each has a picture showing fashions in different decades. The idea is for the students to ask each other questions to find out more about their partner's picture.

(C) 1 📼 Be ready to pause the recording between each example, while the students make up their minds. Make sure everyone concentrates on the first speaker's intonation – not the second speaker's responses.

> **ANSWERS**
>
> 3 ✔ 4 ? 5 ? 6 ✔ 7 ? 8 ✔ 9 ✔ 10 ?

TRANSCRIPTS *2 minutes*

1   WOMAN: Today's the fourteenth, isn't it?
    NARRATOR: She's unsure so put a question mark.
    MAN: No, it's the fifteenth.

2   WOMAN: Today's Monday, isn't it?
    NARRATOR: She's fairly sure so put a tick.
    MAN: Yes, Monday the fifteenth.

3	WOMAN: The capital of the USA is Washington, isn't it? MAN: Yes, that's right.	*sounds sure*
4	WOMAN: And the capital of Canada is Toronto, isn't it? MAN: No, it's Ottawa.	*sounds unsure*
5	WOMAN: There are five oceans, aren't there? MAN: Five? Yes, I think so.	*sounds unsure*
6	WOMAN: And the biggest are the Pacific and the Atlantic, aren't they? MAN: Yes, and of the two the Pacific is bigger.	*sounds sure*
7	WOMAN: Most people in Canada speak English, don't they? MAN: Yes, but there are lots who speak French.	*sounds unsure*
8	WOMAN: Most people in Australia speak English, don't they? MAN: Yes, I think so. It's the official language, anyway.	*sounds sure*
9	WOMAN: Marilyn Monroe was in *Some Like It Hot*, wasn't she? MAN: Yes – great film!	*sounds sure*
10	WOMAN: And it was directed by Michael Curtiz, wasn't it? MAN: No, no, you're thinking of *Casablanca. Some Like It Hot* was directed by Billy Wilder. WOMAN: Oh, yes, that's right.	*sounds unsure*

2 This exercise can be done alone or in pairs. Some of these are difficult!

> **ANSWERS**
> **3** can't it? **4** should they? **5** is there? **6** wasn't it? **7** mustn't they?
> **8** didn't they? **9** haven't we? **10** shall we?

3 & 4 This is open-ended free practice. Follow the instructions in the Student's Book, and make sure you allow enough time to do justice to it. Maybe postpone it till the next lesson if time is short today.

NOTE
Before the next lesson, ask the students to cut some interesting advertisements out of magazines or newspapers and bring them to class to discuss in the last part of 2.5. And cut out some of your own to lend to students who forget to bring any!

2.5 Advertisements and commercials SPEAKING AND LISTENING

Begin by finding out if everyone has remembered to bring some interesting advertisements to class. If several people have forgotten, it's probably best to postpone step D to the next lesson. However, you may have cut out enough of your own to hand out.

A This is an extract from an American mail order catalogue.

B Student A looks at Activity *4*, the other at *32*. They have to describe an advertisement to their partner, who should ask questions to find out more about the product.

C It's not necessary to understand every word – indeed it's unlikely that your students will. During the second playing, pause the recording between each commercial to allow time for writing (and maybe comparing answers). Once the answers have been checked, play the recording again so that the students can **enjoy** them without having to worry about a task.

> **ANSWERS**
> **1** video recorder   stupid/ignorant   Japan   washing machine   2022   understand
> **2** beer   beautiful girl   slips away
> **3** film/movie   mother   elderly people   102
> **4** colour film   hear   symphony

TRANSCRIPTS   *4 minutes 30 seconds*

1 CUSTOMER: Morning, squire.
SALES ASSISTANT: Morning, sir.
CUSTOMER: I'd like a videocaster please.
SALES ASSISTANT: A video recorder, any one in particular?
CUSTOMER: Well, I'd like it to have some specifications, and functions, I must have some functions.
SALES ASSISTANT: I see. Did you have any model in mind?
CUSTOMER: Well a friend mentioned the Harikirikabukikasoonikawhatchamacallit. You know, the Japanese one, the 2000. Because I'm very technically-minded, you see.
SALES ASSISTANT: I can see that, sir.
CUSTOMER: So I want one with all the bits on it. All the Japanese bits. You know, the 2000.
SALES ASSISTANT: What system?
CUSTOMER: Er...w...well, electrical, I think. Because I'd like to be able to plug it into the television, you see. I...I've got a Japanese television.
SALES ASSISTANT: Have you?
CUSTOMER: Yeah, I thought you'd be impressed, the 2000, the Hokikoki 2000.
SALES ASSISTANT: Well sir, there is this model.
CUSTOMER: That looks smart, yeah.
SALES ASSISTANT: Eight hours per cassette, all the functions that the others have, and I know this will be of interest: a lot of scientific research has gone into making it easy to operate, even by a complete idiot like you.
CUSTOMER: Pardon?
SALES ASSISTANT: It's a Philips.
CUSTOMER: Doesn't sound very Japanese.
SALES ASSISTANT: No, Firrips, Firrips – it's a Firrips.
CUSTOMER: Oh it is a 2000 is it?
SALES ASSISTANT: No, in fact it's the 2022.
CUSTOMER: Mm...no no it hasn't got enough knobs on it...What's that one over there?
SALES ASSISTANT: That's a washing machine.
CUSTOMER: Yeah, what...sort of Japanese?
VOICEOVER: The VR 2022: video you can understand. From Firrips.

2 STORYTELLER: (*Irish music*) It was a Saturday and Joe was in the bar with Eddie. But Eddie wasn't necessarily with Joe. He was staring deeply into his glass of Beamish. He fancied he saw the girl with the dark ebony-coloured hair, and the moonlight skin, and the wild, wild eyes. But in no time at all, like his Beamish, she was gone. 'She was beautiful,' said Eddie quietly. 'Buy me a Beamish then,' said Joe, 'so I can have a look too.'
VOICEOVER: Beamish Stout – just slips away.

3 JOHN CLEESE'S MOTHER: Into this?...Hello, my name is Muriel Cleese and I live in a very nice elderly people's home in Weston-super-Mare. My son John is in a new Monty Python film *Life of Brian*. I do hope you'll go and see it because he's on a percentage and he said if it doesn't do well he won't be able to keep me on in the home any longer. So see *The Life of Brian* now because I'm 102 years old and if I have to leave here it'll kill me...Haha.
VOICEOVER: If you want to help Mrs Cleese, please go and see *Monty Python's Life of Brian*. Exclusive presentation at the Plaza from Thursday November 8. Certificate AA.
MRS CLEESE: Haha . . .

4 MAN FROM NEWCASTLE: To prove to you just how clear and vibrant Kodacolor Gold's colours are, I'm going to conduct a little exercise. Imagine for a moment that you can actually hear colour. Now you'll have to concentrate, mind.
Right, this is the sound for blue: (*silence*). I said you'll have to concentrate: (*harps*). Right, thank you. And this is the sound for green: (*violins*). That's it and now let's hear it for yellow: (*flute*). And finally – (*trumpets*) er...wait for it lads, red: (*trumpets*).
Right, I'm now showing you a photograph of a magnificent sunset over the Grand Canyon, as taken on Kodacolor Gold: (*full orchestra playing The Big Country*). And now I'm going to show you that very same sunset taken on ordinary film: (*kazoo*). Well, I suppose it had a certain raw charm.
VOICEOVER: Kodacolor Gold, for a symphony of colour we have the clicknology.

D **1** Remind everyone that in Unit 1 we looked at ways of introducing opinions. Now we're looking at ways of agreeing with someone's opinion and disagreeing **politely**.

If necessary, point out that saying to someone 'You're wrong!' or 'That isn't true!' can be very rude, and may upset someone or make them angry, and turn the discussion into an argument.

Brainstorm some more expressions. For example:

I quite agree.   *I'm not sure that I entirely agree.*
Absolutely!   *I see. But don't you agree that . . .*
I think you're absolutely right there.   *Isn't it also true to say that . . .*

Encourage everyone to **experiment** with different expressions in the discussion that follows.

2 For the discussion students will need their magazine cuttings. You may have to lend out a few to groups who haven't got any – or postpone this discussion to the next lesson, perhaps.

2.6 Position and direction   PREPOSITIONS

To start the ball rolling, if you don't mind putting on a little performance, you could get everyone to imagine that you're pointing at a fly or mosquito as it buzzes round the room, alighting in various positions – but you'd have to do the sound effects yourself. Ask the class to say exactly where it is each time it stops.

Further practice can be given by taking into class a handful of paperclips and putting them in different parts of the room in view of the students. Members of the class then have to say **where** each one is, but they are **not** allowed to point at it or pick it up.

A **1** Make sure there are no problems with this easy part.

2 Tell the students where to add letters **G** to **L**, some of which are **outside** the box.

G is inside the top left-hand corner of the box.
H is standing on top of the box, about a quarter of the way from the left.
I is right in the very centre of the box.
J is to the right of the bottom right-hand corner of the box.
K is below the bottom left-hand corner of the box.
L is just beside the 's' at the end of 'Prepositions' in the title of this section.

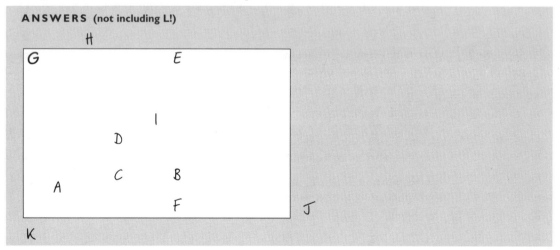

3 Before doing this part, your students may need a bit of help with phrases such as: *just a little, slightly, about a third of the way from, almost touching,* etc. Go round the class while they're doing this and offer help when requested. At the end ask for questions.

B 🎧 Student A looks at Activity **7** and B (and C in a group of three) looks at **35**. One partner has a drawing of a fox, the other a drawing of a rabbit superimposed on the grid. The idea is to explain the **route** that a pencil should take on the grid to draw the same picture.

Make sure that no one peeps at the other's picture and that they explain the route **without** identifying what the drawing is supposed to represent.

Your students may need some help with the vocabulary required to describe different kinds of lines such as: *horizontal, vertical, diagonal, curved, parallel, straight.*

(This activity also practises saying letters and numbers aloud – listen out for students who confuse, for example, A and R, I and E, or G and J.)

2.7 Department stores READING

A This is a first reading task, giving students a purpose to read the texts. If they find it hard to think of any questions, brainstorm questions as a class and write them on the board. Some possible questions that your students might come up with are:

'Which is the cheapest store?'
'Which is the biggest store?'
'What is each big store most famous for?'

B Searching for specific information is the kind of task that students will have to do in the exam. (Harrods is called Harrod's in this text.)

ANSWERS

1 Macy's in New York
2 Harrod's, Harvey Nichols, Fortnum and Mason, and Marks and Spencer in London – and Bloomingdale's in New York
3 Bergdorf Goodman in New York
4 Saks Fifth Avenue, Bloomingdale's and Macy's in New York
5 Bloomingdale's in New York
6 Bloomingdale's in New York (and Harrod's in London?)
7 Most stores in New York
8 All the stores in New York
9 Marks and Spencer

C This group discussion encourages students to use some of the vocabulary they've encountered in this unit.

2.8 Describing a place WRITING

A The questions will help students to prepare for the writing task. Insist that they make notes of the main points that come up in their discussion – you may have to impose a couple of 'breaks' in the discussion to allow time for them to do this.

B Make sure everyone understands exactly what to do. The word limit reflects what is required in the exam, and also forces students to **select** the most relevant and interesting points. The 'target reader' is clearly specified and he or she should be borne in mind when writing (as in the exam).

It will be interesting to see what the effect of careful preparation has on the quality of your students' work compared with the first unprepared written work they did in Unit 1. Look for improvements by comparing the two compositions (if you made photocopies, as suggested).

Remember that encouraging comments (as well as corrections) will help students to maintain their motivation so that they strive to do even better next time.

Friends and relations

3

3.1 Relationships   VOCABULARY AND SPEAKING

The *Voices* video sequence *A wedding* deals with other aspects of this topic.

A In the warm-up discussion, encourage everyone to note down any useful words that come up. Here are some ideas that might come up in the discussion.

1 This looks like a married couple who are doing some paperwork together in their kitchen. The husband's using a computer and his wife's showing him a letter. They both look very pleased. She might be saying, 'Hey, just read this,' and he might be saying, 'Oh, yes, that's great!'

2 The mother and father are having a row while the children are trying not to hear. The mother looks very upset and the father is being aggressive. He might be saying, 'Look, I've had just about enough of this,' and she might be thinking, 'I wish this wasn't happening in front of the children.'

3 The two women look like very good friends (or they might be sisters) who are having coffee together. They're sharing a joke together. One might be saying, 'Listen, you'll never believe this but . . .' and the other might be saying, 'Oh, no, that's amazing!'

4 The little boy and girl are helping their grandparents with some gardening. They seem to be having a really nice time together and they look as if they all love each other a lot. The little girl might be saying, 'How much water should I pour on these plants, Grandad?'

B These gap-filling exercises are similar in style to Part 1 in the Use of English paper. The students could do these alone, and then compare answers in pairs – or do them in pairs and then check their answers as a class. Remind everyone to look at the wrong answers to make sure they know the meanings of the useful words there too.

> **ANSWERS**
> **1** anxious   **2** lonely   **3** on   **4** make   **5** out   **6** sight   **7** engaged   **8** wedding
> **9** got married   **10** anniversary   **11** best man   **12** relations   **13** guests
> **14** reception

C 1 Not all cultures may be familiar with the concept of a family tree. Go round the class while the pairs are doing the exercise, offering any help and suggestions. Dictionaries could be used for this.

> **ANSWERS**
> **2** nephew   **3** grandson   **4** second wife   **5** ex-wife   **6** brother-in-law
> **7** mother-in-law   **8** aunt   **9** (first) cousin   **10** great-grandmother

2 & 3 Students who have lost a parent, or whose families have split up, might find this activity upsetting. It could be skipped in such cases.

D 1   Play the recording twice, allowing everyone time in between to decide what they need to listen out for next time and, perhaps, to compare their answers with a partner.

> **ANSWERS**
> **1** Sarah   **2** Charles   **3** Sarah   **4** Anna   **5** Charles   **6** Lenny   **7** No one
> **8** No one   **9** Lenny

1 CHARLES: Um...my closest friend is...um...someone I've known since I was a baby. Um...our parents were friends and we've always lived in the same sort of neighbourhood. O...originally we lived...er...next door to each other, but now we live exactly three blocks apart. So...er...anyway, we see each other every day, usually in the evening. Um...we have the same interests.

I...I mean, to be friends you have to share the...the same interests, don't you? And you have to be tolerant of each other's moods. I...I think being friends means making allowances for the other person's faults.

2 SARAH: Well, I've got...um...two close friends but they don't get on with each other, which means of course that I have to see them separately! Um...well, sometimes, as you can imagine, that...that's a problem. For example, if there's...um...a new film that I want to see, I have to decide which one I want to go with. And sometimes that means missing the film altogether so...um...neither of them gets upset. It sounds terrible, doesn't it? But, well actually, it's all right most of the time.

I think a friend is someone you can have fun with, um...someone who finds the same things funny, and someone who doesn't take you too seriously a...and stops you taking yourself too seriously.

3 LENNY: Well, I don't have any really close friends, I suppose. I mean, I know a lot of people, you know: people I study with, people I play sports with, um...people I've known since I was a kid. But, you know, no one I could call my 'best friends'.

OTHERS: Oh, that's sad.

LENNY: I mean, well, it isn't really, you see. Friendship isn't really important for me. I think you have to get on well with everyone you come into contact with. I mean, being really close to someone can be...can be dangerous in a way...because, well, you come to rely on them too much and it excludes other people from your...from your social circle. You become sort of unfriendly.

4 ANNA: Well, believe it or not, my best friend is my sister. Um...she's two years older than me and she works in an insurance office. Um...we spend loads of time together. Er...the...it's funny actually because we used to really hate each other when we were younger. Yeah. And then...um...ooh, about three years ago she had a massive row with her...with her boyfriend at the time and...er...she came and actually she talked to me about how she felt for the first time really. And...um...since then, well, we've been really really close.

Um...the most important thing about friends for me is being able to share secrets. Um...and, you know, and to be able to tell each other your problems and share your...your worries, and things like that. And...er...you know, to help each other out.

2 This follow-up discussion gives everyone a chance to use some of the new vocabulary they've encountered in this section. At the end, ask everyone to report on their answers to the last question and, if necessary, suggest any vocabulary items they're searching for.

3.2 The past – 1   GRAMMAR REVIEW

This section covers the main uses of the past, the past continuous, the present perfect and *used to*. 4.6 in the next unit covers the past perfect, the present perfect continuous and some aspects of reported speech. There's more on reported speech in 16.5.

If you anticipate that these points are going to be quite difficult for your students, they should read through the GRAMMAR REFERENCE section on Past tenses on pages 180–181 before tackling the exercises. Alternatively, if they're likely to find the exercises fairly easy, they could refer to it as necessary while doing the exercises.

 This can be done as homework before the lesson and discussed in class, or done in pairs in class, or done alone in class and then discussed in pairs.

ANSWERS

2 *The weather <u>were</u> lovely yesterday and the sun <u>has been shining</u> all day.*	was shone
3 *I <u>have gone</u> to the zoo last weekend.*	went
4 *Where <u>you went</u> on holiday last year?*	did you go
5 *They got married two years ago.*	✔
6 *She <u>has been</u> born in 1980.*	was
7 *Our family <u>was used to living</u> in a smaller flat when I <u>am</u> younger.*	used to live was
8 *Our broken window still <u>wasn't</u> mended yet.*	hasn't been
9 *I've been here for two years but I've only made a few friends.*	✔
10 *The rain started <u>during</u> they <u>played</u> tennis.*	while were playing

B 1 This is one of those 'urban myths' which happened to a friend of a friend. The people who tell these stories swear that they're true, but they never really happened.

SUGGESTED ANSWERS

2 noticed   **3** said   **4** was looking   **5** came   **6** said   **7** said   **8** thought
9 offered   **10** were   **11** went   **12** took   **13** saw   **14** looked   **15** told   **16** could
17 had grown   **18** asked   **19** was going

2 The actual ending was this, but your students may have better ideas. Give them time to write down the words **they** think the woman said:

'My husband and I have separated. He's been having an affair with his secretary. Before he went off on holiday with his new love, he asked me to sell all his belongings and give him whatever money I got for them. So that's just what I'm doing!'

C In the exam this kind of exercise requires two to five words, but some of the sentences in this exercise need more.

ANSWERS

2 We *used to have* a dog.
3 *Have you been here* before?
4 We'*ve studied two* units in this book so far.
5 While you *were away we haven't done* much work.
6 What *were you doing when I phoned you* last night?
7 Although they *had a row yesterday they haven't* stopped being friends.

There's no free practice in this section because the next section provides free practice in using past tenses.

3.3 **Telling stories**   **LISTENING AND SPEAKING**

In the exam, students don't have to tell a story in the Speaking paper. But this **is** a useful skill they'll need in real life, and it's also preparation for **writing** a story which we return to in 3.7 (a skill required for the Writing paper).

A 1 This is a fairly straightforward listening exercise. Its main purpose is to introduce the theme of telling stories, which students themselves will have to do in B and C, and in writing in 3.7.

2 Everyone listens to the two stories and agrees on the correct sequence of pictures (which is not too difficult!).

ANSWERS
The correct sequence of pictures is:
First story: f d b
Second story: a e c

TRANSCRIPTS *4 minutes*

1 MAN: Well, this friend of my brother's called Alex...um...he was a medical student. He was getting married the next day and he was having a night out, you know, with his friends – his last night of freedom before the big day. Well, anyway, he got quite drunk and fell asleep before the end of the party. So his friends, supposed friends, took him back to the hospital and put both his legs in plaster, from hip to toe.

WOMAN: What? Goodness!

MAN: I know, so when he...when he woke up the next morning he was in bed at home, and his best man was there and so he says, 'Well, look, you're very lucky: you had a bad fall last night at the party and, you know, it was a good thing we were there because we were able to get you to the hospital.'

WOMAN: So what happened?

MAN: Well, so he went through the whole wedding ceremony at the church on crutches and then there was the reception, and he was still on the crutches. And it...it was awful for him –

WOMAN: What did his wife say?

MAN: I don't know, I guess she just accepted it like everybody else I suppose. So, I mean, everybody else thought it was hilarious. So, now his...his friends were then going to tell him the truth, but they decided that they were going to wait till he and his new wife got to the hotel in Spain where they were going to spend their honeymoon.

WOMAN: Oh, that's wicked.

MAN: Well, yeah, it gets worse actually. Now, Alex suspected that his friends would play some trick on him – so he gave them the phone number of a hotel in Spain, whereas in fact they were going to a hotel in Greece for their honeymoon. So his friends couldn't contact him till he got back from honeymoon two weeks later. So he spent the entire honeymoon –

WOMAN: Ohh! So he spent the whole honeymoon . . .

2 WOMAN: This friend of my brother called Andrew was going to spend Christmas with his girlfriend and her parents. Now, he hadn't met her parents before, so he was really nervous, like...you can imagine.

Anyway, he was going to drive down to their house from the north and the plan was that he was going to arrive very late on the Christmas Eve. So his girlfriend said that she'd leave the back door open so he wouldn't have to ring the bell and wake people up and all that sort of stuff.

Anyway, what happened was he arrived at the house at about two o'clock, two o'clock in the morning. The street lights were off but he worked out which house was number 31 Forest Avenue, because it was too dark to read the numbers on the front door but it was next to number 29 so he knew of course that it was going to be the right one. OK?

MAN: Right, right. So then what happened?

WOMAN: I'll tell you: what happened, he went round the back, but the door was locked. And because he didn't want to wake them up he saw there was a window open. Now he was just about to...he was just able, you know, to climb in and open the back door to get his things, so that's what he did. Well, after that drive he was quite hungry and everything, so he helped himself to some food from the fridge, like you would –

MAN: Yeah.

WOMAN: and he had a can of beer, a bit of drink, all the rest of it, and then of course he crept upstairs, not wanting to wake anyone up. And the first door he opened was the guest room, OK? So, naturally enough, he got undressed and went to sleep.

Well, the next morning, Christmas Day, he woke up quite late. He was late the night before –

MAN: Yeah.

WOMAN: so he woke up late Christmas morning, went downstairs in his dressing gown to say hello to his girlfriend, meet the parents, have breakfast and give them all their presents. OK? Now listen to this: he opens the kitchen door, he's got his arms full of wrapped presents, calls out: 'Merry Christmas, everyone!' But there was no one in that room that he knew. There was a man and a woman and two little kids sitting at the kitchen table staring at him with their mouths open wide in astonishment.

MAN: So what had happened?

WOMAN: Well, he was at number 27 Forest Avenue!

MAN: Oh no, haha, that's brilliant!

3 🔲 Play the tape again and ask the students to concentrate on some of the story-telling techniques that are used by the speakers. The stories can be treated as 'models' for what the students will be doing in B and C. They should also notice how the speakers involve the listener in each story.

The groups discuss the questions. After the discussion, ask each group to report to the class on what they talked about.

B 1 Draw everyone's attention to the questions that a listener might ask and the reactions that might be shown. Remind everyone that telling a story normally happens as part of a conversation, not a monologue.

2 Maybe change the pairs so that the partners are different from the ones in B1. The students should be concentrating on encouraging and prompting each time.

C Students A and B look at Activity **24**, while C and D (and Student E in groups of five) look at **31**. The pairs prepare their story before splitting up and forming pairs with a student who has prepared a different story. Make sure no one looks at the other's pictures so as to preserve the 'information gap'.

At the end, ask the students for questions and comments. Give them any feedback you think necessary after hearing them telling their stories.

3.4 | Special occasions   READING

A This is a short warm-up discussion.

In some countries, name days are celebrated instead of/as well as birthdays (i.e. everyone called Thomas receives gifts on St Thomas's Day and everyone called Catherine receives gifts on St Catherine's Day). And the sending of greetings cards is still uncommon in some countries – though probably on the increase everywhere.

B 1 These questions give students a purpose to read the text for the first time. They should try to do this task without worrying about unfamiliar words in the text.

> **ANSWERS**
> 1 special days like birthdays, anniversaries, Mother's Day
> 2 44%
> 3 10% of 7.3 billion (730 million)
> 4 It's a matter of opinion, but the one about the untidy room is certainly very strange!

2 These questions encourage students to look for details, appreciate the 'tone' of the text, and examine the text for 'evidence' to support their answers.

> **ANSWERS**
> True: (1) 2 4 5 7
> False: 3 6 8
>
> The relevant phrases in the text are:
> 1 Halloween (October 31st) *in paragraph 1*
> 2 people send fewer cards than at any other time of the year *in paragraph 1*
> 3 (*they sell cards so obviously they don't want people to send letters*)
> 4 a market that threatens to stop growing for the first time since 1945 *in paragraph 2*
> 5 death-of-a-pet card *in paragraph 3*
> 6 (*not mentioned in the text*)
> 7 Others address almost every imaginable calamity *in paragraph 4*
> 8 (*it's ironic*)

3 This is where we look at the vocabulary in the text. This exercise encourages students to guess the meaning of words from the context, but maybe not all of these words are worth remembering. (*Scribe* is less useful than *stay in touch*, for example.)

Encourage everyone to highlight other words in the text which they think will be useful, and which they want to remember.

> **ANSWERS**
> ¶1 reviving
> ¶2 illiterate scribes sentiments
> ¶3 cope (with)
> ¶4 keep in touch calamity
> ¶5 account for saturation

C Here are some questions that might be asked about the photo:

- How old do you think the boy is?
- What presents did he get for his birthday?
- Why do you think he's got his eyes closed?
- What do you think he's wishing for?

3.5 Using prefixes – 1 WORD STUDY

The other sections on prefixes are 4.4 and 5.7.

This word-formation section can be prepared as homework or done by students working together in pairs. You may need to explain some of the meanings, but not unless people are confused – they should be encouraged to work things out for themselves and use dictionaries.

over = too much
under = not enough
re = again
post = after
pre = before

A **ANSWERS**

1 rearranged = to arrange something again, in a different way or in different places
2 overreact = to react in an excessive, unreasonable way
3 underestimate = to fail to guess the real amount, thinking it less than it really is
4 pre-holiday = before a holiday   post-holiday = after it

B Some of the root words in this exercise have been used more than once.

Note that the use of hyphens is slightly problematic and in some cases the words can be written as one word or with a hyphen. Perhaps the best guidance is to say 'if in doubt, use a hyphen'.

Ask everyone to write sentences using the 'new' words in the list in B. (The 'new' words are ones that students haven't come across before which they think will be useful and are worth learning.)

SUGGESTED ANSWERS

re	reappear rebuild reconsider remarry reprint reread
pre-	pre-dinner pre-lunch pre-prepared pre-war
post-	post-dinner post-lunch post-war
over	overcharge overcrowded overexcited overprepared (overpay)
under	undercharge underprepared (underpay)

C **ANSWERS**

2 rebuilt   3 pre-exam   over-confident   4 under-staffed   5 underpaid   undervalued
6 overeat   overweight   7 rewrote   8 overslept

3.6 Looking and seeing VERBS AND IDIOMS

A This section, which can be done by students working in pairs or as homework, deals with some common synonyms of *look* and *see*. Point out that, as we are dealing with synonyms, several variations are possible. If it is done as homework, make sure plenty of time is allowed in class to discuss the problems or queries that arise.

B **1 & 2** The missing phrases (given in Activity *33*) are:

1 looked up to   **2** look out for   **3** looked through   **4** looking forward to
5 look after

3 With this kind of exercise, students should be encouraged to do the ones they know first before trying the ones that are more puzzling. The use of English-to-English dictionaries is recommended here.

Point out that many phrasal verbs can be replaced with equivalent 'normal verbs' – as this exercise shows. Quite often the phrasal verb is more **informal** than its 'normal' formal equivalent.

The difference between 'particles' (e.g. *out* in *look out*) and 'prepositions' (e.g. *after* in *look after*) should only be discussed with students who have very analytical minds! Some of the verbs we have described as 'phrasal verbs' may also be defined as 'prepositional verbs' or 'phrasal-prepositional' verbs! Refer students to the GRAMMAR REFERENCE section on page 181, if necessary.

3.7 **Writing a story**   WRITING

We considered the role of the listener in 3.3, now we consider the **reader** of a narrative. Keeping your reader interested is essential if you're writing a narrative.

NOTE
The instructions to look at Activities *53* and *41* are **not** given in the Student's Book, to prevent students from taking a short cut to the improved versions!

A Brainstorm the first improvement with the class making suggestions. For example, this might be a good second sentence: 'We were on our way home after a marvellous evening out with some friends.'

When everyone has spent enough time making improvements, tell them to look at Activity *53*, where they will see an improved version of the story as well as this analysis of the original version's shortcomings:

The original version of the story contains so little detail that it's impossible to get interested. It's supposed to be a personal story, so there should be personal details to explain why the night was unforgettable. The exact times and distances are irrelevant and distracting.

They then have to highlight the main changes that have been made in the improved version in Activity *53*. There are no 'correct answers' to this as it is a straightforward task designed to draw students' attention to the language used.

Ask if anyone can suggest any further changes which might make the improved version even better.

B 1 Perhaps point out that the plot of a film or book is generally told in the simple present tense, whereas a true story or a fictional short story would usually be told using past tenses.

2 When everyone has spent enough time comparing their improvements, tell them to look at Activity *41*, where they will see an improved version of the story, together with this analysis of the original version's shortcomings:

> The original version of the story uses the past tense, which makes it sound like a true story. But of course it's the plot of a film. The lack of detail also makes it very dull.

The improved version in Activity *41* contains extra information, which has to be highlighted – this is to draw attention to the details. Again there are no 'correct answers'.
Ask if anyone can suggest any further changes which might make the improved version even better.

C 1 Students should write their own composition as homework, but it may be best to discuss the kind of things they could write about in a class discussion beforehand. (In the exam, the target reader and the purpose for writing would be more clearly specified than here.)

2 Before collecting the stories for marking, get everyone to read one or two other people's stories and comment on them.

There is another story-writing task in 4.9.

Time off

4

The *Voices* video sequence *Get in shape! – A morning at a leisure centre* deals with good health and fitness. But you may prefer to link this sequence with Unit 8 *Looking after yourself,* rather than with this unit.

This unit focuses on what people do in their leisure time (including watching and playing sports). Unit 8 focuses on health and fitness (including the health benefits of different sports).

4.1 ## What do you enjoy?   **VOCABULARY**

This is a warm-up discussion, giving students a chance to explore the vocabulary they already know on the topic of this unit.

Here is some useful vocabulary that may come up, or which students may ask about:

competitive   diving   energetic   fresh air   game   match   mountain bike   muddy   soccer/football surf   swimming   underwater   windsurfing

NOTE
The word *hobby* is sometimes over-used by learners. Many activities which we do in our spare time aren't hobbies but *interests* or *sports*.

Maybe spend a little time writing up the hobbies, games and sports that the members of the class are interested in or take part in. Perhaps make four lists:

HOBBIES	*INDOOR GAMES*	*SPORTS*	*ENTERTAINMENT*
stamp-collecting	*bridge*	*basketball*	*watching TV*
painting	*chess*	*athletics*	*cinema*

(And so on depending on your students' real interests.)

Keep the list on the board in case you want to do Extra Activity 2 suggested at the end.

B Some of the sentences have questions within them – encourage your students to answer them.

ANSWERS
1 collecting   taking   **2** active   relax   **3** professional   amateur   **4** team   support
5 match   referee   whistle   cheer   crowd   draw   score   **6** court   course
7 cup   prize   **8** lottery   charity (*or* children!)

C 1 A small translating dictionary probably won't be much use for students who choose more unusual sports.

Perhaps arrange the class into similar interest groups (tennis players together, footballers together, etc.). If the members of the class are quite young, the boys and girls could be in separate groups, perhaps.

2 Obviously not everyone is interested in sports, but those that are should be given a chance to talk about their favourites, even if the non-sporty people are slightly bored for a while. Let them ask the **questions** about the sports and encourage the sporty types to explain **why** they enjoy the sports they do. Alternatively, try one of these extra activities:

EXTRA ACTIVITY 1
Give a slip of paper to each student; they have to speak about why they enjoy/don't enjoy the sport on the paper: hang-gliding, football, tennis, etc.

EXTRA ACTIVITY 2

Students might be asked to grade all the sports, entertainments and games that you wrote on the board earlier. They could put them in order according to how much they like each one or give a number out of five according to whether, in their opinion, the item is extremely interesting/exciting (5) or extremely dull/boring (1).

Ask them this question: 'What do you particularly enjoy or hate about each sport that has been mentioned?'

 4.2 **Leisure activities** **READING**

 A Trying to guess the answers will help everyone to apply their previous knowledge to the theme of the text. Finding the answers in the text gives a purpose to reading the text – normally people only read a particular magazine article out of choice, not because someone has told them to.

ANSWERS

1 walking   **2** swimming   **3** health and fitness clubs   **4** 1,500

B

ANSWERS

swimming	22 million	running and jogging	4 million
snooker and pool	12 million	football	4 million
cycling	9 million	weight training	5 million
keep fit, aerobics and yoga	10 million	badminton	5 million
darts	7 million	squash	3 million
golf	4 million	tennis	4 million
bowling	6 million	fishing	3 million

C This is preparation for the Writing section coming up in 4.9.

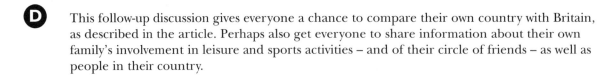

SUGGESTED PARAGRAPHS (Some variations are possible.)

The fitness boom of the eighties led to a big rise in the numbers of people participating in sports. To cater for this boom and provide the up-to-date facilities people want, over 1,500 private health and fitness clubs and the same number of public leisure centres have been built during the past twenty years.

These modern centres, with their swimming pools (22 million people went swimming last year), squash courts, gyms and indoor courts for tennis and other sports, are competing with clubs, pubs and cinemas as places for people to go to spend their leisure time – and their money. Now practically every town has a leisure pool, often with a wave machine, water slides and tropical plants. Families can even spend their holidays at huge indoor water parks, where they can play or relax all day long in warmth and comfort without worrying about the weather outside.

But this may not be helping us to get fitter: we may be becoming a nation of splashers, but not a nation of swimmers. The big question fitness experts are asking is: should sport be taken seriously or should it just be fun?

D This follow-up discussion gives everyone a chance to compare their own country with Britain, as described in the article. Perhaps also get everyone to share information about their own family's involvement in leisure and sports activities – and of their circle of friends – as well as people in their country.

4.3 Sorry to interrupt, but . . .   SPEAKING

A This is similar to one of the types of task your students will encounter in the exam. They may need to hear the recording twice to be sure of all the matches.

> **ANSWERS**
> 1 Amanda   2 Debbie   3 Tony   4 Tony   5 Debbie   6 No one   7 Amanda
> 8 Tony   9 No one

B Play the recording again. The expressions that are used are underlined in the transcript below. Allow time for practising saying the expressions politely and perhaps demonstrate how they should **not** be spoken by saying *Just a minute!* and *Sorry to interrupt* in a rude, peremptory tone.

Note that interrupting also requires eye contact. A would-be speaker has to catch the speaker's eye and receive a signal that he or she may interrupt and have the floor for a few moments.

TRANSCRIPT AND ANSWERS   *3 minutes 10 seconds*
(The expressions used to interrupt are underlined.)

AMANDA: . . . It really really turns me on, I really, really enjoy it.

TONY: Amanda, really!

AMANDA: Well, I know in the long run I don't make a profit but it's great to have something to get really excited about! I enter all the competitions, and my favourite sport is horse racing. I just enjoy the betting and it's so exciting: you've got your own horse there and you're shouting for it – you just want to win.

TONY: <u>Just...just a minute</u>, Amanda.

AMANDA: Yeah.

TONY: I must say...I have to say I am shocked. Right, no, I think gambling is...I think gambling is terrible. No, it's a waste of money and what's worse it's...I mean, it's like a drug. The more you lose the more you want to play a...again and win. I mean, you know, and what about those fruit machines you find in the bars? They're terrible, they're the worst of all. You see people feeding money into them, all in the hope of winning the jackpot. I mean, it's pathetic. I mean, what about...and the people...and I must say –

DEBBIE: <u>Could I say something?</u>

TONY: Yes, Debbie.

DEBBIE: I think you're taking things far too seriously. It's only a bit of fun for most people. Nobody loses anything by it – if people want to spend their money, it's up to them. They may choose to spend their spare cash on drink, or food, or books, or whatever they want to –

TONY: <u>Yes, but</u> if they spend it on gambling it's just money down the drain. Look, the people who bet and, yeah, it's mostly men, right, who are gamblers, you know? Right, they're the ones who can least afford it. And...er...the ones who suffer are...are probably the wives and the children, not them –

AMANDA: Do you know, Tony, what you sound like? You sound like an ex-gambler who has seen the light. Like one of those ex-smokers who's given up smoking and they're passionate about anti-smoking.

TONY: <u>Er...</u> no no no no no no no. I just think it's wrong. It's this association of sport and gambling that I think is just so terrible –

AMANDA: You're a puritan!

TONY: No, sport should be something that you enjoy for its own sake, honestly, you...you –

DEBBIE: <u>I see, what you mean, but</u> I don't think you're being realistic. If Amanda wants to go to the races, that's her business. Personally, I'd never do...go to a betting shop or do the football pools.

TONY: Well, good for you!

DEBBIE: But going in for lotteries seems OK to me. I always buy a ticket for the National Lottery on a Saturday if I can afford it, and I don't see anything wrong with that.

AMANDA: I don't know, I think that *is* a waste of money. I mean, the chances of actually winning the jackpot are a million to one –

DEBBIE: So?

AMANDA: but with horses, right, you've got a question...it's like...you've got control, it's a skill. You know more about the horses, you know the jockeys, you've got more chance to win, you see?

DEBBIE: <u>I'm sorry, but</u> that's not fair. You say it's OK to bet on the horses, but a little flutter on the lottery is different according to you. There's nothing wrong with –

AMANDA: Look, did you know that since the National Lottery started people have stopped going to the cinema, they've stopped giving to charity? Attendances at cinemas are down by twenty per cent – and they say it's because people are spending their spare cash on the lottery. And I bet that if you did win, you wouldn't know what to do with a million pounds, you'd just squander it, you'd waste it . . .

DEBBIE: <u>Well, I'm sorry to interrupt you but</u> I did actually win last week.

AMANDA AND TONY: You won!?

DEBBIE: Yeah. Not the jackpot, just £100.

AMANDA: Well, that's not bad, is it?

TONY: OK, and how much have you paid for tickets over all those months?

DEBBIE: Well, I'd have to work that out –

TONY: Ahh!

Encourage everyone to **experiment** with the phrases in B during their conversation. There's plenty to talk about, and the points can be dealt with in any order.

One member of the group should be an 'observer' who will simply listen to the discussion and give feedback later on how effective other members were at interrupting – and how polite they sounded. Make sure the observer also gets a turn at participating.

This technique of a non-participating observer who will give feedback to the other students in a group may be useful in subsequent group discussions. Not every time, but occasionally. It's a very effective way of making sure that there is a focus on language (rather than just content) in discussions – and making sure that discussions happen only in English!

4.4 Using prefixes – 2 WORD STUDY

This is a quick look at meanings.

> **ANSWERS**
> **1** in the middle of a sentence **2** (approximately) half
> **3** partly retired   works for himself not for an employer

B

> **SUGGESTED ANSWERS**
> **half-** half-afraid half-asleep half-finished
> **semi-** semi-automatic semi-circle
> **mid-** mid-air mid-morning mid-twenties
> **self-** self-defence self-pity self-respect

C

> **ANSWERS**
> **2** mid-fifties **3** half-price **4** mid-winter **5** self-service **6** semi-final
> **7** half-marathon **8** mid-afternoon

4.5 *Make* and *do* VERBS AND IDIOMS

This exercise looks at some collocations with *make* and *do*.

> **SUGGESTED ANSWERS**
>
> **Bill made . . .**
>   Shirley laugh   a cake   a noise   a mistake   an arrangement   a comment   a decision
>   a good impression   me an offer   a promise   a statement
>
> **Shirley did . . .**
>   Bill a favour   the washing-up   her duty   the shopping   an exercise   her homework
>   a good job   badly in the test   her best   very well   nothing at all

B

It may be helpful for students to know the definitions given in the answers which follow. Note that these are rough-and-ready definitions – consult a dictionary for more detail and further examples. This exercise presents just a selection of the myriad idiomatic phrasal verbs with *do* and *make*, but any more would be confusing and discouraging at this level.

ANSWERS
1 (do with = need or want)
2 making up = inventing (a story)
3 doing up = redecorating – We can also do up a shoelace or coat.
4 make out = see with difficulty
5 make up for = repay or compensate for
6 making for = going in the direction of/heading for
7 made off with = stole
8 do without = manage without having something

NOTE
Before doing the exercises in 4.6 remind everyone to look at the GRAMMAR REFERENCE section on Past tenses on pages 180–181 before the lesson.

4.6 The past – 2 GRAMMAR REVIEW

A 1

ANSWERS
Correct sentences: (1) 3 5 8
Incorrect sentences: (2) 4 6 7

2

CORRECTED PARAGRAPH (Some variations are possible.)
It <u>was raining</u> when we <u>arrived</u> at the coast but by midday it had <u>stopped</u>. We thought the rain <u>would last</u> all day and we <u>were</u> very glad it <u>didn't</u> because we <u>wanted</u> to go swimming. We found a café where we could eat outside and <u>had</u> a nice meal. By the time we had finished lunch the sun <u>was shining</u> brightly and the temperature <u>had risen</u> to 30 degrees. We all <u>ran</u> down to the beach and, after we <u>had changed</u> into our swimming things, we dived in the sea.

B 1

SUGGESTED ANSWERS
2 had   3 seen   4 were   5 met   6 had   7 been   8 had   9 finished   10 was
11 were   12 told   13 had   14 was   15 had   16 used   17 went   18 was
19 did   20 have   21 agreed

2

SUGGESTED ANSWERS
2 were/was   3 had   4 was   5 came   6 continued   7 came   8 started   9 had
10 were   11 was   12 scored   13 was   14 was   15 have

C

This is open-ended free practice, starting in pairs and continuing in pairs of pairs. Students with uneventful weekends can use their imaginations and invent a series of surprising and memorable encounters!

4.7 Safety at sea LISTENING

A

Begin by finding out how many people in the class have experience of a water sport: water-skiing, diving, windsurfing or sailing. What do they enjoy about it? How safe is it?

Students should use their previous knowledge and common sense to predict the answers to the questions and then listen to the recording to confirm what they already suspect, rather than receive a huge amount of new information.

B

 Students listen to the recording and answer the questions.

ANSWERS

1 a) 'I am OK.' – picture 3
   b) 'I need assistance.' – picture 1
   c) 'I have a diver down. Keep clear and proceed slowly.' – picture 2
   d) 'Faster!' – picture 7
   e) 'Slower!' – picture 6
   f) 'Speed OK.' – picture 8
   g) 'Back to jetty.' – picture 5

2 nod your head
3 shake your head
4 a) watch the skier   drive the boat
   b) above water
   c) start
   d) let go of the rope and sit down
   e) curl yourself into a ball
   f) they can help to keep you afloat

TRANSCRIPT   *3 minutes 20 seconds*

JENNY: After a series of accidents involving water-skiers, it's clear that there needs to be stricter rules and controls. Andy Brown is a lifeguard. Andy, what advice would you give to people taking part in water sports?

ANDY: Ah, well, Jenny, the first thing you have to know is the signals that you should use if you get into any kind of trouble...because it's difficult to hear, you know, somebody just shouting above the noise of waves and the wind and boat engines, and breathing apparatus or scuba gear if you happen to be wearing that, that kind of thing.

JENNY: Do you have any examples of that?

ANDY: Um...well, if...ah...if you're diving...um...you need to use these signals. You use: 'Now I'm OK' is holding the hand up with thumb and forefinger making an O, like that. You know, like the OK sign. And...um...'I need assistance', that signal is...you put the fist up and you move it from left to right a...above the water, if you can. And, if you're on a boat...um...you should always be flying the...er...correct international signal, which is a flag which is white on the side that's nearest the mast and blue on the other.

JENNY: Oh, what does that mean?

ANDY: Well, that means: 'I've got a diver down, so keep clear or drive slowly' for all the other boats around.

JENNY: I see, how about skiers, water-skiers?

ANDY: OK. Um...anybody who's going to be water-skiing should be taught a...several signs and signals. First of all the signal to go faster: you hold your palm up and you motion upwards or you can just nod your head.

JENNY: Right.

ANDY: And...and the signal for 'Slower' is you hold your palm down, and you motion downwards or you shake your head.

JENNY: Yes, of course.

ANDY: OK, now if you want to indicate that the speed is actually OK, you just give the OK signal with your thumb and forefinger making the O, just like I told you about. Um...and if you want to go back into the shore, you just point your arm downwards. Like that, just down toward your side.

JENNY: I see. Well...um, so much for signals. But water-skiing can actually be quite dangerous, can't it, even if you do know all the signals?

ANDY: Yeah, I guess, but not if you follow some basic safety procedures and you...you have to know what you're doing, like with any sport. There are three points really with water-skiing. There should always be two people in the boat. That's one person to drive the boat and one person to keep his eye on the skier. And before you start your...your ski-tips, if you're the skier, your ski-tips have to be above the water, so you don't get immediately dragged down to the bottom when the boat goes –

JENNY: And go under. Yes.

ANDY: Yes. And...um...if you're the skier, you have to give a clear signal to the helmsman, which is the guy who's driving the boat, when you're ready to start.

JENNY: And I suppose that...um...even the best water-skiers fall into the water sometimes. What do you do if you do fall?

ANDY: Well, no, *when* you fall!

JENNY: Oh, right.

ANDY: Um...well, if you...if you start to fall forwards, you should let go of the rope and try to sit down. If you're falling sideways, you've got to curl yourself up into a ball. And it's very important that if you do fall, you get a hold of your skis immediately because they can help you keep afloat.

JENNY: Yes, of course, right. Well, thank you very much, Andy.

ANDY: Hey, no problem, you're welcome.

C Play the recording again if there are any disagreements to settle, or if the speaker's accent was difficult for your students to understand.

EXTRA ACTIVITY

Ask the students in pairs to make up more hand signals. The others have to guess what they mean.

4.8 Stimulating and satisfying   READING

 A These pre-reading and first reading tasks encourage the students to have a personal purpose for reading the text.

B 1

> **ANSWERS**
> True: 1 6
> False: 2 3 4 5

2

> **ANSWERS**
> gruelling   super-fit   modestly   agony   resentment   exhilaration
> experience   the elements   stimulating

C This is how the article was originally split into paragraphs (but personally I'd start the second paragraph with 'Perched . . .' and continue it until '. . . selves.')

> **SUGGESTED PARAGRAPHS** (Some variations are possible.)
> John Ridgway, the ex-Paratrooper famous for rowing the Atlantic, sailing twice around the world and canoeing down the Amazon, runs the most gruelling survival course in Britain. Perched halfway up a mountain in northern Scotland, overlooking a black lake, the Ardmore Adventure School is cold, bleak and forbidding.
>
> In this week's *Cutting Edge* programme, *Exposure*, it serves as a temporary home for 24 business managers from a multinational company – all in search of their real selves.
>
> The group are not super-fit athletes but very average 28–50-year-olds, ranging from the completely inactive to the modestly sporty. The film follows the men and women as they attempt abseiling, rock climbing, canoeing, orienteering, sea swimming and raft-building in the Scottish wilderness. It's only on the third day that they see their first glimpse of Ardmore House itself, with its relative comfort of bunk beds and cold showers.
>
> Their agony and resentment is clear at the beginning of the course, but, as the days go by, the exhilaration starts to show through. As one participant says, 'It was hell, but it was worth it.'
>
> It's a feeling Ridgway understands. 'I decided to create a small corner of the world where people could experience the confrontation with the elements that I find so stimulating and satisfying.'

4.9 Paragraphs   WRITING

We've already done two exercises on paragraphs in this unit. The idea has been for students to discover some of the reasons why paragraphs are used in English texts.

    Unfortunately, there are no fixed rules about when to start a new
paragraph. Often paragraphs are used simply to split long stretches of text into
shorter, more easily assimilated pieces.
    Or they may be used to emphasise a sentence by giving it prominence. A
new paragraph often signals a change of direction, or a digression.
    The traditional reason for starting a new paragraph is when a new idea is
begun. For example, if you're writing about the advantages and disadvantages
of something, the introduction might be in the first paragraph.
    And the advantages might be in the second paragraph.
    Then the disadvantages would be in the third paragraph.
    If there are lots of disadvantages, there might need to be a fourth paragraph
to contain them all.
    Finally, the conclusion would be in the final paragraph.

In a story, if there is a dialogue, each time a new speaker says something, the words in quotes should be on a new line.
'What are we going to do today?' I asked my friends.
'Let's go swimming!' they all shouted.

In the exam, paragraphs of 40 to 50 words are probably best. A single-paragraph 150-word composition is **not** recommended!

A There are no 'correct answers' to these questions, but any of the reasons outlined above may be relevant. At First Certificate level there's no need to go into great detail on paragraphing, apart from discussing the ideas above. It's best for students to develop a feeling for what seems right, and the tasks in B will help them to do this.

B Follow the procedure shown in the Student's Book, making sure the partners in 1 and 3 are different. Make sure you allow enough time for the discussion questions in 3.

Alternative topic (for students who don't like using their imaginations and writing fictional stories):

Write an article (about 150 words) describing how the people you know spend their spare time. Begin like this: 'Most of the people I know don't have very much spare time, but . . .'

The world around us

5

The *Voices* video sequence *Dartmoor – A National Park* deals with other aspects of this topic, including conservation and protecting the environment.

5.1 Nature   VOCABULARY AND LISTENING

A Here is some useful vocabulary that may come up in the discussion:

autumn/fall   autumnal   blanket   blossom   boiling   cherry tree   chilly   forest   freezing   fresh frosty   icy   meadow   mild   picnic   snowman   spring-like   summery   wintry   wood

B To start everyone off, do a quick brainstorm and ask the class to suggest some mammals, birds and insects they might well see in the wild locally (e.g. sparrows, mosquitoes) – and some animals they'd normally only see in a zoo or on TV (e.g. lions, elephants). Concentrate on creatures that are found in your students' country/countries, not the British Isles.

> **SUGGESTED ANSWERS**
>
> | | |
> |---|---|
> | Fruit: | apple, plum, pineapple, apricot, melon, raspberry, strawberry, blackcurrant, cherry, etc. |
> | Vegetables: | cabbage, cauliflower, aubergine, onion, etc. |
> | Trees: | fir, beech, palm, cypress, eucalyptus, etc. |
> | Flowers: | buttercup, daffodil, crocus, dandelion, orchid, etc. |
> | Wild mammals: | lion, wolf, fox, elephant, deer, monkey, whale, etc. |
> | Birds: | blackbird, robin, stork, crow, swallow, kingfisher, budgerigar, parrot, etc. |
> | Domestic animals: | cow, sheep, chicken, horse, donkey, cat, dog, canary, hamster, gerbil, etc. |
> | Insects: | bee, mosquito, cockroach, beetle, locust, moth, butterfly, flea, etc. |
> | Sea creatures: | sole, sardine, cod, anchovy, red mullet, lobster, mussel, squid, prawn, shrimp, jellyfish, etc. |

Perhaps extend the activity by brainstorming other categories such as:

Young animals:	puppy, calf, chick, cub, kitten, lamb, foal, etc.
Reptiles:	lizard, alligator, snake (adder, python, cobra, etc.), crocodile, tortoise, turtle, etc.

C Play the recording, which is itself a source of further vocabulary on the topic of the unit.

> **ANSWERS**
>
> **1** Steve   **2** Claire   **3** Steve   **4** Steve   **5** Emma   **6** No one   **7** No one   **8** Claire
> **9** Emma

TRANSCRIPTS   *3 minutes*

1 CLAIRE: . . . Well, it seems to me that too many people own dogs in the city. I mean, they keep them in small apartments all day, take them out for short walks maybe twice a day. I mean, some of the dogs in our neighbourhood are huge. I think it's cruel to keep them inside an apartment all day.

STEVE: I think you're being sentimental. I mean, you know, dogs are really good companions, especially for people who live on their own. And they don't have feelings like people, I mean, they don't get lonely if they're alone all day, I mean, they just go to sleep. And then, you know, being alone makes them even happier to see their owners when they get back from work.

CLAIRE: Oh yeah, what do you think, Emma?

EMMA: Well . . .

2 STEVE: . . . I think all this stuff we hear about recycling is exaggerated. We have to put all our waste paper in one place, our bottles in another, and our cans in another, and our plastic in another one, I mean, on and on. I just don't believe that all these things really have to be recycled . . . Well, I'm sure it costs more to recycle them than to make new ones. I suspect some of these things are actually just buried so that everyone *thinks* they're helping the environment.

EMMA: That is a terrible attitude . . . Well, look, to make paper people have to cut down trees, to make bottles they have to use up huge amounts of energy, to make cans, well, they've got to find aluminium and melt it down, you know that. The point about recycling is that it saves energy and it stops us using up the resources that can't be renewed, well, like oil, metal . . . Well, it may not be much cheaper to recycle I agree, but it's much better for the future of the planet.

STEVE: Mm, well, let's find out what Claire thinks. Claire?

CLAIRE: Well, you know, I . . .

3 CLAIRE: . . . Anyway the reason I'm a vegetarian is, well, it's simple really: producing meat is a very wasteful way of producing food. I mean, if you think about it, farmers have to grow crops to feed the animals which people then eat. Now, that land could be used to grow crops to feed the people directly – simple! All the world's problems about lack of food, starvation, would be solved if everyone stopped eating meat and ate beans, nuts, vegetables, fruits instead.

EMMA: Mm, that's all very well but I, personally, don't want to do without meat. Well, you can't make people be vegetarians, can you? . . . I think you've got to be realistic . . .

CLAIRE: Or selfish . . .

EMMA: No, the...I mean...the people I know eat much less meat now than they used to – they eat a lot more pasta and...and more fish. Is it all right to eat more fish, I wonder? Aren't all the oceans being over-fished?

CLAIRE: Steve, what do you think?

STEVE: Well, I think people just . . .

5.2   The weather   READING AND LISTENING

A **2** The original headline for the article was 'Avoiding that unlucky strike'.

3 One or two of the answers given below are clearly implied rather than definitely stated.

ANSWERS

talking on the phone ✔	climbing stairs	sheltering under an isolated tree ✔
washing up ✔	working outdoors ✔	sheltering in a building
watching television ✔	climbing a ladder	sailing ✔
sitting near a closed window	fishing ✔	cycling ✔
looking out of an open door ✔	playing golf ✔	swimming ✔

4 One thing it doesn't tell you is where the **safest** place to be is. The safest place is probably inside a metal box (e.g. car or plane) – but don't touch the metal parts. If you're driving, it's safer to stay inside the car than to get out and become an exposed target.

B   After doing this exercise, discuss what the weather is **really** going to be like during the next few days, according to **today's** forecast.

ANSWERS

	Today	Tomorrow
heavy rain	(S + E)	(W)
dry and warm	W	
cloudy		S
hazy sunshine		W
temperatures above 25°		E
thunderstorms		E
scattered showers		W
gale-force winds		N
light breeze		S
temperatures below freezing and frost	N	

TRANSCRIPT *2 minutes*

PRESENTER: . . . denied that he has been having an affair with his secretary. And now for the weather. Over to Michelle Brown at the Weather Centre. Michelle, what have you got for us today?

FORECASTER: Thank you, Bob. Well it's not going to be very nice in the South today. There's going to be some very heavy rain in the South and also in the East.

In the West today it should be mainly dry and quite warm but overnight the rain will spread to the West and it's going to be very wet there during most of the morning tomorrow. After about lunchtime in the West there may still be a few showers but most of the region can expect some hazy sunshine.

Coming back to the South now, as I said, there will be a lot of rain today but as we move into the evening the clouds will clear and temperatures will fall to about 10 degrees during the night, so you'll need your blanket. Tomorrow a light breeze and cloudy with temperatures around the 20 mark.

In the East today's rain will die out overnight and tomorrow a complete change with temperatures rising to the mid-twenties or even higher, and with this rise in temperatures there may well be the odd thunderstorm during the afternoon and evening.

The North will be much colder today – sorry! – with temperatures falling below zero during the afternoon and a frosty evening and night can be expected. Tomorrow the temperature will be above freezing but it will feel very cold with winds picking up considerably, and some extremely strong winds on the coasts, making it a very rough, nasty day for sea crossings.

And the outlook for the day after tomorrow and the rest of the week: cool and dry in the South, warm and sunny in the West, hot with the chance of more thunderstorms in the East, and foggy in the North.

So that's it from me and back to Bob.

PRESENTER: Thanks, Michelle. And now sport, and good news for Manchester United fans . . .

C These activities give students a chance to use their 'weather vocabulary' and also to think about good attention-catching opening sentences. This aspect of writing skills is taken up again in 7.8.

5.3 Global warming READING

A The topic of the article is quite complex; this pre-reading task lets students discover what they already know about it.

B This is a very tricky exam-style exercise. Perhaps point out that it may be best to do the easy parts first, leaving the harder parts till later. If, after a few minutes, students seem to be finding the exercise too hard, reassemble the class and go through the exercise together, inviting suggested answers from anyone who wants to stick their neck out.

ANSWERS
1 D   2 A   3 B   4 F   5 C   6 E   (Sentence G is not used.)

C Student A looks at Activity *6*, Student B at *34*. They have some more information about global warming to read and discuss.

If you think this may be difficult for your students, divide the class into an even number of pairs so that two students can look at Activity *6* and two (or three) at *34* before combining as pairs of pairs to exchange information.

5.4 Compound prepositions PREPOSITIONS

A **ANSWERS**
1 because of/owing to   2 because of/owing to   3 except for   4 in common with
As well as and *in place of* don't fit anywhere.

B **ANSWERS**
1 (because of *or* owing to)   2 on behalf of   3 because of/owing to   4 instead of
5 as well as   6 apart from/except for   7 apart from/except for   8 according to

Can your students think of any other compound prepositions? Here are some:

out of   away from   up to   in front of   in spite of   together with

Ask everyone to write four sentences using the most useful 'new' compound prepositions.

NOTE
Before starting 5.5 remind everyone to study the GRAMMAR REFERENCE section on Articles and quantifiers on pages 171–172.

5.5 Articles and quantifiers – 1   GRAMMAR REVIEW

This is the first of two sections on articles and quantifiers, the second is 6.4.

A 1 Hopefully, this quick exercise will be enough to deal with this problem area. But be prepared to answer questions from the class and refer them to the GRAMMAR REFERENCE section.

> **ANSWERS**
> This is the only countable noun: disease
> These are uncountable nouns: blood   salt   money   mathematics   health
> These could be either:
> glass – Windows are made of glass. / a glass of milk
> fire – Fire is a great danger. / What a nice fire!
> These are usually uncountable, but they can be countable in these cases:
> food – Hamburgers and frankfurters are fast foods. (i.e. kinds of fast food)
> milk – Three coffees and two chocolate milks, please. (i.e. ordering in a café)

2

> **ANSWERS**
> bread – a slice (*or* a loaf)   education – a lesson   furniture – a sofa (*or* chair, table, etc.)
> information – a fact   homework – an exercise (*or* composition, assignment, etc.)
> luggage – a suitcase   medicine – a tablet (*or* drug, pill, etc.)   money – a dollar (*or* pound, coin, banknote, etc.)   news – a report (*or* article, broadcast, etc.)   traffic – a car (*or* truck, bus, etc.)   vocabulary – a word (*or* phrase, expression, idiom, etc.)   water – a drop (*or* lake, river, bottle, etc.)   weather – a storm (*or* shower, gale, etc.)   wild life – an animal (*or* reptile, bird, mammal, etc.)

B **ANSWERS** (Some variations are possible.)
> 2 More men are involved in politics than women in every country in the world.
> 3 If there were fewer cars in the city, there wouldn't be so many problems with pollution.
> 4 To get to the leisure centre, go along Coronation Avenue and take the first right.
> 5 Education is compulsory – all children have to go to school.
> 6 Anyone can have a look at the/a church even if they don't go to church on Sundays.
> 7 Pollution is a very great problem in the world today.
> 8 Few people realise that using the sun's energy is better than burning fossil fuels.

C **ANSWERS** (Some variations are possible.)
> 2 My work took me all night **because there was so much information** to learn.
> 3 Do you know **how many plants and animals** become extinct every day? Fifty to one hundred!
> 4 There **are so many clouds** that there's sure to be some rain eventually.
> 5 Could **you give me some advice (about what to do)** please?
> 6 Vegetarians **never eat meat, but some (do) eat** fish.

D Perhaps point out that headlines and notes don't obey quite the same rules as normal prose in English. For example, articles are usually omitted ('Queen opens new hospital'), present tenses are used instead of past ('PM makes pro-Europe speech'), passives are just participles ('Princess given warm welcome'), and *to . . .* is used for the future ('President to visit language school'). Perhaps do 2 and 3 with the class first to give them confidence.

SUGGESTED ANSWERS (Many variations are possible.)

2 An escaped tiger has been found in a wood after a search lasting a week.
3 A family is angry because £60,000 has been left to a cat.
4 A man bit a dog.
5 A father lost a £200,000 lottery ticket.
6 A mother has been reunited with her daughter after not seeing her for 20 years.
7 A town is missing from the phone book (perhaps due to a computer error).
8 A golfer who was struck by lightning survived.

5.6 **Talking for a minute** SPEAKING

This section practises a skill that students will need for the Speaking paper in the exam. Here they'll have to speak for about a minute (uninterrupted) about their pictures. The examiner may encourage them, but he or she probably won't ask any specific questions until later.

For more information on the Speaking paper look at UCLES sample papers, or *Cambridge Practice Tests for First Certificate.*

 A Play the recording after students have had time to think of their own ideas. Both speakers sound interesting, but the woman seemed to run out of things to say after her first comment.

They could also have mentioned:
– training animals to perform tricks
– keeping animals in captivity
– killing animals for sport versus killing them for food
– the intelligence and sociability of dolphins.

B Follow the procedure suggested in the Student's Book. Both speakers sound quite fluent because they have disguised their hesitation in various ways.

The phrases used by the speakers are underlined in the transcript. The other technique they both used was **repetition** – also underlined in the transcript.

TRANSCRIPT *2 minutes 30 seconds*

EXAMINER: Now, I'd like you each to talk on your own for about a minute. I'm going to give each of you two different photographs and I'd like you to talk about them. Stephan, here are your two photographs. Please let Gertrude see them. They both show people and animals. Gertrude, I'll give you your pictures in a minute.
Stephan, I'd like you to compare and contrast your two pictures and tell me how you feel about them. Remember, you only have one minute for this so don't worry if I interrupt you. All right?

STEPHAN: <u>Well,</u> OK, <u>well,</u> the first picture is an aerial view of a woman...<u>um</u>...riding through the sea or riding through water on a dolphin. <u>Um</u>...and the second picture is...<u>um</u>...a picture of two men <u>in...in</u> khaki outfits in some sort of bamboo on a boat...<u>um</u>...with a dog and guns, and I would think they are probably hunting. <u>Er</u>...well, the pictures both seem to be about man and animal and their relationships. <u>Um</u>...the men are obviously hunting the animal, I would think for . . . using them to eat them, to eat birds I would think. <u>Um</u>...while the other picture is <u>of...of</u> the closeness of the woman with the dolphin <u>and...and</u> how they can relate to each other and be <u>kind of</u> friends with each other. <u>Um</u>...but I wouldn't want to...<u>um</u>...be very judgmental about this because the relationship you can have with a dolphin is very different <u>to...to</u> what you can have with birds, the relationship you could have with birds . . .

EXAMINER: Thank you. Gertrude, what are your feelings on the subject?

GERTRUDE: <u>Well,</u> yeah, <u>the...the</u> one with the dolphin and the woman <u>is...is</u> a picture of harmony, <u>um</u>...it's humankind and animals living together in harmony, and the other one is...<u>um</u>...the opposite. And so I definitely prefer the one with the dolphin.

EXAMINER: Thank you. Now Gertrude, here are your photographs, please let Stephan see them . . .

C Students A and B look at Activity *10*, while Students C and D (and E) look at *38*. They should begin by preparing what to say about the pictures before giving their one-minute talk.
Go round from pair to pair, listening in. At this stage, encouragement rather than criticism may be the best tactic.

Finally, ask everyone what they found difficult about the task – and reassure them that they don't need to 'make a perfect speech' in order to get a good grade.

EXTRA ACTIVITY
Students can look at the pictures their partners talked about and give a one-minute talk on those pictures while their partners listen.

5.7 Using prefixes – 3 WORD STUDY

Some of these are hard to explain so don't insist on complete accuracy as long as everyone can appreciate the differences in meaning.

ANSWERS
1 a *or* an   the (!)
2 impossible to read   not tidy
3 connected with the topic   not connected
4 behave badly   not follow
5 peaceful   lack of approval
6 put paper round it   remove the paper from around it

SUGGESTED ANSWERS

un-   unable (*but* inability)   uncomfortable   unfair   unfortunate   unnecessary   unpleasant   unusual   unwilling   (unlike)
in-   inaccurate   inactive   inconvenient   incredible   indirect   inexperienced   informal   intolerant
im-   impatient   impossible

un-   unbutton   unfold   unpack
dis-   disagree   dislike   (disable)
mis-   mishear   mispronounce   misspell   (misdirect)

ANSWERS
2 unlock   3 impatient   4 inconvenient   5 unreasonable   6 inefficient
7 misunderstood   8 misspelt/misspelled   9 disqualified   10 disappear

5.8 Making notes WRITING

Give anyone a chance to explain why they're **against** making notes before writing a composition and get the others to convince them they are mistaken. We will continue to emphasise the value of making notes throughout this book – time spent doing so is never time wasted. However, in one's own language this may be less necessary than it is in a foreign language.

Ask everyone to suggest further points that they would make on the topic of recycling: e.g. BOTTLES – recycling glass bottles uses almost as much energy as manufacturing new ones. Plastic bottles should also be recycled.

No particular style of notes is recommended here – students should be encouraged to experiment with various styles to find out which suits them best. The third type, sometimes called a 'mind map', is particularly suitable for making notes on a lecture or on a text you have read.

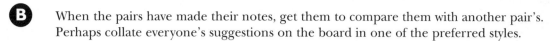

B When the pairs have made their notes, get them to compare them with another pair's. Perhaps collate everyone's suggestions on the board in one of the preferred styles.

C The model notes and model article below are on the topic of zoos. These may be photocopied, perhaps to give students some ideas of how to approach one of the other topics.

Before they hand in their work, give everyone a chance to read someone else's composition.

Discuss what difference it would make to the communicative effect of the composition if the order of the paragraphs is reversed. Does the reader conclude that, on balance, the writer is 'for' or 'against' zoos in the model composition, for example?

Ask the class to look at each other's compositions and comment on how the communicative effect would change if the paragraphs were reversed.

EXTRA ACTIVITY

The model article is approximately 240 words long – too long for an exam answer. What could be cut to bring it down to the right length? Where could each paragraph be split into two shorter paragraphs?

MODEL NOTES

ZOOS

Points against . . .

- unpleasant, depressing – especially old-fashioned zoos
- cruel to keep animals in small cages – lions: Africa, open spaces
- climate – winter: tropical animals
- entertainment (like circus) – people laugh at animals performing (bananas, swinging, etc.) and people make animals nervous – don't respect them

Points in favour . . .

- modern zoo parks – large enclosures
- scientific research
- preserving and breeding rare species – stop some becoming extinct
- education about animals – better than films or books

MODEL ARTICLE

Some zoos are very unpleasant, depressing places. This is particularly true of the more old-fashioned ones where large animals are kept in tiny cages for the amusement of the public. This kind of zoo is cruel – a lion is an animal that lives in the open spaces of Africa and cannot enjoy being a prisoner. In the winter, zoos in colder countries do not provide a warm enough environment for animals from hot countries. Worst of all, it seems to me, is the way that some zoos are regarded as places of entertainment, like circuses, where people are encouraged to laugh at animals as they 'perform' their funny tricks (eating bananas, swinging from rubber tyres, and so on). People often make the animals frightened or angry by teasing them and they don't respect them as our fellow-creatures.

On the other hand, it seems to me that people who say that <u>all</u> zoos should be closed are overstating the case. Many modern zoo parks do keep animals in large enclosures and try to make them feel at home. Some zoos are valuable centres of scientific research, where rare species can be preserved and encouraged to breed. In many cases, this policy has led to the re-introduction of animals into areas where they had almost become extinct. Zoos are also a unique form of education, where children (and adults) can learn about the behaviour of animals in a more effective and enjoyable way than seeing films or reading about them.

6 Going places

Mind how you go!   VOCABULARY AND SPEAKING

A 1 The main message is 'Wear a seat belt' – 'Clunk' is the noise of the car door closing and 'Click' is the noise that fastening a seat belt makes.

Two other pieces of advice for pedestrians might be: 'Don't walk into the road suddenly' and 'If there isn't a pavement, walk on the side of the road facing oncoming traffic'. For cyclists: 'Always look behind before overtaking' and 'Assume every driver can't see you'. And for drivers: 'Always use your indicators' and 'Look behind before opening your door'. But your students may have much better, more heart-felt ideas!

The text here and in the Communication Activities comes from a British Department of Transport leaflet. (30 mph = about 50 kilometres an hour, 20 mph = about 35 kph and 40 mph = about 65 kph)

2 & 3 🔊 Student A looks at Activity *43*, Student B at *51* to see the complete texts. Encourage everyone to summarise these in their own words, **not** read them aloud. At the end, they should look at each other's Activity and **highlight** any useful vocabulary there.

B   ANSWERS

1 seat belts   2 test   licence   3 accident   mirror   overtaking
4 roundabout   way   right   5 lights   lane   6 space   park   meter
7 fine   disqualified   8 pedestrians   pavement/path

C   SUGGESTED ANSWERS

1 trip/journey/flight   trip/journey/flight   2 flight/journey   3 crossing
4 excursions/trips/tours/outings   5 trip   6 cruise   7 excursion/tour   8 Travel
9 transport   10 trip/journey/flight   trip/journey/flight   trip/journey/flight

D   Make sure everyone looks at the wrong answers too and encourage discussion. For example, it would be cheapest of all to walk across London but that would entail going *on* foot not *by* foot – and it certainly wouldn't be the quickest way. Allow plenty of time for this.

ANSWERS

1 motorway (*but US* highway)   2 tube (*but US* subway *and other countries* metro)
3 coach   4 turning   5 brake   6 ticket

E   We end with a discussion to enable students to use some of the new vocabulary freely.

Cars in cities   READING

A   We begin with a warm-up pre-reading discussion to set the scene and help students to build up some expectations about the content of the text.

B 1

ANSWERS

1 D   2 A   3 E   4 F   5 C   (Sentence B is not used.)

2 The original headline was: 'Running out of road'.

3 & 4 Encourage students to look at the words their partner has highlighted before they begin their discussion. Here are some useful words that they might highlight:
congested   squeezed in   hefty   sticker   households   raises   devices   lowers
At the end, continue the discussion as a whole-class activity.

6.3 I don't get it!   VERBS AND IDIOMS

(A) SUGGESTED ANSWERS

1 receive   2 became/grew   have   3 arrived   didn't have   4 buy/obtain   catch

(B) ANSWERS

2 get better   3 get started   4 get a headache   5 getting dark   6 get the joke
7 get ready   8 get into trouble   9 get to sleep   10 get an expert
11 got the sack/got into trouble   12 get lost

(C) ANSWERS

1 (get on with = continue)
2 get out of = avoid
3 getting at = suggesting/trying to communicate
4 got over = recovered from the disappointment or unhappiness
5 get (a)round = solve (a problem)
6 get off = alight from
7 getting on with = managing/progressing
8 get on with = have a good relationship with
9 get (a)round to = find the time
10 get through = get a connection (on the phone)
11 get together = meet
12 getting (me) down = making (me) feel depressed

NOTE
Before starting 6.4 remind everyone to look at the GRAMMAR REFERENCE section on Articles and quantifiers on pages 171–172.

6.4 Articles and quantifiers – 2   GRAMMAR REVIEW

(A) SUGGESTED ANSWERS (Many more are possible.)

Countries in Europe:	Norway Belgium Switzerland
Countries in Asia:	India Thailand China
Countries in South America:	Peru Brazil Colombia
Oceans:	the Pacific the Indian Ocean
Seas:	the Aegean the Mediterranean the Caribbean
Mountain ranges:	the Alps the Andes the Pyrenees
Mountains:	Mount Everest Mount Olympus Mount Fuji
Famous public buildings:	the British Museum the Acropolis the Statue of Liberty
Languages:	Welsh Gaelic Urdu
Cities in North America:	New Orleans Chicago Seattle
Rivers:	the Mississippi the Rhine the Nile
Groups of islands:	the Cyclades the Balearics the West Indies
Lakes:	Lake Titicaca Lake Geneva Lake Constance
Famous streets:	Bond Street Fifth Avenue Broadway
Planets:	Uranus Jupiter Venus

It may not take much thought to come up with 'exceptions' to the rules of thumb implied above and articulated in the GRAMMAR REFERENCE section, particularly when it comes to mountains, streets and buildings (Ben Nevis – the Zugspitze, Buckingham Palace – the White House, Oxford Street – the Champs Elysées, etc.).

(B) 1

ANSWERS (In each case the first alternative is the one that appeared in the original article.)

4 Ø   5 Ø   6 Ø/the   7 Ø   8 a   9 a   10 Ø   11 the   12 the   13 Ø/the
14 Ø   15 the/a   16 the   17 the   18 the   19 Ø/the   20 the   21 Ø   22 an
23 the/a   24 a   25 a   26 the   27 Ø   28 the   29 Ø   30 the/a   31 the
32 Ø   33 the   34 the/a   35 Ø   36 a   37 the

2

3 We end with a short discussion and a writing task.

6.5 **Boring in the Alps** LISTENING

A This pre-listening discussion helps students to familiarise themselves with some background information about Switzerland.

B 📼 This is an exam-style task.

ANSWERS

| 1 60 minutes | 2 30 minutes | 3 400 km/h | 4 675 km | 5 Zürich | 6 4 billion |
| 7 2000 | 8 25 billion | 9 14 million | 10 traffic off the motorways |

TRANSCRIPT *4 minutes 10 seconds*

HELEN: A few years ago the Channel Tunnel seemed like a fantasy. Even while it was being built it seemed hard to believe that it would ever really happen. Now, of course, we take it for granted. Just like the M25 motorway around London it seems as if it's always existed. But now there are plans in the Alps that would make the Channel Tunnel seem like a bypass. Martin Johnson reports.

MARTIN: Travelling in Switzerland seems to most people like an ideal world. The rail system is splendid – the trains are comfortable, they leave and depart on time and the views you get as you ride along are lovely. And the system is brilliantly integrated – bus timetables fit in with train connections, even the steamers on the lakes connect with trains, and little mountain railways and cable cars get you to the nearest mainline station in good time to make your connection to a train that will take you anywhere in the country.

A perfect world? Well, the Swiss themselves seem to think there's room for improvement. There are plans to build a new rail system underground – Swissmetro – which will link all the major cities of the country in at least a third of the time it now takes by normal train. I've been talking to Annemarie Studer, an engineer at the Federal Polytechnic in Lausanne. Annemarie, tell us about the project.

ANNEMARIE: Swissmetro is going to be environmentally friendly, it's technologically feasible and it's going to be profitable too. Let me explain:

The system will link all the major cities in the country: you'll be able to travel from Geneva to Berne in 30 minutes and then on to Zürich in another 30 minutes. That journey takes three hours now. And you'll be able to travel from Basle in the north down to Bellinzona in the south in half an hour too. To achieve this the trains will operate in tunnels which will be bored through the mountains or buried into the countryside.

The trains will fly along, floating on magnetic cushions, so there won't be any friction, and the tunnels will have linear electric motors all along them. Most of the air will be pumped out of the tunnels, so that there will be very little air resistance, just like with high-flying planes. This means that the trains will fly at up to 400 kilometres an hour. The trip will be comfortable and fairly quiet. We already have the technology to build these trains – and the Swiss have the longest experience of boring tunnels in the world. So technologically there would be no problems for us.

The whole scheme will take about 25 years to complete and will involve building 675 kilometres of tunnels. The first part of the scheme will be a line from Basle Airport to Zürich Airport and that will cost four billion Swiss francs. But once we have the go-ahead, this project will start in the year 2000. The whole project, linking all parts of the country, will cost around 25 billion Swiss francs.

MARTIN: Who's behind the scheme? Where's the money going to come from?

ANNEMARIE: A new company called Swissmetro has been set up. About 80 companies are putting up half of the 14 million Swiss francs needed for the feasibility study and the other half is coming from the Swiss government. And both the national airline, Swissair, and Swiss Railways have a five per cent share in the company. We're very confident that the scheme will pay for itself quite quickly because there will be a huge demand from passengers. But the main advantage is keeping traffic off the motorways – by the year 2000 the Swiss motorways are going to be absolutely full and the amount of pollution caused by traffic is getting worse and worse. Something has to be done about it, and Swissmetro is the best solution.

MARTIN: Thank you Annemarie. Well, that's how the future may look in the Alps – if the project goes ahead. Helen, back to you.

HELEN: Thank you, Martin. But are people really going to be in such a hurry to get across Switzerland? I wonder.

Perhaps start off the discussion by relating what the students have heard in the recording to their own experience, by asking the class these questions:

- If a similar scheme was planned linking cities in your country, how do you think it would work?
- If they could build a tunnel between your country and another, which would it be? What would be the consequences?

The rest of this discussion moves well away from Switzerland and tunnels. You'll find that there is a lot of 'mileage' in these questions and consequently you may prefer to postpone the discussion to the next lesson, when you may have more time.

6.6   Can you tell me the way to . . . ?   LISTENING AND SPEAKING

More listening in A, but in this case the emphasis is on following directions. In B students will have to give directions.

A   If students 'get lost', you'll have to play the recording again – or maybe stop it half-way and rewind to the beginning. But it's not very difficult because it's intended to be a model for what they'll do in B.

CORRECT ROUTE

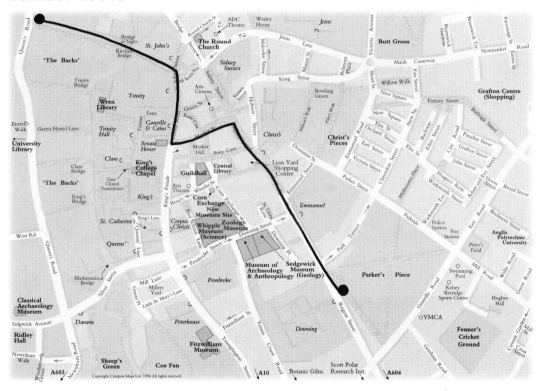

B   Student A looks at Activity *9*, B at *36*. Spend a few minutes looking at the expressions in the speech balloons and practise their pronunciation.

TRANSCRIPT   *2 minutes 20 seconds*

RECEPTIONIST: Regent Hotel, how can I help you?

GUEST: Er...hi. Look, this is going to sound really silly but I'm staying at your hotel...um...except I've forgotten the address.

RECEPTIONIST: Haha, oh I see, it's number 41 Regent Street.

GUEST: OK, I...I wonder, could you...could you give me directions how to get back to the hotel? I had this really nice little pop-up street map but I don't know, I seem to have lost it.

RECEPTIONIST: All right. Where are you now, sir?

GUEST: Um...I'm in Queen's Road. I've just crossed over Kitchen Bridge and I walked straight on till I came to Queen's Road.

RECEPTIONIST: OK, all right. Well, um...first of all you'll need to go back to Kitchen Bridge, you'll see the Bridge of Sighs on your left, cross the river and go straight on till you come to St John's Street – it's a pedestrian precinct.

GUEST: OK, St John's Street. Just a second, I'll write that down. OK.
RECEPTIONIST: OK?...Then you turn right and go down St John's Street and that leads you into Trinity Street. Carry on till you come to the Senate House – that's on the right. Then turn left into Market Street.
GUEST: OK, the Senate House, Market Street. OK.
RECEPTIONIST: Then at the end of Market Street you come to Sydney Street. Turn right and follow that street round a bend past Marks and Spencer's and Boots and eventually it leads into St Andrews Street. Go down there, leaving the pedestrian precinct...and keep walking and soon you'll see the University Arms Hotel on your left.
GUEST: OK, the University Arms Hotel.
RECEPTIONIST: And then just a little way further down you'll find the hotel on your left. It's more or less opposite Downing College.
GUEST: OK, thanks...thanks a lot. How...how long is this going to take me?
RECEPTIONIST: Oh not long. About 20 minutes.
GUEST: Fine. OK, well, thanks a lot for your...Oh, no! you're not going to believe this!
RECEPTIONIST: What's happened?
GUEST: I just found my map. It was inside my passport. I'm so sorry to have given you so much trouble.
RECEPTIONIST: That's quite all right, you're very welcome, sir.

6.7 **Personal letters** WRITING

 Follow the procedure suggested in the Student's Book.

SUGGESTED ANSWERS

This is clearly a matter of opinion, but some of the more helpful bits of the first letter (which students would highlight) are perhaps:
There's a direct bus (number 108)
Ask the driver to tell you
I've drawn a little map (the map itself is also very useful)

And some of the less helpful bits are:
expensive – how expensive?
cheap, but slow – how slow?
you'd have to change twice – where?
Jan doesn't recommend a best option.

Some of the more helpful bits of the second letter (which students would highlight) are:
there is no easy way
I would suggest taking the underground
When you come out of the station . . . etc. – the clear directions
there is a stop opposite Greenwood Park Station
Ask the driver to tell you when to get off
If you get lost . . . phone me at work (the number)

Some of the less helpful bits are:
You'll have to change twice – where?
There's no map.

Three examples of informal style (which students would highlight) are:
Here's a quick note . . .
I've drawn a little map . . .
. . . which could be tricky . . .

Three examples of formal style (which students would underline) are:
Therefore, if you do not have . . .
I would suggest taking the underground.
However, if you have time . . .

 Now students have to write an informal letter to a friend from abroad. Follow the procedure suggested in the Student's Book.

There is no model composition, as the two letters in the Student's Book serve as models in this case, and show how an informal personal letter is laid out.

There's no place like home

7.1 Make yourself at home!   VOCABULARY

A Here is some useful vocabulary that may come up in the discussion:

artistic   blanket   disorganised   duvet   furniture   mess   messy   methodical   musical   neat organised   patterned   plain   radiator   reading lamp   sheet   sporty   studious   tidy   untidy view   wastebasket

B

SUGGESTED ANSWERS

2 floor   **3** block   **4** central heating   **5** air conditioning   **6** accommodation
7 outskirts   **8** suburbs/surroundings   **9** move   **10** cottage   **11** village
12 next-door neighbours   **13** complaining   **14** room   **15** shelves   **16** lounge/living room   **17** wardrobes/cupboards/closets/chests of drawers   **18** mortgage   **19** rent
20 landlord/landlady   **21** spacious/homely/convenient etc.

C Make sure the meanings and uses of the 'wrong' answers are covered while doing this part. For example, with Question 1 you could ask for suggestions like this:

- What's the difference between a *cellar* and a *cave*?
  A *cave* is in a cliff or mountain and a *cellar* is under a house.

- Why are *attic* and *loft* wrong in this context?
  Because they're at the top of a house, not in the basement.

ANSWERS

1 cellar   **2** blinds   **3** drive   **4** shed   **5** lawn

D If this activity catches your students' imaginations, it may take a while to complete. Maybe postpone the continuation to the next lesson. It could be the basis for written work too.

7.2 Town or country?   LISTENING AND SPEAKING

A 🔲 This is an exam-style listening exercise. It's also a 'model' for the speaking tasks in B and C, where students talk about their preferences.

ANSWERS

1 John   **2** Sarah   **3** Sarah   **4** no one   **5** John   **6** Terry   **7** no one
8 Terry   **9** Sarah   **10** John

TRANSCRIPT   *3 minutes 40 seconds*

SARAH: Hello, Terry! Hi, John!

JOHN: Hello Sarah, how are you?

TERRY: Hi Sarah, haven't seen you for a while.

SARAH: Hello, no I've just got back from staying with my uncle in New York. Oh, what a wonderful city! I'd really love to live there. Have you ever been there John?

JOHN: No, I wouldn't want to. I can't think of anywhere I'd want to live less. I've heard all about it and it sounds absolutely terrible – so much crime and violence. Did you get robbed while you were there, Sarah?

SARAH: Of course not. As long as you take care and don't go anywhere you shouldn't go, like into Central Park after dark, or anywhere north of 110th Street, I mean you're perfectly safe. Why in any city you learn which districts to avoid and which are safe.
      What I really love about cities is that there are so many different kinds of people to see, and w...so many different things to do. It's impossible to be bored. I mean, whatever your interests there's something to do: entertainments, artistic events, galleries, historic buildings, museums – I mean, you name it it's there.

JOHN: No, I...I'd rather live in the country because I like living in a...a little village where everyone knows everyone else, and people talk to each other, and they help each other out. In a city nobody knows who you are – everybody's in a hurry and nobody has the time to be friendly. I know Terry agrees with me, don't you, Terry?

TERRY: Err...well up to a point I do but, well, I think you're generalising a bit. Some villages are...are full of unfriendly people and...and some cities are full of friendly people . . . It all depends. Anyway, most cities are actually divided up into smaller neighbourhoods, which...which are sort of like villages within the city . . . Yeah, in a neighbourhood many people do know each other a...and they meet in the shops or the local market and they chat with each other . . . I mean, if you do want to be alone and you don't want to socialise then, well, you can do that, and you have that choice and...and nobody will mind if you keep yourself to yourself. But if you...you try doing that in a village and people will call you unfriendly and unsociable and, well, they'll make life quite difficult for you.

SARAH: Well, that's true. And anyway, what Terry said about neighbourhoods is certainly true of where my uncle lives in New York. I mean, where he lives everyone *does* know everyone else, I mean they're...they're really very sociable.

JOHN: Well, yeah, but I'm sure that's an exception. I mean most people in cities aren't friendly to each other. But y...I'll tell you what: the worst thing of all?

TERRY: What's that, John?

JOHN: The traffic and the public transport. Now, I'd hate to live in a place where the traffic never stops and where you just have to squeeze onto a bus or an underground train just to get anywhere.

TERRY: Oh, yeah yeah. Underground trains are terrible, aren't they? I...it's not so much the crowds as travelling in the dark, without being able to see where you're going, it's frightening.

SARAH: I do agree about the traffic, but the...the subway in New York – a...and the underground or metro in other cities – I mean it's really the best way to get around. I...it's so quick and...and convenient that it, well, it doesn't really matter if you're squashed together because you know you can get anywhere you want in just a few minutes.

TERRY: Yeah yeah, and I do have to agree that cities are exciting places to live in . . . Not like a village where nothing goes on from one week to the next.

JOHN: B...but that's the whole point, as far as I'm concerned, that's exactly what makes a village so great to live in, the peace and quiet!

B Spend some time practising the pronunciation of the expressions in B1 before the controlled practice in B2.

C This develops into an exam-style discussion about contrasting photos.

7.3 Two cities   READING

If possible, encourage students to read the text before the lesson. If they can do the tasks in A, B and C beforehand too, all the better – then the answers and difficulties can be discussed in class. The text – and the questions in B – are quite difficult!

A 1 This could be done as a whole-class activity, if you prefer. Some cities that might be mentioned are: Rome and Milan, Paris and Lyon, Berlin and Munich, Athens and Salonica (Thessaloniki), Rio de Janeiro and São Paulo.

2 The original headline was 'Not as different as they look'.

B

ANSWERS
1 in government offices (*'in the afternoon' is also true, but the joke is about the behaviour of civil servants, not everyone in Madrid*)
2 a newcomer
3 took power away from Barcelona
4 old-fashioned
5 different
6 faster (*this is implied, though it could be argued that Madrid and Barcelona have a similarly fast pace of life*)
7 business centre (*it is also a banking centre, but the term 'business centre' covers this aspect*)
8 resentful of

C ANSWERS
¶2 autonomous   have a dig
¶3 bossed about   squash
¶4 shuttling   plateau
¶5 caricatures   obsession
¶6 pace   cuisine   fanatical
¶8 chip on Barcelona's shoulder

D You may prefer to brainstorm the similarities and differences between two cities your students know about as a whole class, rather than do D1 as a group discussion.

7.4 Have and give   VERBS AND IDIOMS

A SUGGESTED ANSWERS
Note that if more words are added, some different answers are also possible (e.g. Carol gave the information to her friend).

Alex had . . .
a quarrel with Carol   an order   no time to finish   permission to leave   a meal   a drink
a headache   his/her hair cut   a chance   a look   an interview   a good idea
the information   an accident   a rest   a swim   the details   no imagination
better be careful

Barry was having . . .
a quarrel with Carol   a meal   a drink   his hair cut   a look   an interview
a rest   a swim

Charlie gave us . . .
an order   no time to finish   permission to leave   a meal   a drink   his/her opinion
a headache   a chance   a look   an interview   a good idea   the information   a rest
the details

Carol gave . . .
an order   a sigh   a good performance   her opinion   an interview

B ANSWERS
1 (give away = reveal)
2 gave back = returned
3 had given up = had quit/had stopped
4 giving out = distributing
5 gave up = surrendered
6 giving in = handing in
7 gave up = stopped trying (or gave in = admitted defeat)
8 had on = wore
9 have back = returned
10 having round = having a guest/visitor

7.5 A nice place to stay   LISTENING AND WRITING

A 1 Begin by asking everyone to discuss which of the dwellings in the photos they'd prefer to live in and why. The photos show a block of flats (a high-rise tower block), Victorian terrace houses, a detached house on a modern estate and a country cottage – these are **not** the flats described in the recording.

Students with more experience of finding flats and houses (e.g. people who have recently moved) will have more to say about the advertisements. The most important missing information is how much the rent is, but there are other points which may be revealed in the recordings.

Perhaps point out that Windsor, Sandringham and Balmoral (together with Buckingham Palace) are residences of the British Royal Family!

2 Play the recording a couple of times while everyone makes notes.

MODEL NOTES

The new information not given in the advertisements is underlined.

BALMORAL WAY
seen by Bob:
    modern with <u>spacious</u> living room
    two <u>small</u> bedrooms
    <u>tiny</u> kitchen (<u>freezer and dishwasher</u>)
    <u>no TV</u>
    <u>5th floor: nice view</u>
    <u>may be expensive</u>

SANDRINGHAM GARDENS
seen by Louise:
    balcony
    <u>L-shaped bedroom (like two rooms)</u>
    light living room <u>(TV and video)</u>
    <u>2nd floor: view of railway line</u>
    <u>close to centre, station 20 mins</u>

WINDSOR AVENUE
seen by Bob:
    ground floor of <u>old house</u>
    garden: <u>could eat outside</u>
    <u>comfortable furniture</u>
    one <u>big</u> bedroom: <u>two beds (could move one into living room)</u>
    big kitchen <u>with door to garden</u>

WINDSOR AVENUE
seen by Louise:
    <u>full of dirty old furniture</u>
    nice garden
    one bedroom <u>with two uncomfortable beds</u>
    living room <u>with bed (black and white TV)</u>
    <u>close to centre, station 20 mins</u>

TRANSCRIPT   *3 minutes*

BOB: Hello...er...this is Bob. I've been to see two of the places you asked me to look at: er...13A Balmoral Way and 7B Windsor Avenue. Well, first of all the one in Balmoral Way: um...it's quite modern and the living room's very spacious. Both the bedrooms are small though and the kitchen's tiny but it does have everything you'd need, including a freezer and a dishwasher. Um...there's no TV, so you'd have to rent one. It's on the fifth floor and you can see the park and the fields beyond: that's quite nice, but I got the impression that it's quite expensive because it's modern and it's got two bedrooms.

    Now, the other place is quite different. It's the ground floor of an old house and it's got its own garden, with trees and a nice lawn and a patio with a table and chairs so you could...er...eat outside in the evenings. Er...the furniture's comfortable and although it's only got one bedroom it's really big and it's got two single beds which are on separate sides of the room – or, well, you could move one bed into the living room. The kitchen's big and it's got a door onto the garden.

    Ah...that's about it. They're both still free and they're both available from July. Er...well, let me know what you decide to do. Bye.

LOUISE: Louise here. Listen, I've been to see two flats: one was 44C Sandringham Gardens and the other one was 7B Windsor Avenue. I like them both actually.

    Now, the one at Sandringham Gardens: it's got a balcony, which is nice. And the bedroom is quite unusual because it's a kind of an L shape; it's got one bed round the corner from the other. It's almost like two rooms in a way, it's really nice. Um...the living room has a TV and a video and it's very light and it's quite cheerful. It's on the second floor but the view of the railway line isn't what you'd call beautiful.

    Now the one at Windsor Avenue: this is absolutely crammed full of dusty old-fashioned furniture and it's not very clean. The garden's nice, but it was raining when I was there, so I didn't actually go out. There's one bedroom and it's got a couple of beds in it – they didn't look very comfortable. And there's another bed in the living room. And there's an old black and white television.

    They're both quite close to the centre, which is good. You could walk to the shops in a few minutes. The station's about 20 minutes away from both. Um...if you need to know any more just call me. I'll be in tomorrow. Bye then.

B Activity **57** in the Student's Book contains a model letter. This could be looked at **before** writing. Or it could be looked at **afterwards**, when the students compare their letter with it. Students are not told about Activity **57** in the Student's Book instructions, so that you can decide when they should look at it.

NOTE

Before starting 7.6 remind your students to look at the GRAMMAR REFERENCE section on Modal verbs on pages 178–179.

Modal verbs – 2 is in 8.3.

Here are some problems that might occur while doing 7.6 and 8.3:

1 Some students may have difficulty with the use of *was able* rather than *could* in positive sentences. For example:

> He thought he could climb the mountain easily. = He thought it would be possible (but perhaps he didn't succeed).
>
> He was able to climb the mountain easily. = past ability + success

2 The notions of 'certainty' and 'impossibility' can also be referred to as 'deduction' (e.g. You must be joking / You can't be serious). Strictly speaking, if you are perfectly certain about something, you wouldn't use a modal verb at all:

> It will rain today. = I am certain it will rain.
>
> He was joking.   = I knew he was joking.
>
> His plane didn't land on time.

3 Some students may have difficulty distinguishing between the idea of possibility that something is not true:

> That may not/mightn't be correct. = It's possible that it's not correct.
>
> He may not/mightn't have done it. = It's possible that he didn't do it.

and impossibility:

> He can't have done it. = It's impossible that he did it.
>
> That can't be correct. = I'm sure it's not correct.

4 Some students may have difficulty with expressing different degrees of obligation. These are very fine distinctions and may not be worth worrying about, particularly as in many cases *must, have to, have got to, should* and *ought to* are interchangeable.

5 For the benefit of students who require a straightforward (though over-simplified) explanation, the differences could be explained as follows:

Must expresses strong obligation:

> You must go home now. = I am ordering you to go.
>
> I really must leave.   = I am ordering myself.

Have to expresses obligation from 'outside':

> I have to finish this today.   = according to the rules or someone's orders
>
> Don't you have to leave before six? = (perhaps) You've got a train to catch or an appointment somewhere else.

Have got to is equivalent to *have to*.

Should expresses a duty or what is the right thing to do:

> You should be careful on the way home. = I advise you to be careful.
>
> I should work harder.   = It would be the right thing for me to do.

Ought to is equivalent to *should*.

6 Some students may have difficulty understanding the distinction between lack of obligation:

> You needn't do it if you don't want to. = There is no obligation to do it.

and an obligation not to do something:

> You mustn't do it. = There is an obligation not to do it. / You are forbidden to do it.

ANSWERS

1 I can't help you to find accommodation. = I'm unable to help you. (*But all three meanings could be implied in this sentence.*)
2 I don't have to help you to find accommodation. = It's not my responsibility to help you.
3 I won't help you to find accommodation. = I'm unwilling to help you.
4 She can't be joking. = I'm sure she isn't.
5 She can't tell jokes. = She's no good at it.
6 She must be joking. = I'm sure she is.
7 She mustn't tell jokes. = She isn't allowed to.
8 You can't leave now. = I won't let you go.
9 You could leave now. = It would be possible to go.
10 You don't have to leave now. = It's unnecessary to go.
11 You needn't leave now. = It's unnecessary to go.
12 You shouldn't leave now. = It's not a good idea to go.

 ANSWERS

2 *I checked the timetable so I mustn't be wrong about the departure time!*	can't
3 *You needn't to worry if I miss the last bus because I can get a taxi.*	don't need to/needn't
4 *Do I ought to phone for a taxi, or may I pick one up in the street?*	ought I to/should I can
5 *I could get a taxi but I must waiting for five minutes for one to arrive.*	would have to wait
6 *Don't be silly, you ought not to show your passport if you will buy a rail ticket.*	don't need to/needn't want to
7 *You mustn't write anything down unless you want to.*	don't have to/needn't
8 *You need spend as much time as you can on your homework.*	ought to/should/need to

 SUGGESTED ANSWERS (Your students will have better ideas than these.)

• I still can't play the saxophone and I still can't speak Greek. When I was ten I couldn't do either of those things.
• I don't have to go to school and I don't have to do what my parents tell me to. When I was ten I had to do both those things.
• I still have to clean my teeth and I still have to wear glasses.
• One day soon I may visit the USA and I may buy a new car.
• I know I shouldn't laugh at people behind their backs and I shouldn't eat so much.

 To start everyone off with the role-play, act out the start of the dinner-table conversation with two of your brighter students. With groups of four, two students should be local residents.

7.7 **Spelling and pronunciation – 1: Vowels**   WORD STUDY

This section concerns homophones and other spelling difficulties. Note that the examples are all R.P. (Southern middle-class British English: 'Received Pronunciation') and that in other accents some of the words may be pronounced differently. English accents tend to differ most in the way vowels and diphthongs are pronounced, rather than consonants.

Spelling and pronunciation – 2: Diphthongs is in 8.6
Spelling and pronunciation – 3: Consonants is in 9.4

 ANSWERS

worn   meat   one   through

B 1 & 2

ANSWERS

/æ/	scandal flat	marry
/e/	bury/berry weather/whether check/cheque	merry
/ɑː/	laugh castle half	guard
/ɔː/	wore/war source/sauce raw/roar	walk
/ɜː/	turn firm	work
/iː/	weak/week seize/seas wheel/we'll	receive
/ɪ/	guilty witch/which mist/missed	business
/ɒ/	not/knot knowledge quality	wander
/uː/	blue/blew root/route new/knew	soup
/ʊ/	cushion butcher pull	push
/ʌ/	blood tongue country thorough	wonder

3 📟 The recorded answers include correct pronunciations of the examples on the left in the Student's Book, as well as the words listed in the answers above. Play the recording to the class after they have completed the task. Pause for questions every so often – don't play the whole lot remorselessly through (the recording lasts 2 minutes 30 seconds). There are likely to be lots of questions in this exercise about the meaning of the words in the lists.

If there's time in class, or as homework, get everyone to write ten sentences each including two of the words from the lists.

C The mistakes in these sentences include problems with diphthongs as well as pure vowels.

ANSWERS

1 *I am quite <u>shore</u> that this <u>weak</u> is going <u>too</u> be wonderful.*	sure week to
2 *We are <u>truely</u> sorry that you had to <u>weight</u> so long <u>four</u> the delivery.*	truly wait for
3 *He has <u>dredful</u> manners – he <u>paws</u> tomato <u>source</u> on all his food.*	dreadful pours sauce
4 *They couldn't get <u>thier</u> new <u>armchare</u> <u>threw</u> the door.*	their armchair through
5 *<u>Witch</u> of these <u>too</u> alternatives is the <u>write</u> one?*	which two right
6 *He <u>lent</u> the ladder <u>agenst</u> the wall and <u>climed</u> onto the roof.*	leant against climbed
7 *The <u>cieling</u> and walls of this room need <u>peinting</u> <u>ergently</u>.*	ceiling painting urgently

NOTE
For 7.8 C students need to bring their own recent compositions to class. They should be asked to do this.

7.8 Starting and ending well   WRITING

A The best opening sentence is probably number 5: 'G__ is a delightfully unspoilt village surrounded by fields and woods at the mouth of the river.'

B And the best closing sentence is probably number 4: 'Go there before everyone else discovers it!'

C 1 Pick your **own** favourite opening and closing lines from the texts in Units 1–6 and find out how your students' preferences compare.

2 This is an important task which shouldn't be rushed. Encourage students to look at each other's compositions to get ideas from each other.

D Students may prefer to write about a different place from where they actually live, such as a favourite holiday resort (like G__).

8 Looking after yourself

The *Voices* video sequence *Get in shape! – A morning at a leisure centre* deals with other aspects of this topic, and asks the question: 'Do we live in a healthy society?'

Sports have already been discussed in Unit 4, but from the recreational/leisure angle – here sports are discussed as a way of staying healthy.

8.1 How are you feeling?   VOCABULARY

NOTE
Although many people enjoy talking about illness and accidents, others are sensitive about revealing personal information about distressing experiences or embarrassing diseases they may have had. It is probably best not to push your students on this topic.

A Here is some useful vocabulary that may come up in the discussion:

*cholesterol   drink less   get up late/early   give up smoking   go to bed early/late   healthy diet   jog
keep fit   medical examination/check-up   overeat   smoke   stay up late   take exercise   walk*

B Make sure everyone looks at the wrong answers – they contain further useful vocabulary.

> **ANSWERS**
> **2** prescription (*in some countries you can get antibiotics from a pharmacy without a prescription*)
> **3** injection   **4** spots   **5** headache   **6** temperature   **7** sneezing   **8** diet

C
> **ANSWERS**
> **1** off your food   out of sorts   under the weather
> **2** bruise   bump   cut
> **3** physically fit   living a healthy life   in good shape
> **4** affect   damage   ruin
> **5** dizzy   faint   funny

D 1
> **SUGGESTED ANSWERS** (Many variations are possible.)
> **2** leg/arm/collar bone   **3** finger/leg/toe   **4** elbow/knee/heel
> **5** shoulder/back/stomach   **6** ankle/wrist/knee   **7** head/tooth/back   **8** bumped/hit

2 Students should leave plenty of room around their sketch so that there is space for adding vocabulary. You may need to set a time limit for over-zealous students.

Instead of doing this in pairs, you might prefer to draw a body on the board and ask the whole class to tell you how to label the parts. (Be prepared for some potentially tricky requests for vocabulary here!) Alternatively, pairs of pairs could do this task with one pair starting at the toes and the other at the fingers, before forming groups of four to exchange information.

More words that might come up when naming the parts are: *limbs, joints, trunk, knuckles, fist, thigh* and *forearm*.

As a follow-up perhaps get the class to work together in groups and ask each other these questions:

- Have you ever been in hospital?
- Have you ever visited someone in hospital?
- What serious and less serious illnesses have you had?

8.2 Sleep and dreams

LISTENING AND WRITING

A

ANSWERS	
1 Rapid Eye Movement	6 deal with problems
2 deep sleep	7 remember them
3 REM sleep	8 four or five hours/less
4 several minutes	9 (ten minute) nap/short sleep
5 hurt or caught	10 waking up

TRANSCRIPT *5 minutes 40 seconds*

INTERVIEWER: . . . Now, sleep...er...like the way our brains work, is still something of a mystery, but recent research into sleep has given us a few more answers. With me today is Dr William Johnson, who has just published a book called simply: 'Sleep'. Dr Johnson, hello.

DR JOHNSON: Hello.

INTERVIEWER: How many kinds of sleep are there?

DR JOHNSON: Er...well, there are three types of sleep: um...there's light sleep, deep sleep and REM sleep.

INTERVIEWER: REM sleep, what's that?

DR JOHNSON: REM...er...R E M, that stands for Rapid Eye Movement. Now our eyes move about very fast under our eyelids during...um...this particular type of sleep.

Now...er...light sleep is 'optional' – we can actually do without it – and yet quite a lot of our sleeping time is actually spent sleeping lightly. But actually to restore our brains we require deep sleep.

INTERVIEWER: I see, and...er...is it true that dreams occur when you're just about to wake up?

DR JOHNSON: Well, haha, a lot of people actually think this but this is in fact wrong. Dreams take place during Rapid Eye Movement sleep...Yeah, now this type of sleep occurs every 90 minutes or so throughout the night. And...er...it usually goes on for several minutes.

INTERVIEWER: Oh, right...w...is there a...is there a particular reason why we dream?

DR JOHNSON: Um...well, that's a very good question...haha, well there's no...um...easy answer to it. Most of us can remember dreams where we are, I don't know, falling, flying, or being chased or something...Yeah and we wake up just before we hurt ourselves or just before we're caught. It seems that perhaps one purpose of dreams might be to help sleepers to deal with problems that they actually have in their waking lives, um...such as their fears or worries...Um...th...not exactly to solve those problems, but just to come to terms with them.

INTERVIEWER: But i...it's true, isn't it, that not everybody has dreams?

DR JOHNSON: Ah, well, ha, research has in fact shown that, yes, everyone *does* have dreams. The thing is that some people can't *remember* their dreams. Um...in fact, most people forget their dreams very quickly after waking up. For example, um...if I asked you now to tell me about your dreams last night, you...well, you probably couldn't remember, could you?

INTERVIEWER: Mm...well, no no, actually I can't, no.

DR JOHNSON: Haha, but if I asked you as soon as you'd woken up, you probably would have been able to tell me.

INTERVIEWER: Mm, yes, so...er...er...how much sleep do we really need? Um...you know, e...everyone says that eight hours is what...i...is...is the essential amount. Is that...is that right?

DR JOHNSON: Well, y...n...yes, in fact most people actually require *less* than eight hours' sleep a night – um...six or seven is enough for many people. And there are also many successful people who only need...er...a few hours sleep a night. I can think particularly of Napoleon, and...er...there's also Winston Churchill...um...also Margaret Thatcher...they all managed on four hours a night or...or even less – um...leaving them more time to keep one step ahead of their...their enemies, so to speak!

INTERVIEWER: Now then, what about...um...people who have...er...what...well, two sleeps? You know they...they sleep during the day and then they sleep at night as well? Um...now...er...presumably they get more sleep than people who only sleep at night?

DR JOHNSON: Well, if you split your sleep into two parts, you actually need *less* sleep. Um...for example, if someone takes a siesta and sleeps for say an hour, they only need to sleep for four or five hours at night. And presumably that's why people in the Mediterranean countries appear to be able to keep going until, you know, 2 am or...or even later than that.

But...um...a sleep during the day has to be long enough to allow...er...plenty of time for deep sleep. So, for example, the benefit of a ten-minute nap is...is, well, it's only psychological really, it's not physical. It may make you *feel* better, but it doesn't really do you any good at all.

INTERVIEWER: Uhuh, right, so...er...what about things like...um...oh, I don't know, snoring, talking in your sleep, you know, er...are...is there...is there anything you can do about that, are there any cures?

DR JOHNSON: Haha, um...there's only one certain cure for snoring – and that is waking up! . . . Er...but some snorers...um...are cured by sleeping on their sides or by sleeping without a pillow.

And...er...and talking in your sleep is something most people do, I think, at...at some point in their lives, it's, I don't know, it's not a problem exactly and surprisingly it occurs in all types of sleep, not...not just when you're dreaming.

INTERVIEWER: Mm. What about...er...insomnia, people who can't sleep, what...um...is there anything that you can do to help them?

DR JOHNSON: Err...well, there are many different causes for insomnia. Um...there really isn't time to deal with them all now. But if you do have trouble sleeping, the one thing you should *not* do is take sleeping pills.

INTERVIEWER: Oh really?

DR JOHNSON: Yeah, really. If you want to find out more you'll have to read my book.

INTERVIEWER: Haha, oh well, thank you, Dr Johnson, that's...er...that's marvellous, thank you very much.

DR JOHNSON: Thank you.

 Follow the procedure suggested in the Student's Book. Guidelines for writing a report can be found in Activity *58* – you may wish to go through these ideas with the class before they do the writing task.

NOTE
Before starting 8.3 remind your students to look at the GRAMMAR REFERENCE section on Modal verbs on pages 178–179.

8.3 Modal verbs – 2   GRAMMAR REVIEW

Refer to the list of problems that might crop up in 7.6.

 ANSWERS

2 I had to give her my phone number. = I gave her the number.
3 I didn't have to give her my phone number. = I gave her the number.
4 She wouldn't let me give her my phone number. = I didn't give her the number.

5 He can't have gone to hospital. = I'm sure he didn't go.
6 He couldn't go to hospital. = He didn't go, because he wasn't able to.
7 He must have gone to hospital. = I'm convinced he has gone.
8 He needn't have gone to hospital. = He went, but it was unnecessary to.
9 He shouldn't have gone to hospital. = He went, but it was a mistake to do so.

B **ANSWERS**

2 The doctor told me that ***I had to take*** the tablets three times a day.
3 She told me that ***I could stop taking them when I felt*** better.
4 She told me that ***I might feel better*** in a few days.
5 She told me that ***I couldn't expect to get better if I didn't follow*** her advice.
6 She told me that ***I had to take*** some exercise every day.
7 She told me that ***I shouldn't/mustn't/hadn't to*** sit around doing nothing.
8 She told me that ***I ought to/should*** eat less.

 ANSWERS (Some of these require more than five words, so they aren't typical exam questions.)

2 He ***can't possibly need an injection before*** going to America.
3 You ***shouldn't take aspirins if you're perfectly*** all right.
4 Do ***I really have to/need to*** take more exercise?
5 I wonder how long I'll ***have to wait***?
6 He ***had to stay*** in bed.
7 You ***shouldn't have gone/needn't have gone/didn't need to go to the doctor/doctor's with*** a cough.
8 The doctor ***couldn't have/can't have cured*** your cough.

8.4   **What to do about flu**   READING

 A Before reading the text, get everyone to test their general knowledge and common sense. Then they can check if they guessed right by reading the text.

> **ANSWERS**
> 1 True
> 2 False (*They can't kill viruses.*)
> 3 False (*You shouldn't force yourself to eat.*)
> 4 False (*It can become serious for elderly or sick people.*)
> 5 True
> 6 False (*The text would say if this was advisable – but if it helps, why not?*)
> 7 False (*It only gives one year's protection.*)
> 8 False (*winter*)
> 9 True (*Dirty plates and cutlery can spread infection.*)
> 10 True

B **1** This part develops into a straightforward role-play. Here are some questions:

Have you got a headache?
Do you feel weak or shivery?
Are you sweating a lot?
Do you feel sick?
Have you lost your appetite?
Have you got a high temperature?

2 Brainstorm some other ways of introducing advice. For example:

I think you should . . .
You ought to . . .
It's best to . . .
My advice is to . . .

It's best to stay indoors.
You'd better keep away from other people.

3 Students perform two role-plays with the roles reversed in the second one. If necessary, act out the beginning of the first role-play with one courageous student while the rest of the class listen and gain confidence.

8.5   **Smoke-free zones**   READING

A Laws on smoking in public places are moving closer to the ones explained in the article and, in some European countries, even exceeding them.

B
> **ANSWERS**
> **2** c   **3** b   **4** c   **5** c   **6** a   **7** a   **8** c

C
> **ANSWERS**
> ¶1 grimy   consenting adults   ¶3 polls   hazard
> ¶2 harsher   banned   ¶4 hinted   hefty   kicking the habit

D This is the complete table, with the missing figures included.

Number of cigarettes and litres of alcohol consumed per person per year			
	Cigarettes	Litres of beer	Litres of wine
Argentina	1,300	19	58
Belgium	1,700	125	24
Brazil	1,200	34	1
Czech Republic	1,600	130	12
France	1,700	40	70
Germany	2,000	140	23
Greece	2,900	24	24
Hungary	2,500	100	21
Italy	1,600	23	70
Japan	2,500	44	1
Poland	2,600	29	8
Spain	2,200	73	38
Switzerland	1,900	73	47
UK	1,700	110	12
USA	2,100	90	9

8.6 ## Spelling and pronunciation – 2: Diphthongs   WORD STUDY

A ANSWERS

aloud   break   hole   write

B 1 & 2

ANSWERS

/aɪ/	climate by/buy/bye thigh	time
/aʊ/	proud found	frown
/ɔɪ/	destroy employer	point
/eə/	stares/stairs fare/fair pair/pear	share
/ɪə/	cleared atmosphere	sincere
/eɪ/	wait/weight male/mail waste/waist	paint
/əʊ/	folk nose/knows	soap

3 📼 The answers to B1 and 2 are on the recording, which also includes the examples given on the left in the Student's Book.

C 📼 Play the recording while everyone writes the missing words. This exercise should be reassuringly easy. It includes some pure vowels as well as diphthongs. (The recording lasts 1 minute.)

ANSWERS AND TRANSCRIPT

1 The part of your leg above the knee is your *thigh*.
2 What is your *waist* measurement in centimetres?
3 What is your *weight* in kilos?
4 What is your *height* in metres?
5 If you jump out of this window, you'll *break* your leg.
6 The *mayor* of New York is against smoking.
7 Smoking isn't *allowed* in restaurants in Los Angeles.
8 *Walking* to *work* keeps me fit.

8.7 At . . .   PREPOSITIONS

This is the first of four exercises on prepositional phrases. The others are 9.3, 10.6 and 11.5.

> **ANSWERS**
> **2** at last   **3** At first sight   **4** at a profit   at a loss   **5** at war   at peace (*or vice versa*)
> **6** at a time   **7** at least   **8** at once   **9** at the same time   **10** at all

8.8 How to stay healthy   SPEAKING AND WRITING

A Follow the procedure suggested in the Student's Book. This part of the section focuses on the Speaking paper in the exam, using contrasting photographs as the starting-point for a one-minute talk.

If this is feasible, perhaps get the students to record their one-minute talks, so that they have an idea how they sound and can discuss their 'performance' more objectively.

B Activities *16* and *42* give a 'star rating' for the sports listed in B1.

C This writing task is similar to Question 1 in the Writing paper in the exam – again follow the procedure suggested in the Student's Book.

Suggested opening and closing sentences:

I was really pleased to hear from you after all this time.
Let me know how you get on.

NOTE
For 9.1 E ask your students to bring some snapshots of holidays or excursions to class. Bring some of your own too.

9 Having a great time!

The *Voices* video sequence *St Ives – Holidaymakers, artists and surfers* deals with other aspects of this topic. But you might prefer to use it with Unit 18 *Yes, but is it art?*

NOTE
Students should bring snapshots of holidays or excursions to class for Part E in 9.1. They'll need advance warning of this. Bring some of your own too.

9.1 Holidays   VOCABULARY AND SPEAKING

As a warm-up perhaps discuss these general questions about your students' recent holidays:

- What's your favourite kind of holiday?
- What's the worst kind of holiday you can imagine?
- Where did you stay? What did you do? What did you enjoy? What do you remember best about your holidays?
- What are your plans for your next holiday?

A We begin with listening, for a change.

ANSWERS
The first speaker, Susanna, went to Paris (photo 2). Her holiday lasted ten days.
The second speaker, James, went to New York (photo 1). His holiday lasted a week.
The third speaker, Joan, went to Venice (photo 3). Her holiday lasted four days.

TRANSCRIPT   *2 minutes 40 seconds*

SUSANNA: . . . it was wonderful because it was the springtime and it's, you know, traditional sort of romantic place to be in the spring. Er...we went for about ten days, and it was glorious. All the blossom was on the trees and down by the river and...um...the people seem to rush around everywhere all the time and...er...we were just desperately trying to keep up, and didn't, and didn't. But...um...visited the churches and of course the Eiffel Tower – all the...all the old tourist spots, but it was really beautiful, had a lovely time.

JAMES: . . . it's...um...an extraordinary...er...jungle really...um...a fantastic mixture of different kinds of people...um...a...a mixture of different kinds of cultures...um...all sort of packed into a tiny area, considering how many people there are. Er...I was there for about a...a week...um...and it was March and it was beginning to hot up and...um...er...the street life is the thing that instantly hits you. And the number of cabs and the noise on the streets is incredible, there's almost a sort of sense of...a sort of...almost as if there's a permanent earthquake going on under...just under the surface, and you look up and there's just a thin blue strip and you realise that that's the sky and all around you are these incredible tall buildings . . .

JOAN: . . . it was absolutely beautiful. We booked last minute flights and...um...it was a long weekend, which was just perfect actually, we in fact had about four days. Um...and because it was springtime, the weather was ideal for walking, we travelled very lightly, and we just walked miles and miles, and it's just the perfect place to do that really. Um...we did, in fact, have one trip on a gondola, but it's quite a pricey way to...to experience, you know, the sights and sounds of the city. But...um...I loved it and I'd like to go back and spend more time and really explore the city because it's very old and crumbling and the...the artwork is just really quite exquisite, it really is splendid. I took rolls and rolls of film as well, wonderful!

B 1

ANSWERS
1 package   2 agency   3 arrangements   4 brochures   5 guide   6 resort
7 sunbathing   8 beach   9 excursions   10 self-catering   11 view   12 balcony
13 delightful

2 Presumably the reality didn't live up to expectations!

C **ANSWERS**
1 day-trippers   holiday-makers   sightseers
2 bed and breakfast   full board   half board
3 active   busy   energetic
4 lazy   relaxing   restful
5 choice   range   variety
6 gift   present   souvenir

D Here is some useful vocabulary that may come up during the discussion:

*art gallery   castle   crowded   deserted   group   guide   hiking   historical monument
mountains   museum   package holiday   palm trees   path   pedalos   rucksack/backpack
sight-seeing/seeing the sights   sunburn   suntan   track   work of art*

E You may want to postpone this till the next lesson to give everyone a chance to gather up some photos.

9.2 Brazilian Contrasts   READING

A Follow the procedure suggested in the Student's Book.

ANSWERS
2 Salvador   3 São Paulo   4 Rio   5 Rio   6 Rio   7 Brasilia   8 Rio
9 Iguaçu   10 Rio

B 1

ANSWERS
2 Early morning
3 Day 2: afternoon city tour and Days 11–13: Carioca night tour
4 Brasilia
5 No, winding (*streets wind up and down the hills*)
6 By a million new inhabitants every year
7 The noise (*the distant roar of the Falls increases to a deafening crescendo*)
8 Evening

2

ANSWERS
1 Luxor Continental
2 Yes (*290 rooms . . . high rise*)
3 No (*50 yards from . . . Copacabana Beach*)
4 Not necessarily (*rooms vary in size and location*)
5 No (*with shower only*)
6 No (*modern accommodation*)

C Some of the other problems of holidays in exotic places are malaria, yellow fever, snakes, sharks, jellyfish, humidity, long-haul flights, crime, terrorism, etc.

9.3 By . . .   PREPOSITIONS

1

ANSWERS
1 by name   2 by far   3 by heart   4 by accident/mistake   5 by train   by car
6 by day   by night   7 by surprise   8 by chance   9 by all means
10 by post   by hand   11 By the time   12 by yourself

The three superfluous phrases were: *by plane, by ship* and either *by mistake* or *by accident*.

2 Example sentences:

You can cross the Atlantic quickly *by plane* or more slowly *by ship*.
Oh dear, I've put down my old address on the form *by mistake*.

9.4 Spelling and pronunciation – 3: Consonants WORD STUDY

A Pause the recording between each group of words so that everyone can catch their breath and, if necessary, discuss what they've written so far. The correct spellings are in Activity **5**, but students shouldn't look there until they've done all parts of the exercise.

TRANSCRIPT AND ANSWERS *3 minutes 30 seconds*

slipping	He kept slipping on the ice.
sleeping	She was still sleeping at ten o'clock.
trouble	Don't worry, it's no trouble.
robber	The robber stole the money.
total	What's the total amount?
putting	You're putting on weight.
address	What's your name and address?
doubled	Their speed doubled.
request	I agreed to his request.
Christian	Is he a Christian or a Muslim?
angle	Ninety degrees is a right angle.
ignorant	They are very ignorant.
engine	This car has a petrol engine.
average	The average is 50 per cent.
adventure	We had an exciting adventure.
butcher	You get meat from the butcher.
careful	Please be very careful.
million	The population of Britain is 50 million.
often	How often have you seen her?
sudden	There was a sudden noise.
immense	The problems are immense.
coming	Are you coming to see us?
worry	It's all right, don't worry!
railway	I'll meet you at the railway station.
assistant	My assistant will help you.
please	Please don't smoke.
insurance	Don't drive without insurance.
pleasure	It was a pleasure to meet you.
laughing	He kept on laughing.
rough	The surface isn't smooth, it's rough.
convince	They tried to convince me.
live	Where do you live?
theory	In theory that sounds like a good idea.
themselves	They did all the work themselves.
twelve	Six plus six is twelve.
while	I'll wash up while you dry.
university	She's a student at the university.
yawning	I'm very tired, I can't help yawning.

B Some more examples of 'silent letters':

gh	through straight
b	crumb thumb
t	postman fasten
k	know knock knit
l	stalk talk would
r	far father farther confirm (only in RP)
h	honour dishonest exhausted
w	wrestle wrong wretched

C Activities **14** and **22** contain more words that students dictate to each other, but in case of confusion – and there will be plenty – the words should be spelt out.

NOTE

Before starting 9.5 remind your students to look at the GRAMMAR REFERENCE section on *If . . .* sentences on pages 174–175.

If . . . sentences – 2 is in 11.2.

 ANSWERS (The words that show the meaning differences are in bold italics.)

1 We can't go skiing *until* there's more snow on the mountains. = We're waiting for more snow – without more snow we can't go skiing.

2 *Unless* there's more snow on the mountains, we can't go skiing. = There's not enough snow now and there needs to be more snow for skiing (similar meaning to 1).

3 We can't go skiing *if* there's more snow on the mountains. = Too much snow will make skiing dangerous or impossible – there's already plenty of snow.

4 In April, *when* the weather *is* warmer, I *'ll take* a few days off. = I know the weather will be warmer then.

5 I *'ll take* a couple of days off *if* the weather *is* better in April. = I'm unsure whether the weather will be warmer then.

6 *If* the weather *were* nicer in April, I *'d take* a short break. = I know the weather won't be nicer then – I'm just imagining.

7 You'd better take an overnight bag *in case* you have to stay the night. = You may have to stay the night, so be prepared.

8 *If* you have to stay the night, you'd better take an overnight bag. = As you have to stay the night, be prepared.

9 I *'ll go* to Rio for the Carnival *if* I *can* afford it. = I may be able to afford it, and if I can I will go.

10 *If* I *could* afford it, I *'d go* to Rio for the Carnival. = I can't afford it and I can't go – I'm just day-dreaming.

11 I *might go* to Rio at Carnival time *if* I *had* enough money. = I can't afford it, but even if I could I wouldn't definitely go there.

 ANSWERS

2 *If <u>it's</u> my birthday tomorrow, I'd invite my friends out for a meal.*   it was/were

3 *If you <u>will need</u> any help, please let me know.*   need

4 *We'll enjoy our holiday unless it <u>will rain</u> all the time.*   rains

5 *If the sun's shining tomorrow, we'll go swimming.*   ✔

6 *When I'm on holiday <u>I'd like</u> to relax rather than be active.*   I like

7 *Let's go to the mountains <u>if</u> the spring comes.*   when

8 *I'll be arriving on Sunday <u>until</u> there's a change of plan.*   unless

C Most of these sentences require more than five words, so they are not the same as the equivalent part of the Use of English paper.

ANSWERS (Some variations are possible.)

2 If you go to Britain, *you'll be able to practise your English* all the time.

3 If you *stay in the sun all day long, you'll get* sunburnt.

4 If *I didn't have to work this summer, I'd go* on holiday.

5 Unless you book ahead *you won't find anywhere to* stay.

6 Pack a jumper to wear after dark *in case the evenings are* cool.

7 If we *go on holiday together, you'll certainly enjoy* yourself.

8 If *you could go anywhere in the world, which country would you* travel to?

D After the discussion, ask everyone to write down six sentences using *If* . . . .

9.6 An excursion programme LISTENING AND WRITING

A Some things your students might be familiar with are: Loch Ness and the Loch Ness Monster, whisky and kilts.

B Set the scene by asking everyone to imagine that they're in their hotel in Edinburgh on the first morning of their holiday in Scotland. They're having breakfast with the other members of their group (a bowl of oatmeal porridge followed by bacon and eggs and then toast and marmalade). The tour leader is about to make an announcement . . .

Discover Scotland Holidays

Excursion programme

	Departure		Return
Sunday	14:00	Edinburgh city sightseeing *(no need to book)*	16:30
Monday	9:00	(Braemar Castle) and (Aberdeen)	17:30
Tuesday	~~8:30~~ *7:45*	Glencoe and Fort William	17:30
Wednesday	8:00	Inverness and Loch Ness	~~17:30~~ *18:30*
Thursday	14:00	Edinburgh City sightseeing tour	16:30
Friday	*cancelled* 7:00 ~~9:15~~	*Glasgow and River Clyde steamer trip* ~~Galashiels and the Borders~~	*17:45* ~~16:00~~

TRANSCRIPT *2 minutes 30 seconds*

TOUR LEADER: Good morning, everyone. Er...ha...sorry to...er...interrupt breakfast. I've got here a few changes to the excursion...er...programme, which I think you've all got. Um...I might as well go through them all and then you'll know where you are. In fact, they make absolutely no difference to the tours: in fact they...they improve them, which is basically why we've made the changes. Now, your Monday 9 o'clock...um...where you've got the Braemar Castle...er...Aberdeen: what we're going to do is we're going to swop round there and we're going to go to Aberdeen first and then on to Braemar, returning here at 17.30. Now we move to Tuesday. Ah...the only difference there...I'm going to make an earlier start for Glencoe and Fort William: ah...7.45 instead of 8.30. Ah...Wednesday: yes, the...the Inverness and Loch Ness – one of my personal favourites, I think...um...everyone – um...instead of returning at...er...17.30, we'll come back a...a...a little bit later there on that one...er...18.30...give us a bit more time actually at Loch Ness. Hope we spot the monster, eh? Ha! Well...er...Thursday...um...now this is...this is our...our big day in Edinburgh, where we're doing the city sightseeing. Um...also...er...we're going to do an Edinburgh this afternoon – that's today, Sunday, we're going to do an Edinburgh...um...because...er...we...we had nothing planned for today, but we're going to do an Edinburgh as well. Er...same time, no need to book. Er...now unfortunately on Friday we've had to cancel your Galashiels and your Borders. Er...but instead we're substituting Glasgow, leaving at seven for Glasgow and then I think a fitting end to your holiday, one I think you're going to go for: the River Clyde Steamer Trip. Yes, on an actual River Clyde steamer. Re...returning at...at 17...17.45. Er...I hope those are all satisfactory. Sorry we've had to make these changes, but I think you'll find that they'll improve the holiday and make it even better than it already is.

Oh, now I...can I remind you that the...the excursions are of course optional, you know, but I'm sure you'll all want to go on them. Er...and would you decide which ones you want to go on by lunchtime today. Thanks very much, everyone, enjoy the rest of your breakfasts.

C Follow the procedure suggested in the Student's Book. Activity *59* contains a description of one of the Scottish excursions as a model for the students' own written work.

9.7 Use of English: Fill the gaps   EXAM TECHNIQUES

This is the first section where we focus exclusively on exam techniques. From now on, most units will have a special section dealing with a specific paper or part of a paper. The next is 11.7.

A 1

> **ANSWERS**
>
> **2** noun   **3** verb   **4** adverb   possessive pronoun   **5** article   article
> **6** preposition   pronoun

2

> **SUGGESTED ANSWERS**
>
> **1** bad   **2** night   **3** cross   **4** finally   our   **5** A   the   **6** in   myself

B 1

> **ANSWERS**
>
> **1** usual   **2** himself   **3** minute   **4** airport   **5** road   **6** time   **7** lounge
> **8** flight   **9** made   **10** desk

2

> **SUGGESTED ANSWERS**
>
> **12** free   **13** technical   **14** take off   **15** ages   **16** information   **17** night
> **18** expense   **19** happened   **20** asleep   **21** behind   **22** passengers   **23** reason
> **24** imagine

10

Food for thought

The *Voices* video sequence *Enjoy your meal!* deals with other aspects of this topic.

10.1 Mmm, this looks delicious!   READING

A You may prefer to do this warm-up activity with the whole class, so that the useful vocabulary that comes up can be put on the board under headings such as *desserts, cakes* and *fruit*. It's sometimes difficult to distinguish between a dessert and a cake, as in some of the apple recipes that follow.

B Try to resist answering students' questions about vocabulary at this stage. They should attempt the task without understanding every word. Most of the puzzling vocabulary is dealt with in the vocabulary exercise in Part C below.

> **ANSWERS** (Some of these may have to be guessed by a process of elimination.)
> **Dorset Apple Cake:** ingredients C, instructions 3, photo a
> **Somerset Cider Cake:** ingredients D, instructions 1, photo c
> **Apple and Blackberry Pie:** ingredients A, instructions 2, photo b
> **Apple Crumble:** ingredients B, instructions 4, photo d

C
> **ANSWERS**
> A   filling   pastry   C   peeled   chopped (into chunks)   zest
> B   ground   wholewheat flour   D   cider   cored   self-raising flour

D Something completely different! Be prepared to answer questions about what you consider to be good and bad table manners among the examples illustrated. Other examples of bad manners might be talking with your mouth full or eating chicken with your fingers – but not necessarily.

10.2 Cooking and eating   VOCABULARY

A This is the basis for discussion, not a definitive cookery guide. Note that in American English *broil = grill*. Ask the class to suggest other things that can be steamed, boiled, fried, etc.

> **SUGGESTED ANSWERS**
> Chicken can be fried, roasted, grilled or barbecued.
> Potatoes can be steamed, boiled, fried, roasted or baked.
> Rice can be steamed, boiled or fried (after it's been steamed or boiled).
> Fish can be steamed, boiled (to make soup or fish stew), fried, baked, grilled or barbecued.
> Bread can only be baked, or grilled (to make toast).
> Steak can be fried, grilled or barbecued.
> Carrots can be steamed or boiled (and possibly baked).

B Some letters are harder than others to find words for (in italics below). You might want to be kind and put some of the harder ones on the board beforehand, so that your students don't have to waste time fruitlessly searching for them. Students who finish early could start again at A and see how far they get!

> **SUGGESTED ANSWERS**
> aubergine butter chicken duck eggs French fries garlic hamburger ice cream
> jam kiwi lettuce marmalade nuts oranges peaches *quince* radish spinach
> tomato *unleavened bread* vegetables water melon *Xmas pudding* yogurt
> *zucchini* (=courgettes)

C **ANSWERS**

1 hot **2** dishes **3** recipe **4** rare **5** additives **6** wine list **7** greedy
8 helping **9** avoid **10** off **11** still **12** bitter

D Ask the groups to report on their most delicious (and/or most disgusting) dishes to the class.
Perhaps also discuss what kinds of food can be eaten at different times of day and what kinds
of food would only be eaten on special occasions – these vary from country to country, as do
eating habits generally.

EXTRA ACTIVITY
Brainstorm three lists on the board: ten kinds of fruit, ten kinds of vegetables and ten kinds of
drink.

FRUIT: strawberry, raspberry, pineapple, apple, pear, apricot, peach, melon, blackcurrant,
blackberry, banana, grape, grapefruit, plum, greengage, orange, lemon, lime, kiwi,
papaya/pawpaw

VEGETABLES: potato, pea, cauliflower, cucumber, cabbage, carrot, onion, celery, broccoli,
asparagus, artichoke, mushroom, lettuce, spinach, garlic, courgette/zucchini,
aubergine/eggplant

DRINKS: tea, coffee, beer, lager, bitter, wine, whisky, brandy, lemonade, orangeade,
orange juice, tonic water, mineral water, vermouth, cider, milk, apple juice, freshly squeezed
orange juice

NOTE
Before starting 10.3 remind your students to look at the GRAMMAR REFERENCE section on *-ing*
and *to . . .* on pages 175–176.

10.3 *-ing* and *to . . . – 1*   GRAMMAR REVIEW

-ing and *to . . . – 2* is in 12.3.

A **ANSWERS**

2 *I'm looking forward to <u>go</u> on holiday.*   going

3 *<u>To smoke</u> is not allowed in restaurants in New York.*   Smoking

4 *It was kind of you <u>inviting</u> me <u>joining</u> you.*   to invite   to join

5 *At night it's too dark to see without <u>to use</u> a flashlight.*   using

6 *Do you think that cooking for a family is easier than running a restaurant?* ✔

B Some of these sentences require more than five words, so it's not typical of the equivalent
Use of English exercise in the exam.

SUGGESTED ANSWERS
1 I'm looking ***forward to having*** something to eat.
2 It is easier ***to boil eggs than (to)*** poach them.
3 It's ***essential to phone the restaurant to*** book a table for twelve.
4 We got there ***too late to have/for*** lunch.
5 I'm always ***interested in trying*** new dishes from abroad.
6 I was disappointed ***to find that my favourite dish wasn't*** on the menu.
7 ***Drinking*** strong coffee ***at night prevents me from sleeping***.
8 Don't you realise ***that eating sweets is bad for your*** teeth?

C This type of exercise in the exam only requires one word. Moreover, in the exam the same
word wouldn't have to be used four times, as here!

SUGGESTED ANSWERS
1 to visit   **2** seeing   **3** spending   **4** using   **5** to use   **6** to go   **7** sitting
8 eating/to eat   **9** eating   **10** eating   **11** piling/filling   **12** eating
13 sitting   **14** talking/chatting   **15** to stay/to sit

Look again at the fourth paragraph with the class. How could it be rewritten to make it less repetitive? Brainstorm ideas with the class. Perhaps this would be an improvement:

By the time we got back, the table was laid in the garden for lunch and we all began our meal. We went on eating all afternoon! I'm not used to so much food, but grandmother's cooking was so good that I just couldn't help being greedy!

D Follow the procedure suggested in the Student's Book. Write the most amusing examples that come up on the board.

10.4 Eating out   LISTENING AND SPEAKING

A 1 A sophisticated, cosmopolitan class may be able to answer quite a lot of questions before hearing the recording. If so, encourage a class discussion of the ingredients of the dishes mentioned. Reassure them, if necessary, that they won't have to understand or be able to spell French or Italian in the exam!

2 🔲 Play the recording, pausing occasionally to give everyone time to write in their answers. In the exam there will not be so many gaps to fill (but the recording won't be paused while candidates write down their answers).

> **ANSWERS**
> 1 a gin and tonic   sparkling water
> 2 tomatoes   olives
> 3 chopped potatoes   onions
> 4 veal   breadcrumbs
> 5 wine   cream   starter   main course
> 6 grated   bacon   fried eggs
> 7 layers   pasta   meat   oven   cheese
> 8 *moules marinière*   Spanish omelette   green
> 9 Greek salad   lasagne
> 10 orange juice   a half bottle of the house red wine

Before going on to B, students could role-play the same situation.

TRANSCRIPT *3 minutes*

WAITRESS: Good evening. Would you like to see the menu?
AMANDA: Oh, yes please.
WAITRESS: Would you like a drink before you start?
PAUL: Oh, I think so, yes. Um...I'll have a gin and tonic, how about you?
AMANDA: I think I'll just have a sparkling water.
WAITRESS: Oh, right, thank you.
AMANDA: Mm, let's have a look. Oh, I see they've got pizzas.
PAUL: Mm, I think I fancy some fish tonight actually.
AMANDA: Do you? Hey, Paul, what does a Greek salad consist of?
PAUL: Greek salad? Well, it's got cucumber, tomato, olives and...um...you know, that feta goat's cheese.
AMANDA: Oh, I don't like goat's cheese. Oh, what about...um...*Wiener Schnitzel*, what's that?
PAUL: I'm not sure. We could ask the waitress. Oh, hold on, do you know what Spanish omelette is?
AMANDA: Oh yeah, it's an omelette with chopped potatoes and onions in it.
PAUL: Mm, sounds good.
AMANDA: It is.
PAUL: What about *Lasagne al forno*?
AMANDA: Oh, well, I know it's some sort of pasta, but I'm not quite sure. Well, we'll have to ask the waitress . . .
WAITRESS: Um...are you ready to order?
AMANDA: Yeah...um...could you just tell me something: what is *Wiener Schnitzel*?
WAITRESS: It's a thin piece of veal coated in egg and breadcrumbs and then it's pan-fried.
PAUL: And what's *moules marinière*?
WAITRESS: That's...um...mussels cooked in wine with onions and a little cream. You can have those as a starter or as a main course.
PAUL: Mussels, mm, and what's...er...*Rösti*?
WAITRESS: Haha, *Rösti*, yeah, that's...um...grated potatoes, bacon and onions fried together. You can have it with two fried eggs on top as a main course, or you can have it with your main course instead of French fries, if you like.

AMANDA:	And just one more thing: what's *Lasagne al forno*?
WAITRESS:	Oh yes, that's...um...thin layers of pasta and meat sauce with a creamy sauce, baked in the oven with cheese on top.
AMANDA:	Oh, well . . . Um...I'll have mussels as starter, please, and...um...then I'd like the Spanish omelette with a mixed salad . . . No, no, sorry, could you make that a green salad?
WAITRESS:	Sure.
PAUL:	Er...and I won't have a starter. If I could have the lasagne as a main course and a mixed salad to go with it.
WAITRESS:	Right, so that's one *moules marinière* as a starter, a Spanish omelette, a lasagne and two mixed salads.
AMANDA:	No...er...mine was a green salad.
PAUL:	Er...can I have a Greek salad instead of mixed salad. But as a starter, is that all right?
WAITRESS:	Yes, right, that's fine. Anything to drink?
PAUL:	What do you fancy, red wine?
AMANDA:	Oh, no, no, I won't have any wine, I'm driving. Have you got any apple juice?
WAITRESS:	I'm afraid not, but we have got orange juice.
AMANDA:	Oh, that'll be fine, thank you.
PAUL:	Mm. Er...mm...can I have...er...half a bottle of the house red?
WAITRESS:	Oh yes, fine.
PAUL:	Thanks.

B 1 🗣 Don't explain any items on the menu – most of these are explained in the information given in the Communication Activities.

Student A looks at Activity *11*, Student B at *44* and C at *52*. They should spend a few minutes studying the information before beginning the conversation, so that they don't read the explanations out word-for-word but try to remember them.

📼 There is a 'model conversation' on the cassette, which can be played to the class before they take part in the activity in B to give an idea of how their conversation might go. Maybe fade out the recording after 45 seconds, instead of playing it all. Then play the whole conversation at the end.

TRANSCRIPT *2 minutes*

FIRST WOMAN:	Shall we have a look at the menu? I'm so hungry.
MAN:	Yeah, OK. Boy, there are a few things here that I don't understand.
SECOND WOMAN:	There's a lot of this stuff I don't understand. What's all this then?
FIRST WOMAN:	Well, what about the starters? Hey, do you know what 'prawns' –
MAN:	Appetisers.
FIRST WOMAN:	Appetisers, oh. 'Prawns' are what?
MAN:	They're like large shrimps.
SECOND WOMAN:	Oh, they're delicious with avocado.
FIRST WOMAN:	Really? Mind you, I like the sound of 'melon and orange salad'.
MAN:	Hey, hey, look at the main courses. What is 'Lancashire hotpot'?
SECOND WOMAN:	I've heard of that. That's sort of lamb and vegetables cooked in the oven sort of broiled and the potatoes are sliced on top and put in a layer. It's delicious.
FIRST WOMAN:	It sounds good. And what's this one: 'steak and kidney pie', do you know what this is?
MAN:	Yeah, that now is a typical English dish – it's made of beef which is cut up into pieces along with pieces of kidney in a rich brown sauce. It is lovely. And that is traditionally English.
FIRST WOMAN:	Sounds delicious!
SECOND WOMAN:	The one I don't understand is 'cottage pie'.
FIRST WOMAN:	Now, I've come across that before. That's minced beef in gravy and it's got mashed potato on top. I don't know if that's going to be that good, although this does look like a good restaurant, don't you think?
SECOND WOMAN:	OK. Now do either of you know what's this, what's 'nut and mushroom roast'?
MAN:	Well, it's a vegetarian dish...er...hasn't got any meat in it – made of nuts, mushrooms and it's baked in the oven like a cake. Might be quite nice. Er...but the other one I don't know here is 'chicken Madras'. Anyone know that?
FIRST WOMAN:	No.
SECOND WOMAN:	Yes, that's an Indian dish. I can tell you that's...um...it's, I think it's pieces of chicken...

2 Draw everyone's attention to the useful phrases at the foot of the page before they start the activity.

While they are doing the activity, explaining unknown dishes to each other, you could yourself play the role of (head) waiter/waitress, answering any other queries they may have – and if time taking orders for pre-dinner drinks!

10.5 **Compound words – 1**   WORD STUDY

Compound words – 2 in 11.4 looks at more examples that are 'one-offs' and which don't follow a pattern like the ones in A2 here.

A **1**

> **ANSWERS**
>
> **3** He uses his left hand to write with.
> **4** with blue eyes and with red hair
> **5** list of wines
> **6** gadget to open cans
> **7** watch worn on the wrist

2

> **SUGGESTED ANSWERS**
>
> **first**   first floor   first name   first course   (first hand)
> **second**   second-hand   second-best   second cousin   (second floor)   (second name)
> **high**   high-class   high-level
> **low**   low-speed   low-pressure
> **home**   home-grown   home-produced
> **middle**   middle-aged   middle-sized
> **self**   self-respect   self-discipline   self-service
> **well**   well-known   well-off

3 🔲 Play the recording, which includes the examples in the Student's Book and the answers above (apart from the words in brackets). Make sure everyone has a chance to practise their pronunciation. The recording lasts 1 minute 50 seconds.

B This is similar in format to a word-formation exercise in the Use of English paper. But in the exam few, if any, of the words would be compounds – the exercise would concentrate on prefixes and suffixes.

> **ANSWERS**
>
> **2** old-fashioned   **3** fast food   **4** home-grown/home-produced   **5** tin opener
> **6** food processor   **7** self-service   **8** mass-produced   **9** first course
> **10** food poisoning   **11** fruit juice   **12** mineral water

10.6 *On . . . and out of . . .*   PREPOSITIONS

1

> **ANSWERS**
>
> **1** on time   on business   **2** out of order   **3** on holiday/vacation   out of doors
> **4** on your own   **5** on the house   **6** on purpose   **7** on the other hand/on the whole
> **8** out of reach   **9** on duty   **10** On the whole

The superfluous phrases were: *out of work, on the telephone* and *out of date.*

2 Example sentences:

He lost his job last year and he's been *out of work* ever since.
I spoke to her *on the telephone* last night.
Last year's diary is no use because it is *out of date.*

10.7 ## How do you make . . . ? LISTENING AND WRITING

A This isn't an exam-style listening exercise, but looking at the questions before listening is an important exam skill.

Follow the procedure in the Student's Book.

ANSWERS

1 H 2 D 3 G 4 C 5 F 6 K 7 L 8 E 9 I 10 B 11 A
J is the superfluous instruction.

TRANSCRIPT *1 minute 30 seconds*

JOAN: You know those potatoes you cooked for us the other evening?
NEIL: Mm.
JOAN: Well, you said you'd let me have the recipe.
NEIL: Yeah, here you are, I've written it out for you, w...a...at least I've written out the ingredients.
JOAN: Oh thanks...Oh yeah, I see. Um...but what do I have to do?
NEIL: Well it's quite easy . . . Um...right, this is what you do: Um...first of all you boil or steam the potatoes, but make sure you do it...er...in their skins, they've got to be in their skins and you've got to do it for ten minutes, so don't peel them first. Er...and then you drain them, then after you've done that you peel them, you might have to let them cool down a bit because they'll be very hot!
   Er...then you want to cut them into cubes, I'd say about...er...two centimetres square and...er...then let them...let them cool properly. Er...then you heat the...your oil in a frying pan, um...I use just ordinary vegetable oil, I usually find that's fine. And when the oil's hot you want to throw in...um...the sesame seeds. Mm...and then they'll start to pop and as soon as they do that you add the potatoes, and you want to fry them for about...er...I don't now about five minutes. Just keep stirring them, keep stirring all the time so they don't stick to the bottom. Then you add the cayenne pepper, and the salt...er...and...er...you squeeze on the lemon juice. And...um...just keep frying the...er...spuds till they're, you know, crisp and brown.
JOAN: Lovely.
NEIL: And...um...you can serve them with anything really...er...any meat dish, chicken, fish, whatever, or on their own, great.
JOAN: Brilliant, I can't wait to get home to try it.
NEIL: No, good luck.

B Divide the class into an even number of pairs. Half the pairs should look at Activity **55**, the other half at **60**. Remind everyone not to read the instructions out word-for-word, but to use their own words.

C This activity focuses on style. The best way to look at appropriate style is to imagine how the texts would be unsuitable in other contexts. How would you feel, for example, if a friend's letter was written in the style of extracts 3 or 4?

It's important that the style of a piece of writing should suit the imagined reader. No hard and fast rules can be given about this; students should be encouraged to develop a 'feeling' for what seems appropriate in different situations.

SUGGESTED ANSWERS

a letter to a friend: 2 and 5	**a magazine article:** 4 (and maybe 1 and 2)	
a recipe book: 1	**a story:** 3	

1 step-by-step impersonal instructions: 'removing only the rind'
2 personal references: 'our family'; informal language: 'that's the outside part'
3 past tenses
4 information and facts: 'available in cans and bottles'
5 personal references: 'you asked me to send' 'All you need'

D **1** A very complicated dish may be too ambitious. Perhaps encourage students to choose something that is relatively straightforward. Remind them that ingredients and processes they take for granted may be completely alien to a foreigner.

In a multinational class, take advantage of different cuisines represented to get students to share recipes with each other.

2 In this case the 150-word limit may well be exceeded – as in the model composition which follows. The model composition might be clearer if each step was numbered.

3 Guidelines for students giving feedback on each other's written work are given in Activity *61*. Go through these with the class. They should refer to these again when they have to give feedback again in future lessons.

MODEL COMPOSITION

Dear Les,

You asked me to send you the recipe for a typical national dish. The one I've chosen is something I'm sure you'll enjoy cooking and eating, but it's one you've probably never tried before. It's called:

Blackberry Fool
To make it you need:

$\frac{1}{2}$ kilo fresh blackberries (frozen ones will do)
200 g sugar
3 eggs
$\frac{1}{2}$ litre milk
$\frac{1}{4}$ litre cream

Cook the fruit on a low heat with half of the sugar until soft (about 15 mins). Meanwhile, beat the eggs with the rest of the sugar in a bowl. Heat the milk to just below boiling point and pour it slowly onto the eggs and sugar, stirring all the time. Then put the bowl into a pan of almost boiling water and keep stirring until the mixture thickens (about 5 mins). Then remove the bowl and put the custard you have made in the fridge.

Rub the cooked fruit through a sieve and put the purée you have made in the fridge.

When everything is cold, whip the cream. Then fold the cold custard into the purée and then fold in the cream too.

Serve in a large glass bowl or individual glass dishes.

It's quite tricky to make but you'll find it's absolutely delicious!

Best wishes,

You never stop learning

11

11.1   Education   VOCABULARY

A   Here is some useful vocabulary that might come up in the discussion:

active   chemistry   college   discover   experiment   globe   goggles   group work   hands-on high school   information technology (IT)   involved   knowledge   lecture   lecturer   lesson maths/mathematics   overall   passive   physics   primary school   pupil   school uniform   science secondary school   skill   taking notes   tutor   tutorial   university

B **1**

> **ANSWERS**
> 1 state   2 co-educational   3 primary   4 comprehensive   5 curriculum
> 6 pupils   7 head teacher   8 timetable   9 staff   10 exams   11 subjects
> 12 courses   13 compulsory   14 optional   15 sixth form   16 higher
> 17 university   18 eighteen

2   Some students may be mystified by the British system of education. What the text in B1 doesn't mention are the local intricacies of grammar schools, middle schools and public schools (i.e. private boarding schools)!

NOTE
Before starting 11.2 remind your students to look at the GRAMMAR REFERENCE section on *If . . .* sentences on pages 174–175.

11.2   *If . . .* sentences – 2   GRAMMAR REVIEW

A   Discuss the various implications of the sentences with the class.

> **ANSWERS**
> 1 I would have been able to do my homework (*yesterday*) if I hadn't had a headache (*yesterday*).
> 2 I would be able to do my homework (*now*) if I didn't have a headache (*now*).
> 3 I'll be able to do my homework (*tomorrow*) if I don't have a headache (*tomorrow*).
> 4 I'm not doing my homework (*now*) because I've got a headache (*now*).
> 5 I won't be able to do my homework (*tomorrow*) unless my headache has gone (*tomorrow*).
> 6 I would be able to do my homework (*now/tomorrow*) if I hadn't missed the lesson (*yesterday*).

B **1**

> **ANSWERS**   (Some variations, particularly in the use of contractions, are possible.)
> 2 If *I had known where you lived, I could have got* in touch with you.
> 3 He *would have got a higher mark if he had studied* harder.
> 4 If she *had been less lucky/had not been so lucky, she would/might have done badly* in the test.
> 5 If they *hadn't had so much studying to do during the vacation, they could have gone* on holiday.

2   Check your students' answers to the questions in B1 before continuing.

> **ANSWERS**
> 6 I *would have remembered to post the letter if I hadn't been* so busy with my work.
> 7 If she *had done more/some work at school, she wouldn't feel sorry* now.
> 8 I *couldn't have finished the work on time without your* help.
> 9 If he *had been learning English for longer he would/might be able* to speak it better.

C 1

2 would have been **3** wouldn't have **4** would have been **5** would have passed
6 wouldn't have **7** had taken up **8** would have learned **9** would be
10 might not be **11** was **12** would be **13** would be **14** would get
15 might feel **16** might not like **17** would be **18** were **19** am

11.3 Happy days? READING AND LISTENING

Students should read the text and, if possible, do A1 and B before the lesson.

Graham Greene (1904–1991) was one of Britain's most famous novelists. His works often deal with moral dilemmas and the problem of good and evil. He converted to Roman Catholicism in 1926 and many of his books concern religious themes. However, his works are more full of humour than gloom and he is a superb story teller. Among his best-known novels and 'entertainments' (lighter novels and thrillers) are:

Brighton Rock (1938)
The Third Man (1950)
The Quiet American (1955)
Travels with My Aunt (1969)
The Honorary Consul (1973)
The Captain and the Enemy (1988)

A 1

ANSWERS

1 b **2** c **3** b **4** c **5** b **6** c **7** d **8** b

2 It's a matter of opinion which answers seemed unfair. But, in the exam, always choose the best answer. Other answers may be partly correct, but the best one is completely correct.

B

ANSWERS

¶**1** gym shoes recklessly slithered abrupt
¶**6** in (a bit of) a quandary
¶**8** reluctant conceal obscure
¶**10** from hearsay ajar trim

C Ask the groups to report on their answers to these questions.

D 1 📼 This is an exam-style listening task.

ANSWERS

1 Neil **2** Cecilia **3** Nick **4** No one **5** Kate **6** Adam

TRANSCRIPT *3 minutes*

NICK: Um...er...I remember actually getting on a bus to go to secondary school and I did something that was...um...completely against the rules, which was sitting on the back seat...er...where the prefects sit and the whole bus went quiet – actually they were quite nice about it – though they made us all sing a hymn going back...um...from school, back home, because that's what they made all the first years do.

KATE: Yes, I couldn't wait to get to school because my brother was there already, so I wasn't in the least bit unhappy about it. And my first teacher was Sister Francis of Assissi and...er...she was a sweet...sweet woman who squeezed my cheek so affectionately and so tightly it hurt me for the rest of the day.

ADAM: Well I kind of remember my first day at school, but it was a long time ago. It was in New York City and I remember taking a bus across town and...and I was going to a private school so I was wearing a uniform which was like little grey shorts and things, which in New York probably didn't make me too popular. I remember being stared at by the other kids when I was on the bus with my mother. And then we got to the school and my first teacher was called Mrs Norton and she was really really nice on the first day and then for the rest of the year she was just horrible. That's mostly what I remember about school is how nice that nasty teacher was when the parents were there.

CECILIA: Well, I don't really remember too much about the first day, the actual day, but I remember...um...the preparations in the morning, because I was going to school and I was only four and I thought, 'Yeah, I'm really clever, I'm going very early to school'. And...um...my mum made me this huge breakfast and I had everything I wanted that whole morning and I was just really spoilt. And...um...on the way to school we stopped and I said, 'Oh' – and I just felt I was in complete control, I remember that, my mum was doing anything I wanted – and we stopped and I had a cake in the morning. And I never forgot that because I was never allowed to do it again after that.

NEIL: I remember going to secondary school and...um...because it was down the road I went in with my friend Glyn Daley, who also lived sort of...he lived next door to me, and so we walked in together. And all I remember was the pair of us walking in and being surrounded by these *enormous* people...er...most of whom had crew cuts and sort of big bovver boots, and being absolutely terrified – and that was just the girls!

2 Students who are at university should also talk about their first day in higher education.

11.4 Compound words – 2 WORD STUDY

A The answers are all recorded. You may prefer to play them after each part of this exercise or at the very end when 1, 2 and 3 have been completed. (The recording includes the examples and lasts 2 minutes 20 seconds.)

1

> **SUGGESTED ANSWERS**
>
> coffee break computer program exercise book further education
> general knowledge high school higher education instant coffee intelligence test
> personal computer railway station restaurant owner savings account
> school teacher sports ground staff room story telling tea cup television set
> tennis court university professor wholemeal bread
>
> There are many other possible answers:
> general education high ground personal knowledge sports teacher
> university education etc.

2

> **SUGGESTED ANSWERS**
>
> breadcrumbs chairman* classroom headache homework housekeeping
> notebook playground postman* schoolgirl taxpayer timetable toothache
> toothbrush toothpaste
>
> There are many other possible answers:
> housework schoolbook schoolroom taxman etc.
>
> (*Many people prefer to use the terms *chairperson* and *letter carrier* or *postal worker.*)

3

> **SUGGESTED ANSWERS**
>
> blue-eyed brand-new curly-haired good-looking kind-hearted last-minute
> narrow-minded old-fashioned right-handed short-sighted sun-tanned
> well-behaved
>
> There are other possible answers:
> good-hearted short-haired etc.

11.5 ▶ In . . . PREPOSITIONS

ANSWERS

1 in other words   2 in common   3 in a hurry   4 in all   5 In general
6 in tears   in prison   7 in confidence   8 in trouble   9 in public   in private
10 in particular

11.6 ▶ Using your brain LISTENING

A ▶ You'll need to pause the recording occasionally to give everyone time to write their answers and catch up. In the exam, students won't have to write so much information.

ANSWERS

1 right-hand
2 LEFT (rational side)   RIGHT (irrational side)
  language   rhythm
  numbers   *colour*
  linearity   *imagination*
  analysis   *daydreaming*
  logic   space: three dimensions
  lists   seeing *collections* of things as a whole
  sequencing

3 reversed
4 corpus callosum   successful thinking
5 12 multiplied by 137
6 directly above this chair in the room upstairs
7 look to the right   visual information
8 close their eyes
9 do not get worse
10 stimulation   exercise
11 fresh air/oxygen   lifestyle
12 Three Golden Rules:
    a) in an abstract, logical way   visually
    b) both halves
    c) you can't solve a problem   just as good

TRANSCRIPT *5 minutes 50 seconds*

. . . so you see the human brain weighs about $1\frac{1}{2}$ kilos. It contains ten to fifteen thousand million nerve cells. Now, each nerve cell can connect with any number or combination of other neurons – that's what you call a nerve cell, a neuron – the total number of possible connections of course is enormous. Now, if you wanted to type that number so you'd have...get an idea of how many combinations there are, you'd have to start by typing a one, then follow that with ten million kilometres of zeros.

Every human brain has an unlimited potential – only a small fraction of neurons are used for...er...everyday routine tasks like eating, moving, routine work, etc. The rest are constantly available for thought.

Now, our brains consist of various parts, some of which control routine functions. But the important parts that make us into those marvellous thinking machines, we like to think we are, are the two hemispheres or the two sides of the brain: the left and the right. Now, the left hemisphere controls the right half of the body, that's right, the left controls the right, and the right controls the left half. Normally the left half of the brain is dominant.

Now, the left side, which is known as the rational side, controls the...these functions: language, numbers, linearity, analysis, logic, lists and sequencing.

The right side, which is known as the irrational side, sometimes people call it the artistic side of your brain, controls those things...er...which are...well, less specific perhaps: rhythm...er...er...colour, imagination, daydreaming, space: spacial dimension, three-dimensional thought...erm...seeing collections of things as one, as a whole. One interesting thing is that left-handed people often have a dominant right hemisphere, and in this case the priorities of the things I've just mentioned are all reversed.

The corpus callosum is very important. That's corpus CORPUS, callosum CALLOSUM – you should make a note of that, it's very important – that's the link between the two hemispheres in the brain and it's the key to successful thinking, linking the two parts of the brain, so you don't use them independently.

By the way, you...you could try this experiment: you'll see the two halves being used. Ask someone two questions, one to do with numbers – er...you could say 'What's 12 multiplied by 137?', and the other one to do with space. For example, you could say, 'What piece of furniture is directly above this chair in the room upstairs?'. OK? Now, while they're trying to answer the first question, that was the...the numbers one, they'll probably look to the right to prevent being distracted by visual information, and while they're trying to answer the second, that's the spatial one about what's upstairs above the chair, they'll probably look to the left. But of course, some people just close their eyes and that ruins the whole test!

According to experts, as we get older our memories do not get worse. Er...that's just an old wives' tale. In fact, we forget things at all ages. If you *expect* your memory to be bad or to get worse, it probably will. Lack of stimulation, brain exercise and lack of interest can mean that you forget things more easily. Lack of concentration simply.

Ah, lack of fresh air can also lead to your brain being less efficient because it gets starved of oxygen, and an unhealthy lifestyle – take note – can also damage your brain: er...alcohol, smoke, um...pollutants in the air like lead, er...chemicals in food, they can all add to a generally deteriorating condition of the brain.

You've probably heard a lot of people say 'I'm not brainy' or 'That's too difficult for my brain' – but this is not true because everyone's brain has an equal potential.

There are a few rules, Golden Rules of brain power:
One: Use your senses: don't only think in an abstract, logical way. Try to imagine a problem visually.
Second rule: Use both halves of your brain. For example, if you're faced with...er...an abstract, logical problem, try thinking about it imaginative...er...try thinking about it imaginatively. Or if you're faced with a creative problem, try to analyse it. Think logically about it.
And don't ever say you *can't* solve a problem because your brain is just as good as anyone else's.

B Pool ideas on remembering vocabulary (for some suggestions see pages 8–9 of the Teacher's Book Introduction).

11.7 Use of English: Correcting errors EXAM TECHNIQUES

Although we've done exercises in the GRAMMAR REVIEW sections where students have to spot mistakes and correct them, these have not been in the same format as the error-correction exercises in the Use of English paper. In these exercises you have to spot the superfluous word and write it down – or put a tick if there is no superfluous word.

A Allow plenty of time for studying the exam sample. The wrong answer is 5, where the superfluous word is *much*, not *to*.

B 1 Allow time for questions and answers before starting B2. There may be some points in the exam tips that you would like to comment on, or maybe disagree with.

2

ANSWERS									
6 on	**7** still	**8** the	**9** ✔	**10** ✔	**11** we	**12** so	**13** it	**14** with	**15** to

11.8 Advantages and disadvantages WRITING

A Follow the procedure suggested in the Student's Book. In some countries the concept of taking a year out before higher education may be unfamiliar – but it's becoming increasingly popular. If your students can't come up with many ideas as pairs, A1 could be brainstormed with the whole class. Then divide the class (back) into pairs and set A2 as homework.

B Here are some model notes – not all of which can be included in a 150-word article.

> ADVANTAGES
> Everyone gets a chance to speak – not just the more confident students
> You don't feel so self-conscious
> You can express yourself without feeling embarrassed
> Not being corrected helps to develop fluency
> It's more like real life
> You're more active
> You're more likely to remember things you've worked out for yourself
>
> DISADVANTAGES
> Your mistakes aren't corrected
> Some students don't always talk in English
> It can be noisy

New Progress to First Certificate – This document may be photocopied.
© Cambridge University Press, 1996

(See also the Teacher's Book Introduction page 8 for more information about working in pairs and groups.)

C Guidelines for giving feedback can be found in Activity *61*.

What shall we do this evening?

12

12.1 Just for fun   VOCABULARY AND LISTENING

A   Here is some useful vocabulary that may come up in the discussion:

accident   action   adventure   affair   chase   comedy   drama   fall off   fight   get into trouble
motorbike   seduce   sexual harassment   thriller

(In case anyone is wondering, the stills are from *Dumb and Dumber, Disclosure, I Like It Like That* and *Timecop*.)

B 1

ANSWERS	Joan	Chris	Bob	
action films	✗	✗	✓	
old black and white films	✓		✓	(*westerns?*)
cartoons	✗			
horror films	✗		✓	
romantic comedies	✓	✗	✗	
thrillers	✗		✓	
westerns		✗	✓	
dubbed foreign films		✗	✓	
foreign-language films with subtitles	✓	✓	✗	

TRANSCRIPT   *3 minutes*

1 CHRIS: So, Joan, what films do you like?
  JOAN: Mm, quite gentle sort of slow-moving films, I like, such as romantic
    comedies...um...the old black and white films I like very much and some European
    films that are subtitled I like very much. Um...I don't like thrillers, I really don't
    like being frightened in the cinema, I know it's not for real, but I don't like
    thrillers. I don't like action films as well, for the same reason. Um . . .
  CHRIS: Do you like horror films?
  JOAN: No, not at all and I...and I don't like cartoons either.

  JOAN: Now, Chris, tell me: what sort of films do you like?
2 CHRIS: Well, I...I prefer foreign films, by and large, although not dubbed films. I...I can't
    bear dubbed films, I think dubbing is a ridiculous thing to do to a film. I only
    really go and see foreign films...er...they have to have subtitles, although I...I'm
    very fluent in French so I prefer to try and ignore the subtitles if possible and just
    listen to the...er...the language. Um...other than that really I can't bear action films
    or sort of those horrible American romantic comedies, I can't stand. Um...same is
    true of westerns, I'm afraid, they again leave me very cold, I don't like those at all.

  JOAN: So Bob, tell me, what sort of films do you like?
3 BOB: I like action films me, yeah, big ones, the bigger the better...er...you know, specially
    if they've got special effects because I do like special effects. I do like lots of
    sparks, lots of things blowing up, lots of things going up in flames, up in smoke,
    and...er...yeah, that's great, I love that. And I also like...er...westerns, er...er...you
    know, because it's so great actually: big feel to it and great scenery usually, specially
    in, you know, in the old ones. And...er...I like...er...what else do I like? I like
    thrillers, I like...I like a good cop chase, I do with police things and lots of
    suspenseful things, which is the same reason I like...er...I like the horror films.
  JOAN: Could you tell me what sort of films you don't like?
  BOB: Well, I'm not keen on foreign films on the whole. No, I don't...it's just...I don't
    mind them...it's just if they've got those subtitles, I don't like them. Er...I don't
    mind them so much if they're dubbed because at least I can follow the action.
    But...er...what else? Erm...and I don't like, I get a bit bored if they're you know too
    romantic, because I don't really like that much, because I like action.

C

ANSWERS

Ritz Film Centre

5 screens all with Dolby Stereo Surround Sound

DUMB AND DUMBER 12	~~12:45~~ ~~3:15~~ 5:20 ~~8:50~~	(12:30 3:30) 9:00
TIMECOP 12	~~1:05~~ ~~3:25~~ ~~5:40~~ ~~8:20~~	11:20 3:35 5:55 8:10
I LIKE IT LIKE THAT 15	1:15 ~~3:55~~ ~~6:05~~ 8:50	3:45 5:55
DISCLOSURE 18	~~1:20~~ ~~3:35~~ ~~5:55~~ ~~8:10~~	1:05 3:25 5:40 8:35
Movie Classics: ~~SOME LIKE IT HOT~~ U	~~6:20~~ ~~8:55~~	CASABLANCA 6:30 9:00

| recorded information 774112 | credit card bookings 774422 |

TRANSCRIPT   *2 minutes 20 seconds*

WOMAN: Thank you for calling the Ritz Film Centre. Here is information about films
showing from today until Thursday next.

Screen One is showing *Dumb and Dumber* starring Jim Carrey and Jeff Daniels,
certificate 12. Performances begin at 12.30, 3.30, 5.20 and 9 pm.

Screen Two is showing *Timecop* starring Jean-Claude van Damme, certificate 12.
Performances begin at 11.20, 3.35, 5.55 and 8.10 pm.

Screen Three is showing *I Like It Like That* starring Lauren Velez and Jon Seda,
certificate 15.
Performances begin at 1.15, 3.45, 5.55 and 8.50.

Screen Four is showing *Disclosure* starring Michael Douglas and Demi Moore,
certificate 18.
Performances begin at 1.05, 3.25, 5.40 and 8.35.

And in our Movie Classics season Screen Five is showing *Casablanca* starring
Humphrey Bogart and Ingrid Bergman, certificate U. Performances begin at 6.30
and 9 pm.

All seats may be booked and paid for in advance by calling this number 774422
with your credit card details. Thank you for calling the Ritz Film Centre.

D & **E**   These activities explore students' personal preferences.

12.2 Groundhog Day   READING

A 1

ANSWERS

1 romantic comedy   **2** He starts the same day again.
3 He's a weather forecaster and he reports from Punxsatawney on the festival.

B   The answers depend on the questions that the students noted down.

C   **ANSWERS**

True: 2 6
False: 1 3 4 (*at least not in the long run – he gets no satisfaction*) 5

D   **ANSWERS**

¶2 predicament   loathsome   dead-end career   ¶5 fluffs it   rebuffed   jerk
¶3 ingenious   it dawns on him   ¶6 reeling
¶4 be back to square one   ¶7 churlish   dazzling

EXTRA DISCUSSION QUESTIONS

Ask the class these questions:
- If you could relive any day of your life, which day would it be and why?
- If you could have another try at a recent day, what would you do differently?

 Your students will probably be keen to know your own preferences.

NOTE

Before starting 12.3 remind your students to look at the GRAMMAR REFERENCE section on *-ing* and *to . . .* on pages 175–176.

12.3 *-ing* and *to . . .* – 2   GRAMMAR REVIEW

 ANSWERS

Verbs followed by *-ing*:
  imagine   stop   leave   spend time

Imagine having to live your life . . .
you can stop worrying . . .
The horror of Murray's situation leaves you reeling.
and spend his time in the local library, studying Western philosophy

Verbs followed by *to . . .*:
  wake up   try   have   forced

you wake up . . . to discover . . .
if you're trying to make Andie MacDowell fall in love with you . . .
you'll have to start again.
Yet he is forced to live . . .

B 1

SUGGESTED ANSWERS

2 sneezing   **3** to stop talking   talking   **4** to help her (to carry them)   **5** to do it
6 to be ill   **7** to make the speech   **8** to rain/raining

 ANSWERS (Some variations are possible.)

2 I'm *not used to dressing up* when I go out for the evening.
3 Would *you prefer to go* to the cinema or theatre?
4 I can't afford *to go to/to eat at such an* expensive restaurant.
5 They didn't *stop smoking* all through the meal.
6 The drive was so *tiring that we stopped to* have a break.
7 I'll always *remember going to (see)* Walt Disney's *Pinocchio* when I was little.
8 Oh no, I *didn't remember to* phone my uncle!

D Students should write down their five most amusing or memorable sentences.

12.4 **Rewriting sentences**   EXAM TECHNIQUES

This is fairly self-explanatory. (In the exam a contracted form, such as *she's* or *haven't*, counts as two words. However, using or not using a contraction would never bring the total number of words below two or above five in an exam question, as this would be unfair.)

In 3 both answers have changed the word, and the second answer also has too many words. In 4 the first answer has changed the meaning, and the second has changed the word.

> **ANSWERS**
> 1 I'*d rather not* go out this evening.
> 2 You'll find *it impossible to* get a ticket for the show unless you book in advance.
> 3 I *don't approve of* violent films.
> 4 *Some Like It Hot is supposed to be* a really funny film.

B

> **ANSWERS**
> 5 If I *were/was/felt more energetic I would/might* feel like going out for a walk.
> 6 When the film *was over we went* to have a pizza.
> 7 We *arrived early so* that we didn't have to queue.
> 8 There is a *big difference between* watching a film on video and at the cinema.
> 9 After *reading the reviews of* the film I decided not to go and see it.
> 10 You laughed at all the jokes, *so you must have enjoyed* the show.

12.5 **Words + prepositions – 1**   PREPOSITIONS

Words + prepositions – 2 is in 13.6.
Words + prepositions – 3 is in 14.5.

> **ANSWERS**
> 1 for   2 with   3 for   4 of   5 with   about   6 in   7 from   8 for   9 about
> 10 from   11 of   12 on   13 of   14 for   15 of

12.6 **Using suffixes – 1: Adjectives**   WORD STUDY

Using suffixes – 2: Actions and people is in 13.5.
Using suffixes – 3: Abstract nouns is in 14.7.

A 1

> **ANSWERS**
> 1 showing care   not showing care
> 2 not giving pain   giving pain
> 3 unable to help   willing to help
> 4 showing tact   not showing tact

2

> **ANSWERS**
> delightful   endless   hopeful/hopeless   powerful/powerless   restful/restless
> speechless   successful   thoughtful/thoughtless   useful/useless

B **ANSWERS**

-able	comfortable enjoyable fashionable preferable
-al	educational emotional traditional
-ical	geographical philosophical
-ish	foolish oldish smallish tallish youngish
-y	bloody cloudy dirty noisy rainy sleepy

🔊 The answers are recorded, as well as the *-ible* words in the note. (The recording includes the examples and lasts 1 minute 50 seconds.)

C **ANSWERS**

2 thoughtful **3** musical **4** childish **5** sunny **6** readable **7** geographical
8 reddish **9** unreliable **10** unforgettable

12.7 Short sentences? Or long ones?   WRITING

A Although the first paragraph is probably the most interesting to read, perhaps the second is more the kind of paragraph that your students should be encouraged to write – long complex sentences often lead to pitfalls and errors.

Instead of repeating *he* and *she* so much, giving the person a name would reduce the dullness of the second and even the third paragraphs.

There are GRAMMAR REVIEW sections on joining sentences in 13.4 and 14.3.

B Follow the procedure in the Student's Book.

C Perhaps encourage everyone to see the same film **or** split the class into two or three groups (according to their taste in films) and encourage them to go to different films. If this is beyond their means, they should write about a film on TV they have seen.

Refer students to the guidelines in Activity *61* when they look at each other's reviews.

MODEL REVIEW

> 'Barcelona' is an American film set in Spain. It was made on a small budget and there are no famous stars in it – apart from the two main characters all the actors are Spanish, talking English most of the time.
>
> It's about two male cousins who grew up disliking each other. Now, in their twenties, they meet up again. One cousin works for a company in Barcelona and the other, who is an officer in the US Navy, arrives unexpectedly to stay in his flat – and share his life. The story is about how they get on each other's nerves, their involvements with local girls, and the local pro- and anti-American attitudes.
>
> The most enjoyable thing about the film is the dialogue: it's a film full of words and without any violence or anything shocking. You have to listen carefully to catch all the jokes, because the actors are sometimes hard to understand, but it's worth the effort.
>
> The only fault I can find is that the film is rather too long. There are times when you wonder what's going on and where things are leading.
>
> It's an intelligent, witty film which I heartily recommend. The ending will certainly take you by surprise. See it if you can!

13

Read any good books?

This unit is designed to be relevant to everyone (not just students who are studying one of the prescribed books). The activities are suitable for the 'general reader', not for specialists. Not many students are great readers, and it's assumed that all of their reading is in their own language, not English.

For students who **are** reading one of the set books there are special instructions in Activity *19*. The activities suggested there will take up several lessons, preferably spread across several weeks.

13.1 A good read   VOCABULARY

A Tell the students about the last book you read, too.

B ANSWERS
1 literature   2 characters   3 glossary   4 chapters   5 index   6 publisher
7 message   8 well-written   9 favourite   10 put it down   11 minor   12 borrow

C ANSWERS
1 central   main   principal
2 entertaining   readable   true-to-life
3 amusing   believable   likeable
4 convincing   realistic   true-to-life
5 biographies   textbooks   non-fiction
6 bear   enjoy   stand

Look at all the wrong answers in B and C because there's a lot of useful vocabulary there too.

D ANSWERS
1 library   bookshop/bookstore   2 author   3 paperback   4 title   cover
5 biography

E In case your students ask, here's more information about each book:

500 Mile Walkies is an amusing account of the author's walk around England's South-West Peninsula Coastal Path with his dog. It's all about the people he meets and the conversations he has with them.

Alaska is a very long novel about Eskimos and Russian and American explorers and colonists trying to survive in a hostile environment. The action spans thousands of years and it's a blend of historical fact with fictional narrative.

Empire of the Sun is the story of an English boy living in China, who is separated from his parents during the Second World War. He is imprisoned in a Japanese internment camp, where he has many exciting and amusing experiences. It's a semi-autobiographical story, based on J.G. Ballard's own boyhood experiences. (The book was made into a movie by Steven Spielberg.)

The information about the set books is for everyone, even though you and your students may not want to read a set book. The books listed are just examples, not the official list.

For a complete list of this year's books, consult the current exam regulations. A new book on the list usually stays there for two years, and is then replaced by another. There's probably at least one book on the list that would suit your students' tastes.

F. Scott Fitzgerald (1896–1940) is well-known as the chief chronicler of the Jazz Age in the USA in the 1920s.

The Great Gatsby is often considered to be **the** Great American Novel. The story is narrated by Nick Carraway, who rents a small house next door to the mansion of the millionaire, Jay Gatsby. Gatsby rose from obscurity but, at the end of the book, he dies in obscurity. The book expresses the American Dream that anyone in America can become rich and successful, but it also shows that money can't buy happiness and that hedonism can be empty and unsatisfying. The conflict between materialism and idealism is the basis of the book.

Fitzgerald wrote five novels:
This Side of Paradise (1920)
The Beautiful and the Damned (1922)
The Great Gatsby (1925)
Tender is the Night (1934)
The Last Tycoon (1941)
and five volumes of excellent short stories.

 Share your own enthusiasms with the class too.

 The first version (simplified by Celia Turvey), though less poetic than the original version, captures the atmosphere of the story remarkably well, whilst remaining within a 2,000-word vocabulary level (apart from *champagne* and *water-ski*, which are explained in a glossary).

The simplified version omits a great deal of detail, some difficult words and similes:
came and went like moths
scampered like a brisk yellow bug

but there are also some additions:
water-skiing
a dance floor was laid down on the lawn
with dozens of waiters to serve it
I remember the sense of excitement at the beginning of the party.
The party has begun.

(The original version has American spellings: *neighbor, colors* and *center*; the simplified version has British spelling throughout.)

 The main points of the description are given in both versions – though the details may be different. Questions 5 and 6 refer to information that's only given in one of the versions.

> **ANSWERS**
> **2** They swam, lay in the sun or water-skied – *simplified version*
>   They dived, took the sun (or took motor-boat rides) – *original version*
> **3** His big open car – *simplified version*
>   His Rolls-Royce – *original version*
> **4** Eight – *both versions*
> **5** With a special machine – *original version*
> **6** On a special dance floor laid down on the lawn – *simplified version*
> **7** In the main hall – *both versions*
> **8** A big group of musicians – *simplified version*
>   No thin five-piece affair but a whole pitful of all kinds of instruments – *original version*

13.3 Reading habits LISTENING

A 1 & 2

ANSWERS

1 85 electronic noise   2 inexpensive/cheap   portable   3 bookmark
4 one   airport   plane   beach   5 best-selling/established authors   6 John Grisham –
The Pelican Brief (1c)   Barbara Vine – *Gallowglass* (2e)   John Le Carré – *The Night
Manager* (3a)   Judith Krantz – *Dazzle* (4b)   Michael Crichton – *Rising Sun* (5d)

TRANSCRIPT   *4 minutes 40 seconds*

PRESENTER: According to a recent survey, 85 percent of American adolescents quote: 'can no longer take in a printed page if their act of reading does not have an accompanying background of electronic noise' end of quote. And many students nowadays seem to need a background noise of music on headphones to cut out outside distractions. But are we reading less these days? Will the days of books soon be over? I have with me Jason Marshall from the Booksellers' Association.

JASON: Well, there are two questions really. First, will other entertainments – computer games, videos, TV and so on – stop people reading, and second will the new technology – that's CD-ROMs, laptop computers and books recorded on cassettes and so on – will these things provide substitutes for the printed page?

Well, the main advantage that books have over all these media is that they're relatively inexpensive and they're very portable. I mean, you can take a book with you wherever you go, it doesn't break down if you get sand inside it, you don't need batteries and you can put it down and pick it up whenever you like – the only equipment you need is a bookmark.

PRESENTER: Haha, yes – a very good point!

JASON: Now, according to the survey, many people only buy one book a year – as holiday reading. They probably buy it at the airport on their way to the sun and they read it in the airport (while their flight is delayed), on the plane and on the beach of course.

Nevertheless, books by best-selling authors are selling more and more copies every year not fewer.

PRESENTER: That's good, isn't it?

JASON: Mm. All the signs are that people are spending more and more money on books. The most popular books are books by *established* authors – that's writers who've developed a product that their readers know they'll enjoy and whose books they'll 'collect'.

PRESENTER: Who do you mean by 'established authors'?

JASON: Well, for example, John Grisham. He's an American lawyer and the main character in his books is usually a lawyer. Many of his books have been filmed. One of his best sellers was *The Pelican Brief* . . .

PRESENTER: Oh, what was that about?

JASON: It's about a beautiful young law student who is trying to find out why two judges have been murdered.

Another established author whose books are always best sellers is Ruth Rendell. Her books are also about crimes and about strange people who commit crimes or who find it hard to live in society – her characters are never glamorous.

PRESENTER: Yes, she's very popular, isn't she?

JASON: Mm. She writes books under her own name and also under the name...um...Barbara Vine as pen name. For example *Gallowglass*, which is about a clever young man's plan to kidnap a rich young woman. The story teller is rather pathetic, a stupid young man, who becomes the clever one's partner – or more like his servant really.

PRESENTER: Anyone else?

JASON: Yeah, John Le Carré: he's British and his books are mostly about spies – he used to be a spy himself. For example, *The Night Manager* is about a man who used to be a spy who now works as a hotel manager. He has to catch the world's most dangerous arms dealer. Now . . .

PRESENTER: Mm, sounds interesting.

JASON: Mm, yes, it's a great book, a great book. Judith Krantz i...er...completely different, is another established writer. Now, she lives in California, is married to a movie producer and used to be a fashion editor. All her books are best sellers. *Dazzle* is about a rich and beautiful woman. She's a world-famous photographer and three different men are in love with her. Her enemies are the members of her own family.

PRESENTER: So those people are really writing from their own experience?

JASON: Well, partly yes. Or they're using it as a background, you know, I'm not saying it's all completely accurate.

Then there's Michael Crichton, who used to be a doctor. Now, his books are thrillers, many of which have been made into films. For example, um...*Rising Sun?*

PRESENTER: No, I don't know it.

JASON: It's about a man who is trying to find out why a young woman has been murdered in an office in a Japanese company.

Now, apart from making their authors millionaires, the one thing that all these books have in common is that they're all 300 to 700 pages long, which is fine if you're used to reading . . . But the problem is that many people aren't. Now, reading tends to be something you enjoy more as you get older – but if you don't develop a taste for it when you're young, you may never discover the pleasures of getting involved in a good book.

PRESENTER: Mm, that's right.

JASON: Now, technology and its influence on reading is, as I said, another question. Will people who study need to buy textbooks in the future? Or will they just sit in front of computer screens and get all the information they need on the Internet? . . .

 B Allow the experts among your students to give everybody the benefit of their knowledge!

NOTE
Before starting 13.4 remind your students to look at the GRAMMAR REFERENCE section on Joining sentences and relative clauses on page 177.

13.4 Joining sentences – 1: Relative clauses GRAMMAR REVIEW

Joining sentences – 2: Conjunctions is in 14.3.

 A **ANSWERS**
2 Agatha Christie, who wrote detective stories, died in 1976 when she was 86.
3 Her books, some of which have been made into films, have all been best sellers.
4 Hercule Poirot, who is Belgian, is Agatha Christie's most famous creation.
5 ✓
6 ✓
7 The victim's elder brother, who lived in Paris, was an accountant.
8 ✓

B **ANSWERS** (Several variations are possible.)
2 New York, *which is a wonderful city, is a place I'd love to go to one day.*
New York *is a wonderful city, which I'd love to go to one day.*
3 Ms Fortune, *who was a writer, was found dead in the cellar.*
Ms Fortune, *who was found dead in the cellar, was a writer.*
4 My friend, *who is a great reader, told me all about a book he'd just read.*
My friend, *who told me all about the book he'd just read, is a great reader.*
5 The car *which was stolen was found at the airport.*
The car *which was found at the airport was stolen.*
6 Science fiction, *which is about the future and space travel, is loved by some people and hated by others.*
Science fiction, *which some people love and others hate, is about the future and space travel.*
7 The book *(which/that) you recommended to me was very good.*
The book *was very good which/that you recommended to me.*
8 A simplified edition, *which is easier to read than the original, is shorter.*
A simplified edition, *which is shorter than the original, is easier to read.*

C Remind everyone that they read an extract from this book in 11.3. This is an exam-style exercise.

ANSWERS
1 which **2** about **3** whose **4** who **5** who **6** whose **7** After **8** who
9 but **10** During **11** between **12** but **13** until **14** When **15** after

13.5 Using suffixes – 2: Actions and people   WORD STUDY

A

ANSWERS

1 very loud, loud enough to make you deaf
2 a person who is an expert in psychology (the study of how the mind works and human behaviour)   a doctor who is an expert in psychiatry (the study of mental illness), or who treats mentally ill patients
3 made simple
4 person who invented
5 given a subsidy (money to support)
6 person who takes photographs   person who creates works of art

B

ANSWERS

-ise/-ize	generalise memorise personalise summarise
-en	deafen loosen straighten weaken
-ify	intensify simplify

 The answers are recorded – practise the pronunciation of the root words (*bright* to *weak*) if necessary too. (The recording includes the examples and lasts 50 seconds.)

C

ANSWERS

-er	driver painter reporter speaker
-or	collector director editor inspector supervisor visitor
-ant	accountant assistant
-ent	correspondent
-ist	artist guitarist novelist pianist scientist violinist

 The answers are recorded – practise the pronunciation of the root words (*account* to *visit*) if necessary too. (The recording includes the examples and lasts 1 minute.)

D

ANSWERS

1 scientist(s)   assistants   **2** widened   motorist   **3** pianist   violinist   **4** sharpening
5 rider   cyclist   **6** inhabitants   immigrants   descendants   **7** narrator   writer
8 classify

13.6 Words + prepositions – 2   PREPOSITIONS

ANSWERS

1 (introduce you) to   (involved) in   (hope) for   (confidence) in   (lack) of   (deal) with
2 (engaged) to   (married) to   (forgive Bill) for
3 (depends) on   (exchange it) for   (borrowed it) from
4 (insisted) on   (interfering) with

13.7 Writing against the clock   EXAM TECHNIQUES

This might be a good time to start marking your students' written work using the same marking scale that is used by the examiners. Band 3 and above in this general mark scheme, supplied by UCLES, is classified as a pass:

Band 5	• Good range of structure and vocabulary within the task set [a] • Minimal errors of structure, vocabulary, spelling and punctuation • Points covered as required with evidence of original output • Text suitably set out and ideas clearly linked [b] • Register appropriate to task and sustained [c] → Very positive effect on target reader
Band 4	• Good range of structure and vocabulary within the task set but text not always fluent • Errors only when more complex vocabulary/structure attempted; spelling and punctuation generally accurate • Points covered as required with sufficient detail • Text suitably set out and ideas clearly linked [b] • Register appropriate to the task and sustained [c] → Positive effect on target reader
Band 3	• An adequate range of structure and vocabulary to fulfil the requirements of the task • Some errors which do not impede communication • Points covered but some non-essential details omitted • Text suitably set out and ideas clearly linked; linking devices fairly simple • Register on the whole appropriate to the task → Satisfactory effect on target reader
Band 2	• Range of structure and vocabulary too limited to meet all requirements of the task • Errors sometimes obscure communication/distract the reader • Some omissions or large amount of lifting/irrelevant material • Text not clearly laid out; linking devices rarely used • Some attempt at appropriate register but no consistency → Message not clearly communicated to target reader
Band 1	• Range of structure and vocabulary very narrow • No evidence of any systematic control of language • Notable omissions in coverage of points needed and/or considerable irrelevance • Poor organisation of text; lack of linking • No awareness of appropriacy of register → A very negative effect on target reader
Band 0	• Too little language for assessment (fewer than 50 words) or totally irrelevant or totally illegible [d]

NOTES
[a] Task achievement entails completing the task within the word limits.
[b] Conventions of paragraphing, letter format, etc., expected here, with cohesion maintained as appropriate for FCE level; additional notes for specific tasks are provided for examiners.
[c] Fine-tuning of register is not expected at this level but some distinction between semi-formal (neutral) and informal needs to be demonstrated and **sustained** to fit into Bands 4 and 5.
[d] Poor handwriting is penalised.

To find out how the scales are implemented and to get a feeling for the levels you should look at *Cambridge Practice Tests for First Certificate* Teacher's Book and *Specifications and Sample Papers for the Revised FCE Examination*, available from UCLES (address on page 7). For more guidelines on marking students' work, see the Introduction pages 14–16.

Discuss the instructions with the class. Perhaps some of them have already timed themselves.

There are special instructions for students who are reading one of the set books in Activity *19*. The activities suggested there will take up several lessons, preferably spread across several weeks.

For students who aren't reading a set book, follow the instructions on page 111 of the Student's Book.

MODEL LETTER

Dear Peter,

   I felt I simply had to write to you about the enclosed book, which I'm sure you'll enjoy reading.

   As you'll see from the cover it's by David Lodge and it's called 'Nice Work'. It's all about two people who live close to each other in the same city. One is a female university teacher who lectures about English literature, the other is the male managing director of a factory. They have nothing in common but they are thrown together when the teacher becomes the industrialist's 'shadow' and spends one day each week with him as part of a scheme to increase co-operation between the university and local companies. I won't spoil it by telling you what happens in the end!

   You'll enjoy the humour of the relationship and the contrast between the world of the university and real life in the factory.

   When you've read it, let me know what you think.

                                        Best wishes,

All in a day's work

14

The *Voices* video sequence *A family airline* deals with other aspects of this topic.

Throughout this unit the discussion questions assume that students don't have jobs and are in full-time education. If your students **are** working, adapt the questions accordingly, and ask them to talk about their work.

 14.1   **Earning a living**   VOCABULARY

 A   See the note above.

 B
> **ANSWERS**
> 1 profession   2 career   3 in   4 employee   5 permanent   6 promoted
> 7 training   8 pension   9 a salary   10 routine

C
> **ANSWERS**
> 1 company   firm   organisation
> 2 makes   manufactures   produces
> 3 dismissed   fired   sacked
> 4 experience   personality   qualifications
> 5 department   staff   team

Discuss the wrong answers in B and C before starting the group discussion in D.

 14.2   **Paper 5: Speaking**   EXAM TECHNIQUES

A   Most of the information you'll need is contained in the panel in the Student's Book. But you may have to field some questions arising.

Here are some typical questions that students may ask – and suggested answers:

If there are an odd number of candidates at an examination centre, will someone have to do the exam one-to-one with the examiner?

— No, the last three candidates will do the exam as a group of three. Candidates will not normally be examined on a one-to-one basis.

What if the other candidate is so hopeless or nervous that he or she doesn't say anything?

— The examiners are trained to take account of any imbalance between the students when they're working in pairs. But don't ignore the other candidate: remember that marks are given for interactive communication.

What if the other candidate is much more talkative than me and I can't get a word in edgeways?

— The examiners are trained to take account of any imbalance between the students. You will be given your chance. If you can't break in, the examiner will interrupt for you.

What if I can't understand what the other candidate is saying?

— Make it clear to the examiner that you don't understand. The examiner will intervene and explain, if necessary.

Will I know in advance who I'm paired with in the exam?

— Local examination centres are responsible for pairing candidates. You should know who you are going to be paired with in advance, at the discretion of the local centre.

What if there's a student I just don't get on with and I'm paired with him or her?

— You could try asking your teacher to ask the centre to change your pairing, but this may not be possible to do at the last minute. By the way, it doesn't really matter if you disagree with everything the other candidate says – it may give you more to say than if you agree with everything.

Reassure everyone that the examiners are fully aware of students' worries and concerns about this paper. They are trained to take account of any problems that may arise.

There is a video of the Speaking paper available from UCLES. Your students may find it helpful to watch this as part of their preparation for the Speaking paper. Contact UCLES for further information.

B The procedure for the two mock exams is fairly complicated. It's important to familiarise yourself with what's going to happen by looking at Activities *25* and *47* before the lesson starts. If possible, decide in advance who's going to be in which group.

Divide the class into groups of four. If you don't have exactly 12, 16, 20, 24, 28 or 32 in your class, maybe form one or two groups of five. Then there can be three 'Examiners' (two assessing and one participating) in the first part, but in the second part there will have to be three 'Candidates' (which is unrealistic), or three 'Examiners' again (which means one student doesn't get a go at being a 'Candidate').

Alternatively, with one or two groups of three everyone will get a go at being a 'Candidate', and someone will have two goes. But the 'Examiner' will have a lot of work to do.

Or, if there are 11, 15, 19, 23, 27 or 31 in your class, you could be the fourth member of one of the groups.

If you run out of time, step 2 could be postponed to the next lesson.

NOTE

Before starting 14.3 remind your students to look at the GRAMMAR REFERENCE section on Joining sentences on page 177.

14.3 Joining sentences – 2: Conjunctions   GRAMMAR REVIEW

A **ANSWERS** (Some variations are possible.)

1 She's been looking for work	since leaving university.
2 She sent in her application	as soon as she saw the advertisement.
3 She felt very nervous	before the interview.
4 She didn't do well in the interview	even though she is intelligent and charming.
(**5** She didn't think she'd get the job	after the interview had gone so badly.)
6 The other candidates were well qualified	so she wasn't very optimistic.
7 She was amazed that they offered her the job	before she had even left the building.
8 She got the job	because she had such good qualifications.

B **1**

ANSWERS

2 I've brought my dictionary with me ***even though it is (very/so)*** heavy.
3 I phoned the office ***to let them know*** my time of arrival.
4 My friends were ***having fun while*** I was working.
5 If I ***have enough time, I'll*** go for a swim at lunchtime.
6 I'm going to try to get to work ***despite the bus drivers' strike*** tomorrow.

2

> **SUGGESTED ANSWERS** (Many variations are possible.)
> 1 Getting *a part-time job would help you to pay for your course besides giving you useful experience.*
> 2 She can't *decide what kind of job she wants to do until she has finished her studies and got her degree.*
> 3 Although *some school subjects such as history seem irrelevant to the world of work, other subjects such as languages have a direct relevance and are likely to be useful in work.*
> 4 He's probably going to take *the new job that he has been offered in another city because, even though moving there would mean leaving his family, the job itself sounds really interesting and living in another city would be interesting too.*

> **SUGGESTED ANSWERS** (There are lots of possible variations.)
> 2 A teacher who saved a kitten from drowning has been given a reward by its grateful owner.
> 3 Although the liner sank all the passengers and crew were rescued and there were no casualties.
> 4 After heavy rain in the mountains a landslide might destroy several villages.
> 5 A huge victory for the ruling party in the forthcoming general election is predicted because the President has promised to reduce taxes.
> 6 Due to a fall in the value of the pound sterling and a rise in the value of the US dollar, exports have risen during the past month.
> 7 The teachers have called off their threatened strike because the government has agreed to give them a pay rise.
> 8 Five hundred new jobs have been created now that a new factory has opened.

14.4 First jobs   LISTENING

A 📼 There are two separate conversations – you may wish to pause the recording at the point indicated in the transcript below.

> **ANSWERS**
> 1 b   2 a   3 c   4 c   5 b   6 c   7 b   8 a   9 a   10 c

TRANSCRIPT *4 minutes*

DAVID: Do you remember the...er very first job you ever had?
JILL: Yes, I certainly do. I wasn't very good at it actually. Um...it was as a secretary, I was supposed to be a secretary but I hadn't done very much secretarial training, and I went along – it was a design studio – and in fact I wanted to be a designer, so I used to sit around doing drawings all the time when I should have been typing letters, shorthand and typing. And...er...my boss went away for three weeks' holiday and there was...um...a horrible woman put in charge and she was very very nasty and got me into terrible trouble with my boss, who came back and gave me a big lecture and I ran home in tears and then I didn't go back and then several...several weeks later I had a letter from him saying: 'Please come back because the...' – now what did he call her? Something horrible, anyway, haha – 'She's gone' he said.
DAVID: So you went back?
JILL: 'And would you like to come back?' – No, I didn't. Tell me about yours.
DAVID: Oh mine, oh, straight out of school I worked in a library for six months, which was so boring it was untrue and the...the only excitement we got out of the day was seeing people come in the door which was at the far end and we would all decide between ourselves what sort of book they were going to take out, right? So they'd come up to the desk and you'd...you'd sort of say: 'Oh, she's going to get an Agatha Christie.' 'No, no, no she's into cars,' you know. And then of course it would turn out to be something totally different. We...we used to have a point system, you know, you'd score points according to... But apart from that I would never ever go back to work for a library, but what I do know now is how to get...how to find my way round in a library. So if you find yourself in a library you don't know, you can find your way around. That's the only part I enjoyed about it.

(pause tape here if necessary)

RICHARD: Well, the first job I had and certainly one of the best was straight after school and before I went to university, I had some months off, and I was fixed up with a job in Berlin as a postman in...in a...a quarter of Berlin called Spandau...Spandau. Er...and it was a lovely job. I find postmen the world over tend to be very friendly sort of people and the...there were a group of us Englishmen in there and the German postmen were wonderful, they sorted all our mail for us and everything, and took us round, got drunk with us after the round and... And...er...it was strange for me because I'm not used to getting up quite that early but I lived about an hour and a half away, the other side of the city, I had to get up at five in order to be there for half past six, do the round and I was back in bed by about one o'clock in the afternoon. Haha.

JOSCELYN: Was it well paid?

RICHARD: Well, it...for someone who had just left school it was quite well paid, yes. Er...it was...um...a German postman has to do far more than an English postman. They have to take the old-age pensions round and hand them out and collect various moneys and things, so it's a much more responsible job and I was amazed that they were giving me all this responsibility – an English schoolkid, basically, carrying thousands of pounds around with me, accountable for it in theory. But it was great fun.

JOSCELYN: My first job was about the same time really, I suppose, I was leaving school, but I made a lot of money but it was an awful job: it was selling encyclopedias door-to-door in the United States and the pressure to sell was incredible. I mean, you had to go back every night and...and...and produce the goods and I found that I just used to burst into tears. They would drive you into an area that...where you didn't know the streets, you didn't know where you were, and they said: 'Well, we'll pick you up in four or five hours,' and there was no sort of steady wage, you had to sell in order to make any kind of money at all. And at first I was so timid I'd, you know, ring the doorbell and I'd expect them to slam the door in my face and of course they did. And after a while I thought: 'The only thing that's going to save me is a sense of humour here'. So I would make jokes, I would run through the sprinklers on the lawn and this seemed to....um...interest them. Haha. So I found myself getting asked in and I would spend the evening talking about everything else other than encyclopedias and then sort of towards the end I'd say: 'Oh by the way...' And they would buy them. It would be...yeah...

RICHARD: So you made a living out of it?

JOSCELYN: Yeah, I did, I did. Well, I put myself through college on it.

RICHARD: Fantastic!

 B Four possible questions are:

- What did you have to do?
- What was enjoyable/dull about the work?
- How hard did you have to work?
- Would you like to do the same work again? Why/Why not?

If your students are working, this would be a good time for them to give one-minute talks about **their** first jobs.

14.5 **Words + prepositions – 3**   PREPOSITIONS

> **ANSWERS**
> 1 (preparations) for   (suffering) from   (thank them) for
> 2 (reminds me) of   (related) to
> 3 (rely) on   (provide you) with   (tired) of   (waiting) for
> 4 (suspected the man) of   (stealing the goods) from   (paid) for
> 5 (share them) with
> 6 (welcome you) to
> 7 (succeed) in   (revise) for
> 8 (worked) for   (responsible) for   (complaints) from   (resigned) from

14.6 **How to create a good impression . . .**   READING

Begin by finding out if anyone in the class has had a job interview. Ask them to speak about it.

 A Vocabulary is dealt with in B – to answer the questions in A students don't need to understand every word.

2

> **ANSWERS**
> DOs   1 3 4 5 6 7 8 9
> DON'Ts   2 10

3

> **ANSWERS**
> DOs   12 15 16 18 19 20
> DON'Ts   11 13 14 17

B 1

> **ANSWERS**
> 1 b   2 b   3 c   4 b   5 a   6 b

2

> **ANSWERS**
> 1 c   2 a   3 c   4 c   5 a   6 b

4 The article was written for school-leavers who are going to attend their first interview, not for experienced job-seekers.

Some more DOs:
- Look your best
- Send a good photo of yourself
- Appear to be confident: body language and good eye contact

Some more DON'Ts:
- Move your chair closer to the interviewer
- Offer the interviewer a cigarette
- Stand up and start walking around the room

C In the FCE Speaking paper you don't need to take your certificates with you (point 7) – but you do need to take your identity card or passport to prove you are who you say you are, and that someone else isn't impersonating you.

The other DOs that are relevant to the FCE Speaking paper are probably: 5, 6, 8, 9, 12 and 18. And DON'Ts 2, 10, 13 and 14.

The other points are probably irrelevant, but suggest that if an examiner holds out her hand to shake the candidate's, it's a good idea to be polite and respond!

14.7 Using suffixes – 3: Abstract nouns   WORD STUDY

A 1

> **ANSWERS**
> **-ment**   agreement astonishment employment encouragement entertainment
>   improvement replacement retirement
> **-ance**   insurance resistance
> **-ence**   insistence preference
> **-ion**   collection creation decision direction protection
> **-tion**   production
> **-ation** imagination
> **-al**   approval proposal survival

2 🔲 The answers are recorded. (The recording includes the examples and lasts 2 minutes.)

B 1

ANSWERS

-ness carelessness happiness loneliness nervousness politeness rudeness selfishness
-ance importance significance
-ence patience presence
-ity formality popularity possibility reality security simplicity
-cy efficiency fluency privacy proficiency

2 The answers to B1 are recorded. (The recording includes the examples and lasts 1 minute 40 seconds.)

3

ANSWERS

anxious free strong wise bored proud hungry thirsty

C This is an exam-style word formation exercise.

ANSWERS

1 difficulties 2 modernisation 3 useful 4 retrained 5 computerisation
6 knowledge 7 employment 8 awareness 9 recognition 10 replacement

14.8 Including relevant information   WRITING

A 1 You may prefer to brainstorm this part with the whole class.

2

SUGGESTED ANSWERS

Missing information in Letter 1:
– previous experience
– languages

Irrelevant information in Letter 1:
– height
– missing lectures and attendance record
– the question about working hours is answered in the advertisement itself

Other faults in Letter 1:
– the writer isn't 'selling' him/herself hard enough: 'I wonder if I might be suitable', 'my typing is quite good', etc.

Missing information in Letter 2:
– perhaps a bit more detail of previous experience?

Irrelevant information in Letter 2:
– 'at top of page 13'

B Instead of the advertisement in the Student's Book, you might prefer your students to write a letter applying for a real job they've seen advertised. Or which you've photocopied from a newspaper.

There is no model composition in this case: refer students back to Letter 2 in B, if necessary.

Can you explain?

15

15.1 Science and technology VOCABULARY

A The photos show:

1 a remote control (or 'zapper')   **2** the sticky part of a Post-it™ note, seen under a microscope   **3** a computer keyboard   **4** a TV satellite dish on the roof of a house

B Some of these questions are deliberately open-ended to provoke discussion.

> **ANSWERS**
> **1** hydrogen   oxygen   **2** chemistry   physics   biology   **3** practical
> **4** experiments   laboratory   **5** practice   **6** hardware   software
> disk/hard disk/floppy disk   **7** adjust/lower/increase/control   button
> instructions/manual   **8** serviced   break down   repaired/fixed/mended
> **9** carpenter   chisel/screwdriver/drill/plane/sander, etc.
> **10** screws/nails/glue – and various tools, presumably

C Maybe start everyone off by describing the parts of your classroom cassette player, and its various controls, buttons and facilities.

NOTE
Before starting 15.2 remind your students to look at the GRAMMAR REFERENCE section on The passive on page 179.

15.2 Using the passive GRAMMAR REVIEW

A
> **ANSWERS**
> It *was done* yesterday.
> It *was being done* last week.
> It *has already been done.*
> It *will be done* eventually.
> It *will have been done* before long.
> It *had been done* earlier.
> It *had to be done* at once.
> It *may not have been done* yet.

B Generally, the information given at the **beginning** and **end** of a sentence is the important or emphasised information. The last thing mentioned (at the **end** of the sentence) is usually more important.

However, in conversation, if you place a stress on information **within** the sentence you can emphasise that instead:

Camcorders were marketed by <u>Sony</u> in 1982.   (stress on <u>Sony</u>)
Camcorders were <u>first</u> marketed by Sony in 1982.   (stress on <u>first</u>)
. . . and so on!

> **SUGGESTED ANSWERS**
> **1** Emphasis on *by an expert.*
> **2** Emphasis on *be repaired.*
>
> **3** Emphasis on *camcorders.*
> **4** Emphasis on *the year* (and Sony is unimportant).
>
> **5** Emphasis on *New York.*
> **6** Emphasis on *restaurants.*

C ANSWERS (Some variations are possible.)

2 These particles **can't be seen without** a microscope.
3 Computers **are being used everywhere** nowadays.
4 Dangerous **chemicals must be kept** in a secure place.
5 Both Scotch Tape and Post-it™ Notes **are made by 3M.**
6 Intelligent life **will probably not be discovered** on other planets.
7 This room **hasn't yet been** cleaned.
8 No one is sure who **President Kennedy was shot** by.

D This is a discussion task, and students aren't expected to know the right answers – but you might be:

ANSWERS
aeroplane (1903)   bicycle (1840)   camcorder (1982)   computer (1943)
compact disc (1982)   light bulb (1878)   margarine (1869)   Post-it™ Notes (1980)
telephone (1876)   television (1926)   thermometer (1593)

15.3 Paper 4: Listening   EXAM TECHNIQUES

A For further information on this paper consult *Cambridge Practice Tests for First Certificate* Teacher's Book and *Specifications and Sample Papers for the Revised FCE Examination*, available from UCLES.

B   These are the first two parts of a mock exam paper. The second recording is unlike Part 2 in the exam because it contains some information which students might already know – such as the answers to Questions 9 and 10. In the exam, this recording would give an unfair advantage to people who have previous knowledge of the subject. Parts 3 and 4 are in 16.4.

1 Play each of the eight short situations **twice** in turn – don't play all eight all the way through non-stop. (In the exam, each situation is heard twice on the tape, but here we have only recorded each situation once, so you'll have to rewind each one to play it again.)
2 Allow 45 seconds for everyone to read the questions for Part 2 then play Part 2.
3 Rewind Part 2 and play it again.

ANSWERS
Part 1   1 B   2 C   3 C   4 B   5 B   6 B   7 A   8 C
Part 2   9 ships   10 aircraft   11 weapon   12 cooling systems   13 by-product
14 substitute for rubber   15 stick properly/permanently   16 more sticky
17 less sticky/leave a mark   18 sang in a (church) choir

TRANSCRIPTS   *11 minutes 20 seconds* – but if you play each part twice and pause for the specified time between playings, the whole sequence will take about *25 minutes*

PART 1
NARRATOR: These are the instructions that you will hear in the exam.
ANNOUNCER: Hello. I'm going to give you the instructions for this test and tell you about what you are going to hear. I'll introduce each part of the test and give you time to look at the questions.
     Remember, while you're listening, write down your answers on the question paper. You'll have time at the end of the test to copy your answers onto the separate answer sheet.
     The tape will now be stopped. Please ask any questions now, because you must not speak during the test.
NARRATOR: Then you'll be told to open your question paper and look at Part 1. Each piece is played twice.
ANNOUNCER: Look at Part 1. You'll hear people talking in eight different situations. For questions 1 to 8 choose the best answer: A, B or C.
NARRATOR: In the exam you'll hear each question and the three possible answers read out in full. (But we won't bother reading all the possible answers out now.)

ANNOUNCER: One. Listen to this woman talking to a friend. Why was she angry?

WOMAN: Well, they said that they'd send someone round on Monday, which was OK because...um...I don't work on Mondays. The only trouble was it was a beautiful day, really sunny and...er...I could have gone out for a walk, or gone shopping or something. Anyway, I waited in until 5.30 and nobody came, so I telephoned them and all I got was a recorded message telling me to call during office hours. And there was this programme I really wanted to see that evening. But the doorbell rang, and would you believe it, it was him. And I tell you I really gave him a piece of my mind!

ANNOUNCER: Two. You've taken your camera to a shop for repair. When is it going to be ready?

MAN: Mm, well, let's see, five days from today is Monday the 27th – ah ah ah, but that's a public holiday so...er...the workshop will be closed over the weekend. So...ah...let's say a week tomorrow, no no a week on Wednesday, but you'd better phone us on the Tuesday...um...just to make sure, I...I wouldn't want you to have a wasted journey.

ANNOUNCER: Three. Listen to this woman talking to a colleague. Why is she upset?

WOMAN: Well, you see, I left it on my desk during the lunch-hour and...er...and then when I got back it had gone. Well, to be honest actually I didn't notice it had gone till...er...Max brought it back later that day. Well, he said he'd just borrowed it for an hour or so. Er...he said he would have asked me but he couldn't find me. Anyway, he said he bought his own tape to use and that he took it out in the park to film his girlfriend and...er...and then when it started raining he...he said he put it back in the bag and it couldn't have got wet. Well that's what he said anyway. Well, I used it myself at the weekend and...and now the tape keeps going slow.

ANNOUNCER: Four. Listen to a man talking about a gadget. Why do the batteries need replacing?

MAN: No it'll probably be all right for a while but before too long it'll stop working. What's worse is that if you go on using it you may do permanent damage to the motor and replacing that will cost a lot of money. Did they put these batteries in for you in the shop?

WOMAN: Mm.

MAN: Well in that case it's their fault, they should have known they were wrong. My advice is to take it back to them and tell them that rechargeable batteries shouldn't be used – as it says in the instructions here, look.

WOMAN: Mm.

ANNOUNCER: Five. You're in the kitchen at a friend's flat. What does he want you to do?

MAN: Um...could you give me a hand please? Er...look I've tried opening it using this but it's stuck now. I think there must be some kind of special trick or knack you have to know – I've already made all this mess, look, and now I've cut my finger too. Ow. Could you take over and see if you can do it please? I should have asked you in the first place but...um...because you're much stronger than me.

ANNOUNCER: Six. Listen to a man talking to a colleague. What is he talking about?

MAN: Well, this red light keeps coming on and it makes a sort of buzzing noise. It was working all right earlier today. I...I've had it for a couple of months and I've never had any problems with it before. Look. I...I'll show you. I...if I feed the document in it, well, it grips it all right, then when I dial the number the red light will come on and I won't be able to send it, then this light will come on and, well, it won't go off again till I press the red button . . .

ANNOUNCER: Seven. Listen to a woman talking to a man. She's an expert, but what is she an expert in?

MAN: So...er...what do you think I should do?

WOMAN: Let's see. Have you tried turning it off and on?

MAN: Yeah, yes, but it...it still prints out like this. Look, look at this document. I can't send this to a customer, can I?

WOMAN: No, I see what you mean. Well it looks to me as if the cable connection may be loose . . .

MAN: No no no no, it's OK I've checked it.

WOMAN: Really? Then it must be the driver software. Could I just sit down and try it myself? It's probably corrupted or something . . .

ANNOUNCER: Eight. Listen to this man talking. Who is he talking to?

MAN: So you see all you have to do is put a very small amount of the liquid on a damp cloth – only this much, no more. And then you rub the surface ever so gently, like this. And after just a few seconds the whole surface is sparkling. Now this remarkable product is only on special offer . . .

ANNOUNCER: That's the end of Part 1.

PART 2

ANNOUNCER: Part 2. Now you're going to hear part of a radio programme. For questions 9 to 18, complete the notes which summarise what the speaker says.

PRESENTER: . . . and good luck plays a part in scientific research too. In this case it's often referred to as serendipity, which, according to my dictionary, is 'the natural talent that some people have for finding interesting or valuable things by chance'. Debbie Charles has been looking into this for us. Debbie.

DEBBIE: That's right, Jenny. In fact, you know, most important discoveries in the world of science and technology came about by some sort of lucky accident. Starting with the wheel, presumably.

Now let's just look at a few of these, starting with...er...penicillin. Now, Alexander Fleming found some mould growing on a laboratory dish which he'd...er...absent-mindedly left on a window-sill. Now, he found that this mould stopped the spread of bacteria, which as you know is the cause of illnesses like pneumonia. And modern antibiotic drugs based on penicillin save millions of lives every year.

And then there's radar. Now, all sea and air transport depends on radar for navigation and safety – and armies depend on it for defence as well, of course. Radar was discovered during the war while British military scientists were trying to find a death ray, which was...er...some sort of radio wave that could be used to kill people. They didn't find a death ray, but they did find a technique.

And then there's...er...Teflon, which is a substance which is used in non-stick frying pans. Now, this was discovered by accident in a laboratory by DuPont scientists, who were doing research into gases to use in refrigerators. Now, they discovered that a plastic coating had formed on their equipment and this was unaffected by heat and it was also very slippery. Now, no use was found for this until some time later a French researcher used it in a frying pan – and...er... Teflon's also used in space vehicles.

And then there's artificial sweeteners: now, from saccharine to the more modern sweeteners, all of these (for example...ah...Cyclamate, Nutrasweet, etc.) were discovered by accident. The usual pattern was that scientists were...were doing another experiment and they happened to taste one of the by-products, which they found to be sweet. Some of these sweeteners are thousands of times sweeter than sugar, you know.

And then there's chewing gum, which was discovered while scientists were looking for a substitute for rubber. And again there seemed at the time to be no apparent use for this product of the...er...Mexican Sapodilla tree! But serendipity made this product – there's no country in the world where chewing gum isn't available...

PRESENTER: Haha, no, but...er...I'm not sure that that is quite as beneficial to mankind as the others you've talked about!

DEBBIE: Oh, maybe not. But here's one more very useful product. You know those...er...little yellow stick-on notes we use in the office and...er...for leaving phone messages and so on? Um...Post-it™ Notes, they're called I think. Well, a researcher at 3M (which is the firm that makes Scotch Tape) was doing research into adhesives and glue, and...er...he discovered a substance that seemed to be completely useless. I mean, it was...was quite sticky but it wouldn't stick permanently to anything. You know, that's what adhesives obviously are supposed to do. And in fact, however long he left the adhesive sticking to various surfaces, it didn't make a mark on the surface and the bond became no more and no less effective. All other adhesives either get more sticky or less sticky with age, you know. Now, he was a member of a church choir and he always had to use slips of paper to mark the place where each of the hymns was in his hymn-book – and the slips of paper kept falling on the floor. So he used these bits of sticky paper with this...er...'useless' adhesive on to mark his place in the hymn-book. And then he realised that other people could find a similar use . . .

PRESENTER: Brilliant!

DEBBIE: No, just serendipity!

PRESENTER: Haha. Yah. Thank you, Debbie.

C The follow-up discussion is in two parts: about exam skills and techniques, and about the topic of the second recording: good luck and bad luck.

15.4 Effortless cycling   READING

A **Sir Clive Sinclair** was famous as the inventor of the pocket calculator back in the sixties. He was also responsible for the boom in home computers in the seventies. But he's probably best known for one of his failures: the Sinclair C5 – a one-person electric vehicle which became something of a joke.

ANSWERS
1 F   2 E   3 G   4 H   5 B   6 A   7 I   8 C   (D is the odd one out.)

B If time is short, or if this section doesn't appeal to your students, the writing task could be omitted.

You may prefer to brainstorm the pros and cons, as well as questions to ask Sinclair Research as a whole-class activity.

NOTE
For 15.5 students will need to bring some gadgets to class: TV or video remotes, digital alarms, Walkmen, digital wristwatches, etc. Bring some of these yourself, so that students who forget have something to talk about.

15.5 How do they do that?   LISTENING AND SPEAKING

A 1 The correct sequence is shown here:

How to juggle

You will need:
three bean bags, balls or any other small evenly-shaped objects of the same size

Facing a bare wall, imagine two spots about 30cms away, in front of your forehead. Keep concentrating on them at all times.

1d Practise tossing one ball from your right hand so that it passes through the imaginary spot on the left and is caught by your left hand.

2c Then toss it back to the right hand, making sure it passes through the spot on the right. Repeat this until you can toss one ball in an even figure-of-eight.

3b With a ball in each hand, start as before. When the first ball reaches the spot on the left, toss the second ball. Repeat this until both balls move evenly and you catch them every time.

4a Hold two balls in your right hand and one in your left. Begin as for two balls, but toss the third ball when the second one passes through the spot on the right as it makes its way to your right hand. Do not worry about catching the third ball at first. It is more important to learn when to toss it, aiming for the spot on the left when it leaves your right hand. Keep practising and you will improve.

TRANSCRIPT   *2 minutes 30 seconds*

JULIET: OK, now imagine that you've got two spots...er...about 30 centimetres away from your eyes...Yeah?

NICK: What, straight out in front?

JULIET: Straight out in front of you, yeah. Now I want you to con...keep concentrating on them at all times. OK, is that clear?

NICK: Right...yeah yeah.

JULIET: Right, now take one ball in your right hand and just practise throwing it from your right hand to your left hand, passing through that imaginary spot.

NICK: Wh...which one? The one on the –

JULIET: The one on the left-hand side.

NICK: So with the right hand through the –
JULIET: Through the left-hand spot...OK.
NICK: OK, like that...yeah...and then back.
JULIET: Now, take...the...the ball is now in your right hand, yeah? And you throw it back to the...um...left hand.
NICK: To the right hand.
JULIET: Oh, sorry, it's in the left –
NICK: It's in the left hand now, yeah.
JULIET: Oh right, it's in the left hand. So you throw it back to the right hand making sure it passes through the spot on the right...
NICK: On the right-hand side, OK, I see.
JULIET: Right, OK so far?...Now you repeat this until you can...you can toss the ball from one hand to the other in a...in a figure of eight, in an even figure of eight...Just keep doing that for a bit.
NICK: Is that right?
JULIET: That's good, yeah. That's OK so far. Right, now take the other ball...so you've got one ball in each hand now and then what you have to do is, when the first ball reaches the spot on the left, you then throw the second ball up.
NICK: Right, so I throw the right hand first, when it reaches the spot on the left, then I throw the left-hand ball and it's got to go through the spot on the right.
JULIET: Exactly, exactly, and you just repeat that until you've got both balls moving evenly and you catch them every time.
NICK: One, two...They've both got to go up, haven't they?
JULIET: Yeah. So when that one hits that point over there, at that point the other ball...yeah...but you want that one to go up as well.
NICK: One of them's going straight across, isn't it?...Hm...that was better, wasn't it?
JULIET: That was much better, yeah. You've got it, haven't you?...OK, that's great, great. Now, with two balls in your right hand...and one ball in your left...now what you're going to do is . . .

2 To start things off, ask one student to explain her/his gadget to you – and pretend to be ignorant so that she/he has to explain some of the more 'obvious' points.

B   Divide the class into pairs of pairs. Students A and B look at Activity *15* while C and D (and maybe E) look at *39*.

Activity *15*, which continues in Activity *23*, is an explanation of how a microwave oven works. Activity *39*, which continues in Activity *45*, is an explanation of how a computer mouse works.

After studying their explanations, the students form pairs with a different student and tell each other what they've discovered. They shouldn't read the text aloud but should rely on their memory.

15.6 Opposites   WORD STUDY

A **1** We begin with some revision of negative prefixes.

> **ANSWERS**
> dishonest   unkind   illegal   unlucky   immature   unnecessary   impersonal
> unpleasant   impolite   irregular   irrelevant   unsafe   untrue   invisible   unwilling

2

> **ANSWERS** (Many variations are possible.)
> modest   ugly   expensive   kind   safe   empty   well/healthy/fit   confident
> quiet/silent   modern/up-to-date   polite   hard/rough   fresh   loose   fast asleep
> right/correct

3

> **ANSWERS**
> lose   lower   fall   lie   lose   break   finish/end   turn off

B **ANSWERS**
> **2** wet/rainy   **3** easy   **4** soft   **5** heavy   **6** dark   **7** calm   **8** smooth   **9** pass
> **10** succeeded   **11** rich/wealthy/well-off   **12** good   **13** Lucky   won   **14** found
> **15** gained

15.7 Coming and going VERBS AND IDIOMS

A ANSWERS

1 come   2 go   3 take   4 Come   bring   5 take (*or* bring)
6 delivered (*or* taken/brought)   7 fetch   8 carry (*or* deliver/take/bring)

B ANSWERS

2 came across   3 go with   4 comes in   goes out   5 gone off   6 gone off
7 went off   8 went in for   9 Come on   10 go on   go over

15.8 Describing a process WRITING

A The first paragraph lacks detail and the second has rather too much irrelevant detail. These faults are ones to avoid when writing the composition in B.

B Decide with the class who the intended reader of the explanation is to be: maybe an English-speaking friend who comes from a country where the gadget in question is not commonly used, or no longer used because it's so old-fashioned?

By the way, make sure everyone knows what's wrong with the examples at the foot of the page – and how they should be corrected! It may be necessary to check this, rather than just assuming that everyone has spotted all the mistakes.

MODEL EXPLANATION

MICROWAVE OVENS

Microwaves are a type of short-wave radiation, rather like radio waves. They are produced by a device called a magnetron which is housed inside the oven. The microwaves are reflected by metal surfaces but absorbed by food. They cause the molecules of the food to vibrate billions of times a second, making the food heat up and cook. Larger amounts of food take longer to cook so microwaves are especially effective when cooking small portions.

The advantages of microwave cooking are that it is both quicker and cleaner than conventional cooking. Food that has already been cooked can be re-heated at any time without loss of flavour or juices, and frozen food can be de-frosted and cooked very easily.

Microwave ovens use less energy than conventional methods of cooking and are very safe. As soon as the door is opened, they automatically switch off and microwaves cannot normally leak out of the door while they are operating – despite some frightening stories about this!

---

16 Keeping up to date

The press, politics and crime   VOCABULARY

Bring a selection of English-language newspapers to class; this will help the topic to come alive and will help to jog students' memories when they get to Part C below.

A   Get a consensus from the class on their sources of news and attitudes to it. In this discussion, remember that many people hardly ever keep up to date with the news – give them a chance to say why.

B   ANSWERS

2 article   report   3 editorial   leader column   4 hostages   people
5 civil war   revolution   6 earthquake   explosion   7 election   referendum
8 PM   prime minister   9 arrested   caught   10 seized   stolen   11 gaol   jail
12 convicted   found guilty

C   To prepare for this (and prove that it is possible) make your **own** chart of events that have happened in the past seven days.

If you can, take newspapers for the last seven days to class – students can pass them round to help them to remember the stories. Encourage students to think of events that have happened in other countries than their own.

At the end of the discussion, ask each group to report to the whole class. Perhaps ask these questions:

- What was the most awful event?
- What was the most amusing event?
- Why is so little **good** news reported – can you remember any from the past week?

Alternatively, either compose a chart on the board, brainstorming ideas from the class or set this task as 'research' for students to prepare for homework and then discuss in pairs in class.

16.2 ## What happened?   WRITING

A   🗬 The stories these headlines are from can be found in Activities *3, 8,* and *12.*

B & **C**   Follow the procedure in the Student's Book.

MODEL STORY

We received this fax from St Lucia: 'One of our workers dropped her wedding ring in one of the boxes. Please can you find it?'

When the shipment arrived it was my job to open up the crate and start searching. Just laying the bananas out on the floor took all morning. Then I had to pick up each bunch, shake it and then put it back into the box. By 6 o'clock there was just one more bunch to check.

I picked up the bananas and shook them hard. There was a little ringing noise on the concrete floor. Success! I went straight to the office and sent a fax with the good news.

The next morning, when I got to work, there was a fax waiting for me: 'Thank you! As a reward, we'd like to invite you to come to St Lucia for a free holiday.'

16.3 **Shoplifting in America** READING

 1 As a lead-in to the reading passage, you could ask your students how serious a problem shoplifting is in their country and brainstorm possible means of deterring shoplifters.

2

> **ANSWERS**
> **A** matches paragraph 3
> **B** matches paragraph 4
> (**C** matches paragraph 1)
> **D** matches paragraph 7
> **E** matches paragraph 6
> **F** matches paragraph 2
> **G** has no match
> **H** matches paragraph 8
> **I** matches paragraph 5

 B

> **ANSWERS**
> ¶1 bust   euphemism
> ¶4 merchandise   policing   weird
> ¶5 gimmicks   bonus   snatch
> ¶6 communal   collude
> ¶7 stunts   mock   sticky-fingered villain

 C This follow-up discussion leads from shoplifting to more serious crimes. The 'right answers' are in Activity *56*.

16.4 **Paper 4: Listening** EXAM TECHNIQUES

A Allow students 30 seconds to look at the questions in Part 3. Play the whole of Part 3 through, then rewind it and, after a ten-second pause, play it again. Then, after a pause of 30 seconds, play the whole of Part 4 twice with a pause of ten seconds between each playing.

> **ANSWERS**
> **Part 3**
> 19 C   20 A   21 E   22 D   23 B
>
> **Part 4**
> 24 BB   25 MM   26 MM   27 MM   28 TT   29 BB   30 MM

TRANSCRIPT   *4 minutes 20 seconds (not including pauses)*

PART 3

NARRATOR: You're going to practise Parts 3 and 4 of the Listening paper.
ANNOUNCER: Part 3. For questions 19 to 23, choose from the list A to F the best summary of what each speaker says. Use the letters once only. There is one extra letter which you do not need to use. You have 30 seconds to look at Part 3.
SPEAKER 1
(WOMAN): . . . Well, um...I...came back in the...er...er...in the middle of the afternoon and I saw a...a red Ford Fiesta it was, um...parked outside the building. I...I didn't recognise the car at all but the only reason I noticed it was because it was...er...because it was parked...um...at quite an unusual angle, you know, as if it had been abandoned or something. Anyway I...er...I called the lift and when it came these two young men got out, each of them was...was carrying a shopping bag. Well, I..I got upstairs and I...I opened my front door and everything was...was upside down. I...it was a real mess and...er...it took quite a long time to work out exactly what was missing. But...um...at least they didn't get away with the video.

SPEAKER 2 (MAN): . . . I was on my way to town and I stopped outside the bank to get some money. There was a parking space just outside, which was lucky, but...er...when I got into the bank this shopkeeper was in front of me paying in all his takings – thousands of pounds. And it all had to be counted. Well, I only wanted to cash a cheque. And while I was waiting, I...I couldn't help noticing this, well, rather dirty-looking man with long hair reading a newspaper, standing away from the queue. And, when the shopkeeper had finished, this man sort of looked around him and followed him out. Well, I...I cashed my cheque and went outside. And there was another car in the space where I'd left mine and I didn't realise at first what had happened because . . .

SPEAKER 3 (WOMAN): . . . got away with a hundred thousand pounds, which is an incredible amount, I mean, more than most people earn in a lifetime. I mean, when I think of that man i...it makes my blood boil. And all the publicity he's got in the papers make...makes him out to be some kind of hero, wh...when in fact he's committed a terrible crime. I mean the trouble is with people like that i...if they go to prison, when they come out they've invested all the money somewhere and i...it earns interest while they're inside, and . . . Still people like that can pay for the best lawyers and they usually get away with it, don't they? I mean it's just not really very fair . . .

SPEAKER 4 (MAN): . . . and I mean that's a really dreadful thing. A man's car is...is something special, you know. To do that to it and...and for no reason! I...I don't usually leave it in the street and...er...never again, I can tell you, but this time I did. I mean, I should have realised when I heard these guys outside in the night. I...I opened the curtains and I looked out to see what was going on and...and they must have seen the light from the window and th...they ran off. But it wasn't until I...er...went out the next morning to drive to work that I noticed the mark all down the side – I mean, they must have used a key or something. Honestly, if I catch those guys, I . . .

SPEAKER 5 (WOMAN): He was driving down the road when this car overtook him, then it braked so suddenly that he nearly crashed into the back of it. Well, he jumped out and he was going to start swearing at the driver when this really glamorous young woman got out of the driver's seat and smiled at him so sweetly. Well, all his anger sort of vanished. She walked towards him and took hold of his arm and pushed him down onto the ground. Then she bent down, kicked him hard and put her hand in his pocket and grabbed his wallet. Then she drove off. He was so shocked he didn't even get the number of the car.

ANNOUNCER: That's the end of Part 3.

TRANSCRIPT   *3 minutes 30 seconds (not including pauses)*

PART 4

ANNOUNCER: Part 4. For questions 24 to 30, write 'TT', 'BB' or 'MM' in the boxes provided. You have 30 seconds to look through Part 4.

PRESENTER (KATHY): The resignation of the minister for the family has raised again the topic of the press and what their role is in telling the world about the private lives of the rich and famous. I have with me Tony Towers, editor of the *Sunday Globe*, Bill Brown editor of the *Daily Echo* and Mary Matthews editor of *Hi!* magazine. First of all, Tony, good morning.

TONY TOWERS: Hello, Kathy. Yes, well it seems to me that there's absolutely nothing wrong with what we've been doing. The minister was having an affair with his secretary, his marriage was about to break up and this is the man who was standing up in public talking about the importance of family and threatening to reduce benefits to single-parent families. He deserved what he got.

PRESENTER: Mary Matthews.

MARY MATTHEWS: Well, ...er...it seems to me that people who are in the public eye and who are making their living from appearing in public can't start making a fuss when...um...a magazine publishes photos of them lying by their swimming pools or...er...kissing the people they love. Well, after all in the end it's the public who are paying them and I...they don't really have the right to say when the public are allowed to see them and when they aren't. I believe that public figures can't really expect to live private lives.

PRESENTER: Bill Brown.

BILL BROWN: Y...yes, well I can't agree with Tony or Mary. First of all, the Minister's private life was his own affair . . . No, no, there's no reason, there is no reason why the things he does in private should affect his work. He was doing a perfectly good job and I don't see . . . I don't see why he shouldn't still be in office – in countries like...like France or Italy he still would be.

But...um...now as I see it you have to separate people's lives into a public side and a private side, whoever they are – famous people or members of the public. And, I mean, how famous do you have to be to...er...to forgo the right to privacy? Do *slightly* famous people like soap opera actors or...or newspaper editors lose their right to privacy? Now, I...I assume that even Tony would agree he himself has a right to privacy?

PRESENTER: Mm. Tony?

TONY TOWERS: Not if the public are interested, no . . . No! We don't publish details of Mr Jones having an affair with Mrs Smith next-door, simply because that wouldn't sell papers . . . Nobody would be interested (except Mrs Jones and Mr Smith!) . . . Ha. We try to report what our readers want to know about. They do want to know about soap opera characters and film stars, they don't want to know about my private life.

PRESENTER: Mary Matthews.

MARY MATTHEWS: Well, I...I don't actually agree there. People *are* interested in how other people live however ordinary they are. You know, one of our best-selling issues was the one where we interviewed the man who won the...er...lottery jackpot of £20 million and...er...didn't want anyone to know who he was or where he lived. But...er...he was happy to talk to my magazine and...er...let us photograph him and his family in their new villa in Spain. And, you know, our readers really loved that article, and...er...he...he was pretty pleased too. Th...the point is that every person likes to be treated with respect, and...er...well, they have every right to object if they aren't.

ANNOUNCER: That's the end of Part 4.

NOTE
Before starting 16.5 remind everyone to look at the GRAMMAR REFERENCE section on Reported speech on pages 184–185.

16.5 The past – 3: Reported speech   GRAMMAR REVIEW

A

SUGGESTED ANSWERS

2 What's the time? / Do you know what the time is? / Could you tell me the time?

3 Have you had lunch yet (by any chance)?

4 Would you like to come for a walk with us? / Do you feel like coming for a walk with us? / How about coming for a walk with us?

5 Don't forget to make the/that phone call. / Remember you've got to make a phone call.

6 I've just got back from holiday.

7 Can you meet me here tomorrow? / Please meet me here tomorrow.

8 Do you think you could possibly help me with my work? / Would you mind giving me a hand with my work?

B Verbs used to introduce reported speech are listed in the GRAMMAR REFERENCE section on Reported speech in the Student's Book (pages 184–185).

SUGGESTED ANSWERS

2 He asked her when she had set off.

3 He wondered how she felt now that she was home again.

4 He asked her what the worst moment of her voyage had been.

5 He asked her if she was pleased to be home.

6 He wondered if she would like to sail round the world again.

8 She told him (that) she had said goodbye to her family on 1 April and (that) she hadn't seen them again until that day.

9 She admitted (that) she felt very tired, but she was proud of what she had achieved.

10 She told him (that) the worst moment had been when the sails were torn in a storm.

11 She said (that) she was delighted to be back home because she had missed everyone terribly.

12 She told him (that) if she did it again, she would take her family with her on the trip.

14 She advised them not to spend so long on their own as she had just done.

15 She warned them not to expect her to be the same person she used to be.

16 She invited them to/She offered to take them to a fancy restaurant to celebrate her return.

17 She asked them to lend her some money and promised to pay them back the next day.

18 She told them to open the champagne because she wanted to celebrate.

C Perhaps begin by brainstorming some newsworthy events: swimming the Channel, cycling around the world, saving someone from drowning, etc. Then the students can choose an achievement they can identify with.

The two steps of the activity can be repeated with changed roles.

16.6 Pauses and stress SPEAKING

Students will **not** have to read aloud in the exam. But reading aloud is an excellent way of focusing on pronunciation in class – in conversation students are concentrating on what to say next and can't be expected to pay attention to their own or each other's pronunciation. Reading aloud gives everyone a chance to concentrate on pronunciation.

Nonetheless, it should be pointed out to students that speaking in a conversation and reading aloud are different skills. In real life most students will rarely need to read long texts aloud – but they may well have to read out a sentence or even a short paragraph to someone, over the phone for example.

In 17.5 we look at stressing the right syllable in polysyllabic words.
In 18.5 we look at catenation (joining up words).

A There is no single correct way to read any sentence. The pauses and stresses in the recordings are model readings. Moreover, some syllables are more strongly stressed than others.

1 📼 The first item is read aloud in a monotone with equal stress on each word and pauses in the wrong places. (The recording lasts 30 seconds.)

2 📼 The recording begins with an improved reading of the news item in A1:
A láwyer | who arríved láte for his cáse at Léwes Crówn Coúrt | explaíned that he had been áccidently lócked úp with the prísoners.
The recording then continues with the four news items in A2. Pause the recording after each sentence to give students time to mark the **pauses** they heard. (The recording lasts 1 minute.)

3 📼 Play the recording again pausing after each sentence to give students time to mark the **stresses** they heard.

4 The marked-up versions of the items are in Activity **46**.

B 📼 Student A looks at Activity **17** while B looks at **20**. They each have three more short news items to read to their partner. But **before** they read them, they have to mark the pauses and stresses they intend to place in the sentences.

📼 Model readings of these items are recorded for students to listen to after they've done the activity. (The recording lasts 1 minute 20 seconds.)

16.7 *Put* VERBS AND IDIOMS

ANSWERS
(**1** put on = switch on)
2 put out/off = switch off
3 put up = provide accommodation
4 put off = distract
5 put off = postpone
6 put up = raised
7 put on = gained
8 put down = write down
9 putting back = replacing
10 put away = remove to proper place
11 put forward   put back = change to later/earlier time
12 put through = connect to phone extension
13 put up with = tolerate
14 put off = discouraged

16.8 Paper 1: Reading   EXAM TECHNIQUES

A For more information about the Reading paper see *Cambridge Practice Tests for First Certificate Teacher's Book* and *Specifications for the Revised FCE Examination*, available from UCLES.

B Choose a suitable test paper for your students to do. You may prefer to do this in class (under exam conditions), or set this for homework. As the test takes 1 hour 15 minutes, you may not have time to do all of it in class.

16.9 Giving your opinions   WRITING

A (Neil Postman is the author of the passage on Etiquette in Unit 1.)

B You may want to choose one or two of the opening lines and brainstorm continuations with the class on the board. For example (opening line 6):

> The only solution to terrorism is to call for world action against terrorists so that there is nowhere they can be safe. If this is done, and every government enforces this law, terrorists will become outlaws in every country.

C Rather than have everyone do all three topics, you may prefer to assign different topics to different pairs, who could later combine and tell the others what their points would be.

D Perhaps reassure everyone that, in the exam, they don't need to write a brilliantly argued article – all that's required is that they communicate their ideas and justify them to some extent. Students who don't have strong opinions should, perhaps, avoid this kind of topic in the exam.

17

It's a small world

17.1 Other countries   VOCABULARY

 A   Here are some adjectives that can be used to describe each photograph:

1 *comfortable   domestic   harmonious   uncomfortable   traditional*
2 *busy   colourful   crowded   lonely   urban*
3 *intimate   kind   polite   private   thoughtful*
4 *active   independent   happy   lighthearted   uninhibited*

B 1   This is a discussion activity. Students shouldn't worry if they don't recognise some of the countries – but their names in English (spelt correctly) are important. The countries are: (top row, left to right) Portugal, Turkey, Japan, Spain, Poland, Germany, Australia, (bottom row, left to right) Italy, China, Switzerland, Ireland, Canada and Greece.

The two largest countries are Canada and China.

The two smallest countries are Ireland and Switzerland.

2

> **ANSWERS**
>
> Japanese   Spanish   Polish   German   Australian   Italian   Chinese   Swiss   Irish
> Canadian   Greek

C 1

> **ANSWERS**
>
> **1** important   **2** century   **3** image   **4** employed   **5** modern   **6** blocks   **7** cities
> **8** thinking   **9** become   **10** whether   **11** safety   **12** problems   **13** understanding
> **14** chance   **15** unique

2 & 3

> **ANSWERS**
>
> **1** what   **2** where   **3** For   **4** with   **5** found   **6** by   **7** what/which/how/that
> **8** as   **9** on/about   **10** what   **11** country/place   **12** for   **13** as
> **14** need/want/require   **15** language

4 & 5   This is the first of two writing tasks in this unit. You may prefer to brainstorm ideas instead of having students do this in pairs.

NOTE
Before starting 17.2 remind your students to look at the GRAMMAR REFERENCE section on Comparing and contrasting on page 173.

17.2 Comparing and contrasting   GRAMMAR REVIEW

A The eight sentences can be written in pairs, or as homework. Encourage everyone to use a **variety** of the structures shown in the examples in the GRAMMAR REFERENCE section, and not just 'more . . . than'. Here are two examples:

> In 1950 there were far fewer retired people in Britain than now.
> In 2025 there will be over twice as many retired people in Japan as there are now.

Make sure any mistakes are spotted and corrected. As this exercise is open-ended, no model answers are given.

B The sentences in B and C all refer to the information in the 'World Weather Guide' chart.

> **ANSWERS**
>
> 2 *The daytime temperature in Tokyo in July is the same <u>than</u> New York.*   as
> 3 *There <u>are not much differences</u> between the weather in New York and Warsaw.*   is not much difference
> 4 *The weather in Athens in July is <u>more warmer</u> than London.*   warmer
> 5 *New York is <u>more cold</u> in winter <u>as</u> London.*   colder   than
> 6 *There are <u>much less</u> wet days in Tokyo than in Warsaw.*   far fewer

C

> **ANSWERS**
>
> 2 There isn't **as much rain in** Buenos Aires as in New York.
> 3 More **rain falls in Athens than** in Tokyo in January.
> 4 In July Buenos Aires **is much cooler than** New York.
> 5 About the same amount **of rain falls in London** as in New York.
> 6 Summer nights in London are **not as hot as in** Cairo.
> 7 Warsaw **is a colder place than** New York in winter.
> 8 New York and London **have the same number of** rainy days as each other.

D After the discussion make sure everyone writes a paragraph (probably for homework) to consolidate what has been revised in this section.

17.3 A nice place   READING

A To start everyone off, point out where Norwich (pronounced /nɒrɪdʒ/) and all the places mentioned are on a map of the UK. Alresford (pronounced /ɔːlsfəd/) is a few miles west of Winchester. Ask students to predict what the article is about from the headline. Prompt the students by asking the following questions:

- How does Norwich feel?
- Why might the city be pleased with itself?

> **ANSWERS**
> 1 a   2 c   3 d   4 d   5 d   6 c

B

> **ANSWERS**
> ¶2 courteous   ¶5 award   ¶8 citizens
> ¶3 squeezing   ¶6 manners   ¶9 consolation
> ¶4 agents   ¶7 needless to say   ¶10 reasonably

C This discussion gives an opportunity to explore what kinds of behaviour are considered polite in different countries. Concepts of what is rude and what is polite differ from country to country.

Students are invited to compare different countries and regions – this topic may be delicate, explosive, controversial or amusing! In some classes you may want to avoid allowing your students to express their prejudices if they are going to upset each other. (You may want to postpone the discussion until after everyone's read the article about Miami in the next section.)

17.4 **Not such a nice place**   READING

This is a long article and more difficult than students will encounter in the exam. If possible, it should be prepared (and the tasks in A and B both done) as homework before the lesson.

Ⓐ The original headline was: 'How to visit Miami and survive'.

Ⓑ **ANSWERS**
1 G   2 F   3 D   4 C   5 I   6 E   7 A   8 H (Sentence B doesn't fit anywhere.)

If there's time, ask the students to compare Norwich and Miami with a big city in their country. And make sure everyone highlights any new vocabulary they want to remember in the article.

17.5 **Stressing the right syllable**   WORD STUDY

Ⓐ **1**

ANSWERS

verbs and *-ing* forms	**nouns and adjectives**
(They expórted the goods to the USA.	Tourism is an invisible éxport.)
(These bananas are impórted.	Ímports have risen this month.)
He insúlted me.	That was a terrible ínsult.
They perfécted a new method.	Your work is not quite pérfect.
Smoking is not permítted.	You need a pérmit to fish in the river.
His work is progréssing well.	New Prógress to First Certificate.
They protésted about the situation.	They held a prótest meeting.
Listen to the recórding.	Have you heard their new récord?
He is suspécted of the crime.	He is the main súspect.

2 📼 The sentences are recorded. (The recording lasts 1 minute.)

Ⓑ **1**

ANSWERS

(emplóy   emplóyer   employée   emplóyment   applý   applicátion)   ádvertising   advértisement   attráction   certíficate   cómfortable   communicátion   députy   désert   dessért   desírable   détails   devélopment   expérience   gírlfriend   informátion   intélligence   machíne   pérmanent   phótograph   photógraphy   qualificátion   recéptionist   reservátion   secretárial   sécretary   télephone   teléphonist   témporary   themsélves   tóothache   végetable   yoursélf

2 📼 The words are recorded. (The recording lasts 1 minute 10 seconds.)

Ⓒ 📼 Pause the recording after each sentence to give everyone time to catch up. (The recording includes the first sentence and lasts 1 minute.)

ANSWERS AND TRANSCRIPT
2 It takes móst péople a lóng tíme to perféct their pronunciátion in Énglish.
3 Nórwich is pléased to púll óff a níce óne.
4 We fóund Nórwich to be a cíty with a smíle.
5 We're réasonably níce to éach óther, but I'm súre that mány óther tówns are équally as níce.
6 Sáve the gréen Bermúda shórts and yéllow pólo shírts for Orlándo.
7 Hów to vísit Miámi and survíve.
8 Tínted wíndows would be níce. Só wóuld a cár phóne.

17.6 *Bring, call and cut*   VERBS AND IDIOMS

ANSWERS
1 brought about   2 brought up   3 bring down   4 bring back   5 called off
6 call in   7 call off   8 call for   9 call back   10 cut down   11 cut out   12 cut off

17.7 **When in Rome . . .**   LISTENING

As the speakers don't mention the name of the country they're talking about, it might be fun for everyone to guess which country each one is talking about. There's plenty more information and interesting ideas in each speech which your students might like to comment on and discuss.

ANSWERS
1 D   2 F   3 A   4 B   5 C   (Sentence E is not used.)

TRANSCRIPT   *3 minutes 30 seconds*

NICK: (*talking about Uganda*): Well, I was amazed, I don't know, I think I was expecting somewhere very dry and barren for some reason and in fact it's the most incredibly lush and rich place. And it...the soil is a deep red and it looks as if you threw a seed in the ground it would grow into a tree by the next day. And the people are incredibly friendly...er...very welcoming.

SUSANNA: (*talking about Switzerland*): Well, I know it quite well because my grandparents live there, so as a child I used to go there every year. And it's very clean and there are a lot of flowers, but all the same flower: geraniums, red geraniums. And they're in every window box on every house so wherever you go you see these flowers, bright red. Um...there's cows in the mountains and you hear...you hear the cow bells going and...and the grass is very green, and little tiny chalets sort of nestling. Um...it's kind of too good to be true, and the people are a bit like that too.

NEIL: (*talking about Poland*): . . . and I couldn't get anywhere because they have their own code of politeness and behaviour, you have to understand it and I...I couldn't make myself understood, I would go to a canteen and I would ask for...like...a piece of lemon to go in my tea and I wouldn't get it. And I asked my friend...um...who came from...came from the local place...um...what I should do about this because it was driving me nuts. And he said, 'Ah you must remember,' he said, 'We do things differently in this country, you must . . . everything's done with charm, between man and woman is charm.' So the next day I went into the canteen and I said to this enormous woman, who must have been at least 90 years old, 'Could I please have a bit of lemon?' And she gave me a bit with a big smile on her face and she kissed me and it was great.

GERTRUD: (*talking about Japan*): Well, it's quite extraordinary because...um...it's really like a different planet, it's so alien to everything you know when you come from the West...er...so it's quite overwhelming. Apparently it takes eight years to learn the basic rules of behaviour, which is a bit daunting really. And everything's just so different: the smells, the colours, um...the food, the taste, the music even. And...um...everything is very aesthetic, they're very aesthetic people, and so the way the food is arranged is very beautiful, and...um...for instance you can apparently even give someone a glass marble but it's got to be beautifully wrapped and you can give that as a present to your boss.

NIGEL: (*talking about the USA*): One of the things that struck me really was the portions of the food when you go into a restaurant. You get this huge quantity of food that everybody seems to manage to finish. And when you look at some of the people, most of the people, they're either very thin and terribly health-conscious or they're grossly overweight, obviously from eating these huge portions of food.

A For more information on the Writing paper see *Specifications and Sample Papers for the Revised FCE Examination,* available from UCLES and the Teacher's Book of *Cambridge Practice Tests for First Certificate* – in particular the sample compositions and examiners' comments and evaluation.

The examiners' marking scheme is reproduced on page 111 and was referred to in 13.7.

B The written work should be done under exam conditions with a time limit of 45 minutes.

MODEL LETTER

Dear Yoshi,

Thank you for the lovely postcard.

I'm afraid that there's a slight problem because I'll be away when you arrive.

So what I've done is book a room for you in a nice hotel called the Hotel Comfort. I'm sending you the brochure so you can see what it's like. Then, when I get back on Monday 16th, you can come and stay with me.

From the airport take the bus which says CITY CENTRE on it. It goes non-stop to the rail station, and the Hotel Comfort is directly opposite.

But it would be better if you could change your flight date – is it possible to do that, or is it too late?

Now for your questions. The same clothes you'd wear at home will be fine here. And about £200 spending money will be plenty – if you do run out, I can lend you some.

And some great news! My brother is free during your second week. He's offered to drive us around in his car so that you can see some of our lovely mountains, beaches and historic buildings.

I'm really looking forward to seeing you!

Best wishes

New Progress to First Certificate – This document may be photocopied.
© Cambridge University Press 1996

Yes, but is it art?

The *Voices* video sequence *St Ives – Holidaymakers, artists and surfers* deals with other aspects of this topic.

This unit doesn't assume a 'high-brow' knowledge and appreciation of art and music. It covers popular art and entertainment – and students are encouraged to talk about the things they don't like, as well as the things they like.

18.1 The arts   VOCABULARY AND SPEAKING

A **1 & 2** Here are some suitable adjectives to describe the pictures:

1 *calm   massive   monumental   puzzling   serene*
2 *beautiful   classical   harmonious   lyrical   melodic   quiet*
3 *deafening   exciting   exhilarating   loud   modern   noisy   tuneful*
4 *colourful   jolly   rhythmic   traditional   festive*

3 & 4 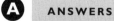 The purpose of this activity is to encourage students to compare their musical tastes. The instruments heard on the recording are: **1** a violin, **2** a saxophone, **3** an acoustic guitar, **4** an electric guitar, **5** a piano, **6** a flute, **7** a trumpet, **8** an organ, **9** drums **10** a clarinet. (The recording lasts 3 minutes 40 seconds but it only needs to be played once.)

B **1**

> **ANSWERS**
> **1** actor/actress/dancer/performer   **2** pianist/piano player   **3** guitarist/guitar player
> **4** violinist   **5** conductor   **6** soloist   **7** potter   **8** sculptor   **9** dramatist/playwright
> **10** genius

(Musicians themselves sometimes talk about playing 'trumpet' or 'piano' rather than '*the* trumpet' or '*the* piano'.)

C The paintings, which illustrate the styles in Question 5 of the survey, are:

Murnau with Church (1910) by Wassily Kandinsky – abstract, 20th century
The Morning Walk (1785) by Thomas Gainsborough – portrait
Dance at Bougival (1883) by Pierre-Auguste Renoir – French impressionist
The Poppy Field (1873) by Claude Monet – French impressionist, landscape
Playing chess (c 1400) by Elwes? – medieval
Self portrait (1669) by Jan Rembrandt van Rijn – great master, portrait
The Wizard (1951) by René Magritte – surrealist, 20th century

18.2 Mozart   READING

A

> **ANSWERS**
> **2** 3   **3** 5   **4** 5   **5** 7   **6** 0   **7** 7   **8** 5   **9** 2½   **10** 1   **11** 0   **12** 14   **13** 1791

B Point out that this discussion needn't focus on composers. If students know more about popular musicians, that's who they should talk about.

NOTE
Before starting 18.3 remind your students to look at the GRAMMAR REFERENCE section on The future on pages 173–174.

18.3 **The future** GRAMMAR REVIEW

A These are the most likely answers. Instead of the answers given here, *going to* will fit in the gaps where *will* is used.

SUGGESTED ANSWERS

1 will pass   **2** is going to   **3** are coming   **4** rises/will rise   **5** arrive   will have been
6 get   'll make   **7** are you going to tidy/clean it   **8** will pay back   can

Perhaps point out that, in conversation, the contracted form *'ll* is often used after names and question words:

> Thomas *'ll* be there.
> Alison *'ll* know the answer.
> Who *'ll* tell us?

but usually only written after pronouns:

> Thomas *will* be there.
> Alison *will* know the answer.
> Who *will* tell us?
> He *'ll* be there.
> She *'ll* know the answer.

An extra point on *will* v. *shall*:
Point out that, in these examples, either can be used, but *won't* and *will* are more common:

> I won't/shan't tell anyone our secret.
> We will/shall never know the answer.
> We won't/shan't forget your birthday next year.

B **ANSWERS**

2 *If the telephone rings, I'll answer it.*   ✓

3 *After the floor <u>will have</u> been cleaned, I'll polish the furniture.*   has

4 *By the time you get home we <u>will finish</u> dinner.*   will have finished

5 *We'll be waiting for you when your plane <u>is going to land</u> at the airport.*   lands

6 *Liz <u>has</u> a baby next month.*   is going to have/is having

7 *The new bypass <u>shall</u> be finished in the spring.*   will

8 *You won't be able to unlock the door if you <u>won't remember</u> your key.*   don't remember/ haven't remembered

C Make sure everyone realises that they have to transform the formal announcements into **informal** style. (This is not an exam-style exercise.)

ANSWERS (Many variations are possible.)

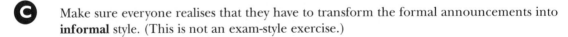

2 This weekend the weather *'s going to get worse and it's going to* snow.
3 Nobody seems to know *why there aren't going to be* any lessons next week.
4 They*'re holding an exhibition* of students' work in the main hall next week.
5 We *won't find out the* exam results until the end of September.
6 The performance *is going to start in* five minutes' time.

D This is an open-ended practice activity. Students with uneventful lives should invent some unusual plans.

At the end, perhaps ask everyone to write a paragraph (about 50 words) summarising their plans.

18.4 Art in New York   READING

A This exercise requires students to search for specific information, but the difficult part is spotting the places where two or more answers are correct.

> **ANSWERS**
> **A** 4   **B** 2, 4 and 6   **C** 5   **D** 5   **E** 1   **F** 6   **G** 3 and 6   **H** 2   **I** 5   **J** d   **K** b

B If your students really know nothing at all about local museums, you might prefer to suggest that they talk and write about local clubs, discos, or maybe cinemas.

18.5 Joining up words   SPEAKING

A 1 🔲 The examples (including the strange-sounding one) are recorded, and the marked up sentences in the Student's Book reflect the recorded readings. Alternative readings are possible. (The recording lasts 2 minutes.)

3 MODEL VERSION

These are the consonant-to-vowel catenations that the two readers made in the recording. Alternative readings are possible.

SOUND⌣OF MUZAK SOOTHES PATIENTS

IT'S heard⌣in supermarkets, cinemas, lifts and⌣on the telephone⌣as callers wait to be connected. But – muzak⌣in the doctor's consulting room?

A family doctor trainee has found that background music relaxed patients, allowing them to absorb more information during⌣a consultation.

Dr Jonathan Kabler, of St Helier, Jersey, played continuous music during consultations with⌣a hundred⌣and two patients. He chose Mozart's piano concertos seven⌣and twenty-one.

Sixteen patients reported not hearing the music. Of the rest, one felt the music⌣interfered with the consultation, eighty-three per cent found⌣it relaxing, and sixty-seven per cent said⌣it helped the consultation.

'The result⌣appears to be a more⌣enjoyable surgery with lower levels⌣of stress for patients,' Dr Kabler writes⌣in⌣a letter to the British Journal⌣of General Practice.

New Progress to First Certificate – This document may be photocopied.
© Cambridge University Press, 1996

Here are some points which more advanced or musical students might ask you about:

1 Some consonants can be catenated with other consonants. In these examples the /t/ at the end of the first word is lost as it joins with the first consonant of the second word:

  last⌣sound /lɑːsaʊnd/   first⌣time /fɜːstaɪm/   next⌣word /nekswɜːd/

2 Vowel-to-vowel catenation can happen in some cases by adding an extra /w/ or /r/ or /j/, as in these examples:

  to⌣absorb /tuːwəbzɔːb/   to⌣understand /tuːwʌndəstænd/

  law⌣and⌣order /lɔːrəndɔːdə/   over⌣and⌣over /əʊvərəndəʊvə/

  be a more enjoyable /biːjəmɔːrɪndʒɔɪəbl/

3 Catenation usually only happens within clauses. If there's a comma between two words, catenation doesn't usually happen. Similarly, if you pause between phrases catenation doesn't happen 'across the pause'.

B   This activity simulates the more realistic situation of quoting from a text, which is one of the most common situations where people do read aloud to each other in real life.

18.6 *Fall* and *hold*   VERBS AND IDIOMS

> **ANSWERS**
>
> 1 falls for (= is attracted to)   2 fell out with (= quarrelled)
> 3 fell over (= fell on the ground)   4 fallen through (= failed before completion)
> 5 fell in (= fell in the water)   6 held up (= robbed)   7 hold on (= hold firmly)
> 8 hold on (= wait)   9 held up (= delayed)   10 hold against (= allow a bad opinion to influence a decision) – there is a famous old play on words: 'If I say you have a beautiful body will you hold it against me?'

18.7 Works of art?   LISTENING AND SPEAKING

A   The illustrations show two of Christo and Jeanne-Claude's works: 'Surrounded Islands, Biscayne Bay, Greater Miami, Florida, 1980–83' and 'The Pont Neuf Wrapped, Paris, 1975–85'.

B   📼 There is plenty to discuss in the recording besides the information required to answer the questions.

> **ANSWERS (Some variations are possible.)**
>
> 1 1935   2 $23 million   3 1995   4 trivial and dull   5 14   6 40 km
> 7 temporary/ephemeral/not permanent   8 discussing it/arguing about it
> 9 next projects   10 take things for granted/be cynical

TRANSCRIPT *5 minutes*

PRESENTER: Christo Javatcheff is the Bulgarian artist who is famous for wrapping things – not small things like birthday presents but huge things like buildings and islands. Although they stay wrapped for only two weeks these creations are hugely expensive and take years to plan. Julian Morris has been looking at his work.

JULIAN: Actually, it's *their* work, um...Christo is actually two people: Mr Javatcheff and his French wife Jeanne-Claude have been working together since...ooh...since the 1960s. They...in fact they were born on the very same day in 1935.

Their most expensive project so far was called *The Umbrellas*, which was in 1991, and that cost $23 million. There were 1,340 yellow umbrellas, which were stuck in the ground in California, and then 1,760 blue ones in Japan. And the umbrellas were opened simultaneously by 810 workers.

PRESENTER: That's amazing. Now the wrapped buildings are what he's best known for, aren't they?

JULIAN: Yes. Perhaps most famous of all is the *Wrapped Reichstag*, um...when Christo wrapped the Reichstag in Berlin in 1995. The idea was first developed in 1972, but it wasn't until 1994 that they finally actually got permission. And that project cost $7 million.

And another famous landmark they wrapped was the Pont Neuf across the River Seine in Paris – this was covered in 40,000 square metres of a very beautiful gold fabric, which was tied down with 13,000 metres of rope. Even the lamps and statues along the bridge were wrapped. Millions of people came to see it in 1985 and to discuss it. And it was...it was a marvellous sight. For 14 days the bridge remained wrapped, and...um...during those days, well, everything around the bridge looked somehow trivial and...and dull. The bridge was the focus of everyone's attention – it was a wonderful sight.

PRESENTER: I've always admired his . . . their work with coastlines and landscapes.

JULIAN: Yes, yes, well, their wrapped landscapes are famous: *Surrounded Islands* (which was...um...actually Jeanne-Claude's idea in the first place) um...consisted of 14 islands in Florida surrounded by sheets of bright pink nylon. That was in 1983 – it...it was a wonderful sight and the islands seen from the air looked like...um...tropical flowers floating in...in a blue sea.

And the *Running Fence*, which was a 40-kilometre long fence in Northern California running down in wonderful curves, following the curves of the hills to the Pacific Ocean. And the fence was made of...of sheets of fabric, over five metres high and supported by thousands of steel poles.

PRESENTER: Now, what inspired him, do you think?

JULIAN: Well, in 1920 the surrealist artist Man Ray wrapped a sewing machine in a blanket, gave it a title, and created a new work of art and this may have been Christo's original inspiration. His first works, which now are worth a small fortune, were wrapped bottles and cans, but nobody wanted them when he created them in Paris in the sixties.

PRESENTER: Now, most people judge works of art by whether or not they stand the test of time and are still considered to be works of art by future generations. Christo's work isn't like that, is it?

JULIAN: No, the Christos say that their art is all about challenging the immortality of art – the whole point is that the creation is temporary. They borrow a space for a couple of weeks and create a...well, a gentle disturbance. Their works are ephemeral, not permanent. And yet for years before, while the project is being planned, people all over the world are discussing it, disagreeing about whether it's a beautiful idea or a terrible one. And then the public take an active part in the Christos' creations in a way that...that visitors to an art gallery looking at a painting or a...or a statue can't do.

And the other thing is that the Christos' works don't *belong* to anyone – they aren't paid for by businessmen or millionaires – they're for everyone and no one has to pay to go and see them. They raise the money themselves and...and pay for the works by selling their sketches and models and plans. And all the money they make is used to pay for their next projects.

PRESENTER: So, why do they do it?

JULIAN: To make people think, to make people discuss them, to make people see things in a new way, to make them aware of the...the shapes and textures of buildings or...or landscapes they might otherwise take for granted or simply not notice at all. To persuade people not to be cynical, I suppose and encourage them not to take things for granted. To make them wonder – to remind everyone of something we tend to forget nowadays: 'If you don't wonder at the wonderful, it stops being a wonder.'

PRESENTER: Julian Morris, thank you very much.

(The publishers have recently been informed by Christo and Jeanne-Claude that their most expensive project to date 'The Umbrellas, Japan–USA, 1984–91', cost $26 million and not $23 million as stated in the recording.)

C 🎧 Student A looks at Activity *18*, Student B at *21*. Each has a painting to describe and explain his or her reactions to: *Madame Charpentier and Her Children* by Pierre-Auguste Renoir (1878) in Activity *18* and *Eagle Head, Manchester, Massachusetts (High Tide)* by Winslow Homer (1870) in Activity *21*.

NOTE

In 18.8 B, students will be asked to look at the last two compositions they have written. Ask them to bring them to class for the lesson.

18.8 **We all make mistakes**   EXAM TECHNIQUES

The activities in this section all focus on the Writing paper – but they are also relevant to the Use of English paper where students have to write answers (and written answers in the Listening paper too).

A

SUGGESTED ANSWERS **(Several variations are possible.)**

I enjoy **visiting** galleries **because** I'm really interested **in** art. My favourite paintings are modern **ones, (delete 'painted')** by painters like Picasso and Matisse. Whenever I visit another city I **always** try to find time to **spend** an afternoon looking **at** paintings in an art museum. Some quite small cities have an art gallery, which may not contain any really famous or **valuable** works of art, **but** every museum has **its** surprises and there are often **fascinating** things to see – especially works by local artists who are unknown in **other** countries.

But I must confess that sometimes it's the people **(no comma)** who are more interesting **than** the paintings. As you wander round a museum it's wonderful to watch different people looking at the exhibits and reacting in different ways. It's a bit like sitting in a pavement café because you can watch other people without feeling **embarrassed** about **staring** at them.

So, I'd recommend a visit to a museum next time **you have nothing** else

B Follow the procedure in the Student's Book. Step 4 of this may be set for homework.

C A 'visit to a show' could be any form of public entertainment – it needn't be particularly 'artistic'.

Other people

19

19.1 It takes all sorts . . .   VOCABULARY

(The signs of the zodiac are: Capricorn, Aquarius, Pisces, Aries, Taurus, Gemini, Cancer, Leo, Virgo, Libra, Scorpio and Sagittarius.)

Ⓐ Some more derogatory adjectives are: *arrogant, fussy, lazy, touchy, miserable, intolerant, unsociable, unreliable* and *mean*.
And some more complimentary adjectives are: *sincere, reliable, practical, modest, cheerful, tolerant, loyal, sociable* and *generous*.

Ⓑ **ANSWERS**
1 cheerful   **2** bad-tempered   **3** sensitive   **4** likeable   **5** sympathetic (= *showing sympathy to people who have problems*)   **6** jealous   **7** naughty   **8** generous
9 self-confident   **10** spoilt

Ⓒ To start things off, take some pictures of people cut from magazines into class and brainstorm ideas for describing their appearance – and what kind of person they seem to be. Try to find a selection of ages, races and smartness – not all film stars and fashion models.

EXTRA ACTIVITY
Write these words on the board and ask the class to discuss the questions below:

ambition   creativity   good looks   honesty   independence   intelligence   loyalty   sense of humour.

- What qualities do you admire most in other people? Put the qualities into order of importance.
- What other important qualities are missing from this list? (*strength, tenderness, understanding, warmth,* etc.)

Ⓓ If you ask everyone to read the advertisement before the lesson, there will be more time for discussion in groups.

Another question for students who don't find this topic embarrassing is:
Is it possible to find a perfect partner for life by an arranged marriage (where your spouse is chosen by your parents)?

NOTE
Before starting 19.2 remind your students to look at the GRAMMAR REFERENCE section on Adverbs and word order on page 170.

19.2 Adverbs and word order   GRAMMAR REVIEW

The points covered here are quite tricky. There are no firm rules, and concepts like 'frequency adverbs' tend to be confusing. Hopefully, by now, students will have developed a 'feeling' for the position that adverbial phrases can be placed in a sentence. Some places feel 'just right' or 'comfortable', others feel 'not quite right' and others feel 'wrong'.

By doing these exercises, students who are mystified will probably come to realise that, in fact, they do already have this 'feeling'. Tell everyone to rely on this feeling for what sounds right.

Ⓐ **ANSWERS**
2 ✓
3 ✓
4 He ran into the room very suddenly.
5 I had toothache really badly yesterday.
6 She tripped over the cat and nearly fell over.
7 He had completely misunderstood what I told him to do.
8 ✓

B There are three possible ways of dealing with this exercise – the one you choose will depend on the level of your students and the time you have available.

Three possible procedures:

1 In class, divide students into pairs and get each pair to decide on just one position that each adjective can be placed in for each sentence. Go through this as a class later, accepting any positions that seem 'comfortable'. Point out how the emphasis may change, according to where the adverbs are placed.

2 As homework, get everyone to decide on just **one** position that each adjective can be placed in for each sentence. Go through this in class later, accepting any positions that seem 'comfortable'. Point out how the emphasis may change, according to where the adverbs are placed.

3 In class, write up the sentences on the board, perhaps with numbers as shown below. Ask everyone to call out which positions each adjective can be placed in in each sentence. Point out how the emphasis changes, according to where the adverbs are placed.

Don't point out any possible positions that the class have missed – only any ones they have got wrong. The whole topic is confusing enough as it is, without adding further details!

1

ANSWERS

1 position c for all adverbs
2 position b for all adverbs

2 In many cases other positions are possible – especially if commas are added (or, in speech, pauses). The suggested answers show the most 'comfortable' (i.e. most common) positions and don't take account of cases like these:

She was, as usual, able to finish her meal.
She, as usual, was able to finish her meal.
She was able to finish her meal – really!

SUGGESTED ANSWERS

In both sentences **all** the adverbs can be used in position **a** at the beginning of the sentence. The other 'comfortable' positions are as follows:

as usual 1d 2d   *certainly* 1c 2b   *definitely* 1c 2b   *maybe* (only a)   *normally* 1b or c or d 2b or d   *obviously* 1c 2b   *often* 1c 2b   *on Friday* 1d 2d   *one day* 1d 2d *perhaps* 1c or d 2b or d   *possibly* 1c 2b   *probably* 1c 2b   *really* 1b or c 2b   *still* 1c 2b *surely* 1c or d 2b or d   *usually* 1c or d 2b or d   *yesterday* 1d 2d

C

SUGGESTED ANSWERS

2 You *hardly ever meet such* charming people.
3 The task *took an unexpectedly long* time to finish.
4 130 km of spaghetti *is eaten annually by* the average Italian.
5 She *rarely loses her* temper.
6 By now you *(will) have probably* already done some FCE practice tests.
  By now you *(will) probably have* already done some FCE practice tests.
  By now you *probably (will) have* already done some FCE practice tests.
7 You *definitely must/must definitely do some thorough* revision before the exams.
8 You *will certainly/certainly will* do well in your exams.

19.3 Use of English: Tricky questions   EXAM TECHNIQUES

This section gathers together some grammar points that have not been dealt with in previous GRAMMAR REVIEW sections. These are some typical points that 'discriminate' between good candidates and excellent ones.

ANSWERS

1 You *had/'d better be* more careful.
2 I *wish I wasn't/weren't* so unhappy.
3 I *would/'d like you to* use a dictionary.
4 It *was Tony who* told me to do that.
5 I *suggest (that) you* arrive a few minutes early.
6 It *is time to do/you did* the work.

ANSWERS

Sentences 1, 3, 5, 6, 9, 10, 11, 12, 13 and 15 are correct. These contain errors:

2 *You had better to do some revision.*   do
4 *I suggest you to read the questions very carefully.*   (that) you read
7 *Would you rather being healthy or rich?*   be
8 *I would rather to wear a sweater than a jacket.*   wear
14 *He wishes he is more intelligent.*   was/were
16 *If only I have worked harder.*   had

ANSWERS

1 I'd *rather you didn't* interrupt me when I'm speaking.
2 I *suggest (that) you* phone and ask for information.
3 It's *better to be tactful than* frank.
4 I'd *prefer you to tell/give* me your decision now.
5 I *would/'d like you to* fill in this questionnaire.
6 It *is/'s time we found out/to find out* how much it's going to cost.
7 I *wish I didn't have* so much to do today.
8 If *only you had/'d told* me earlier.

19.4 First impressions   READING

Christopher Isherwood (1904–1986) is best-known for his novels set in Berlin in the thirties: *Mr Norris Changes Trains* (1935) and *Goodbye to Berlin* (1939). The musical *Cabaret* is loosely based on the latter. He was a close friend of the poet W. H. Auden and emigrated with him to America in 1939. Most of his books are indirectly or directly autobiographical, including:
Down There on a Visit (1962)
A Single Man (1964)
A Meeting by the River (1967)

ANSWERS

¶1 scared   startled   instinctively   pace
¶2 collided   reassure him
¶4 conveyed   agitation
¶6 delicately   disclosed
¶13 atmosphere   exaggerated   respective   doubtful   foresaw   utter

B **ANSWERS**

1 a   2 c   3 c   4 b   5 c   6 c   7 a   8 a   9 c   10 d

C A description of the stranger:

The stranger seems very nervous, as though he is scared of the narrator. He is wrapped up in his own thoughts and rather unwilling to talk. He is smartly dressed, has small, pale, well-manicured hands and a charming smile. His teeth are 'like broken rocks'.

D Student A looks at Activity **37**, Student B at **62**. It's important that they don't look at each other's picture by mistake (or deliberately) – if you look at the pictures yourself you'll see why!

19.5 People talking . . .   LISTENING

To simulate what will happen in the exam, play each situation **twice**.

ANSWERS

1 b   2 c   3 c   4 c   5 a   6 c   7 b   8 a

TRANSCRIPT *6 minutes*

NARRATOR: One. Listen to these two friends talking. What kind of document is the man filling in?

WOMAN: You're not really going to fill that in, are you?

MAN: Yes, why not?

WOMAN: Well, I think it's a waste of time.

MAN: It may be, but it doesn't cost anything, look. Anyway, as you're here you can help me. Right, now the first bits are name and address and so on, so I'll do those later. Right, now what about personality? How would you describe me? Serious? Reliable?

WOMAN: Serious and reliable? Hardly! Put down 'silly and unreliable'.

MAN: I can't do that, those aren't the alternatives. What about 'fashionable'?

WOMAN: In those shoes? Haha!

NARRATOR: Two. Listen to this woman talking about a man called Bill. Why can't she describe him?

WOMAN: Well everyone says he's a really nice guy, you know, intelligent, friendly. But even though I've been doing work for him since, what, November, I've only met him once. The problem is that the...the first time I met him I hardly paid him any attention because he'd just joined the company and my meeting was with Laura – w...we were introduced but I thought he was just one of Laura's very many assistants, you know? Um...then Laura left and...er...he took over. And then for months we only ever communicated by...by letter or fax – and...um...you know, the odd phone call. And on Tuesday I'm due to meet him again about six months after that first meeting and, do you know, I can't even remember what he looks like!

NARRATOR: Three. Listen to this man talking about a friend called Jane. What is Jane's greatest fault?

MAN: Oh, yeah, we go way back, I've known Jane for years. We've fallen out from time to time – that...that's not surprising because we're both quite strong characters. She has her views and I have mine – and we don't usually agree! But still we do get on surprisingly well. The problem is that she goes on trying to convince you, even though it's obvious that you're never going to agree with her. I mean, her...her frankness I don't mind, that's reasonable most of the time. Er...and there used to be times when she wouldn't talk to me for days when she thought I'd won one of our arguments.

NARRATOR: Four. Listen to this woman talking. When must the work be finished?

WOMAN: You told me it would be ready on Friday, but it's now Monday and you still haven't finished.

MAN: Well, I'm sorry but there have been other calls on my time, you know.

WOMAN: All right, but you did promise. Look the point is that the deadline is in two days' time and if everything isn't ready by then, then, well, I'm the one that's going to be in trouble.

MAN: I'm sorry. It'll be on your desk first thing tomorrow. I promise.

NARRATOR: Five. Listen to this man talking. Who is he speaking to?

MAN: It's very nice, very good. Who's that person on the right? It looks like me – oh it is me! I don't have such a long nose surely? Well, even if you think I do, I...I don't mind. I'm really quite flattered that you've included me. Um...listen, what I'd love to do is show it to Mrs Maycock – if you don't mind me borrowing it for a day or two. Would that be...um...would that be OK?

NARRATOR: Six. Listen to this man talking to a friend. Why is he late?

WOMAN: Here you are! You said you'd be here at half past.

MAN: I'm sorry I'm so late. I was running late all afternoon and then I...well, then I had this call just as I was leaving. It was Gary and he went on and on and I couldn't get him to stop. Anyway, by the time he did stop it was...well, it was already half past and it takes at least ten minutes to get here. I'm sorry, I would have been here earlier if it hadn't been for Gary.

NARRATOR: Seven. You're staying at a friend's flat. What does she want you to do?

WOMAN: Oh, hello, you're up already. Sleep well? I'm just going out to the supermarket. I've left the breakfast things on the table, there's coffee in the flask and the milk's in the fridge. I should be back in an hour or so. See you later . . . Oh, um...I nearly forgot. Tony may phone – he wanted me to give him Chris's phone number, which is on a yellow Post-it™ Note next to the phone. So if he calls, can you let him have it? See you!

NARRATOR: Eight. You're sitting in a restaurant when you overhear this conversation. How many pizzas are ordered?

WAITRESS: Are you ready to order?

ALAN: Er...yes, I'd like a pizza with ham and mushrooms.

BRENDA: Um...I...I'll have one with tuna and anchovies, please.

CHARLIE: Just a plain one for me, please.

DEBBIE: Um...I don't feel like pizza. What kind of fresh pasta do you have today?

WAITRESS: Er...today's special is home-made spaghetti with tomato and mushroom sauce.

DEBBIE: Oh that sounds nice. I'll have that please.

ALAN: Um...I'm going to change my mind . . . C...can I have the same as her instead please?

CHARLIE: Yes, me too. Sorry.

WAITRESS: That's all right. So that's...um . . .

 19.6 **Synonyms**   WORD STUDY

There is, of course, no such thing as an exact synonym. Even words which have very similar meanings usually have different connotations or are used in different collocations or different contexts.

Ⓐ 2

SUGGESTED ANSWERS	
nice	pleasant attractive satisfying friendly likeable agreeable
good	splendid excellent terrific perfect fine great marvellous wonderful
bad	terrible dreadful awful
thing	object topic article item subject
like	love appreciate enjoy value
dislike	hate loathe detest dread despise

3

large	big enormous huge immense great
small	little tiny unimportant
important	serious vital essential
intelligent	clever bright brainy smart
interesting	exciting entertaining fascinating
strange	unusual unfamiliar odd
unpleasant	nasty disgusting annoying terrible frightening
beautiful	attractive good-looking pretty

B This part deals with hyponyms (words like *vehicle*, which includes the meanings *bus*, *car*, *tram*, etc. or *flower*, which includes the meanings *rose*, *dandelion*, *chrysanthemum*, etc.).

SUGGESTED ANSWERS

3	plants	14	currencies
4	animals/mammals	15	sports equipment
5	meat	16	sports/games
6	vehicles	17	hobbies
7	buildings/dwellings	18	professions
8	birds	19	pets
9	metals	20	cereals
10	meals	21	flowers
11	seasons	22	insects
12	clothes/garments	23	publications
13	food	24	(musical) instruments

19.7 *Leave, let, pull* and *run*   VERBS AND IDIOMS

A ANSWERS

1 let   2 pulling   3 pull   4 leave   5 leave   6 let   7 leave/run   8 ran/runs
9 left   10 run   11 let   12 runs/ran

B ANSWERS

1 leave out (= omit)   2 left over (= remaining)   3 left behind (= forget)
4 let down (= disappointed)   5 let in (= admit)   6 let off (= allow to explode)
7 pulls up/is pulling up (= stops)   8 pulled out (= removed)
9 pulled down (= demolished)   10 running over (= killing or injuring)
ran into (= collided with)   11 run out of (= have no more)   12 run after (= chase)
13 ran into (= met by chance)   14 run off with (= left secretly or unexpectedly)

19.8 Describing people   WRITING

A SUGGESTED ANSWERS

1 He is a slightly overweight man in his mid-30s. He is terribly selfish and even dishonest but his worst feature is that he loses his temper whenever people disagree with him.

2 She is a very thin lady in her late 50s. She does tend to be rather absent-minded but she has a delightful sense of humour and is always ready to help other people with their problems.

3 He is 18 years old and very athletic. He really loves sport and his favourite game is football. In his spare time he enjoys going out with his friends and particularly going to the cinema.

4 She is 16 years old and a very studious young woman who enjoys reading. She has four brothers and two sisters. When she leaves school, she hopes to go to university, where she wants to study engineering.

There is a wide choice of topics here. You may prefer to discuss with the class the pros and cons of choosing each one before they do the task.

THREE MODEL COMPOSITIONS

1 The two people I admire most are my aunt and uncle. They are my mother's sister and her husband and they have a small farm in the country about 200 km from where I live.

   My aunt is quite tall, she has wavy black hair and wears glasses. She has a round, friendly face and smiles quietly to herself while she's working – even when she's cooking or washing up! She has two children who are two and four years old. Amazingly, she is able to look after them and do all her work in the home and on the farm and she never, never loses patience or gets cross. That's what I admire in her.

   Her husband is quite a short man with attractive brown eyes who always behaves charmingly even when people are not pleasant to him. He's busy every day of the week from morning till evening. Whenever I go to visit them he encourages me to help with the work, and with him even routine jobs seem fun. That's what I admire about him – he makes work seem a pleasure.

2 I'll never forget the first time I met Chris. He was sitting on a bench in the park, looking very depressed and cold. He had no coat on and it had started to rain quite heavily.

   Normally, I wouldn't have dreamt of stopping to talk to a complete stranger who looked like that – not that he looked like a tramp or anything: his shoes were well polished and his clothes were quite smart. But on an impulse I stopped walking and said to him, 'Are you OK?' in a sympathetic voice.

   He said he was but I sat down beside him and he started telling me how his wife had just locked him out of the house after a row and so he was sitting in the rain waiting for her to calm down and let him in again. I suggested that we went somewhere warm and dry, so we found a nearby café and continued our conversation.

   And that was how I met Chris – the man who was later to become my worst enemy.

3 Dear Maria,

   As this is my first letter to you, let me begin by introducing myself: my name is Susan Underwood and I live with my parents in Brompton, which is a little town about 40 km north of London.

   I have curly fair hair, blue eyes and a round freckled face. I'm quite tall and a bit overweight at the moment! I enjoy listening to classical music and going to the cinema. Of course, I also watch television and I particularly enjoy watching old movies.

   I'm still at college and I'm studying for a diploma in hotel management at Brompton College. If I pass my final exams next summer, I hope to get a job somewhere abroad for a year to get experience of foreign hotels, and also learn a foreign language. I'm really looking forward to starting work, even though the course I'm doing is excellent.

   That's about all I can think of to tell you about myself. Do write back and tell me all about yourself. I'll write again soon.

   Yours truly,

20 Memories

In this section there are exam-style test papers and exam tips covering each of the five papers. 20.2 and 20.3 contain complete exam-style papers which can be done in exam conditions. For the other papers only part of each paper is presented. For more information about each paper consult *Specifications and Sample Papers for the Revised FCE Examination* or the Teacher's Book of *Cambridge Practice Tests for First Certificate*.

Although the exercises in this unit can be used for a mock exam, it would be more realistic to use test papers from *Cambridge Practice Tests for First Certificate* for this, especially as regards the length and timing of each paper. The exercises in this unit are best used as revision rather than tests.

20.1 Paper 1: Reading   EXAM TECHNIQUES

A For the answers to these questions, see 16.8 in the Student's Book.

B This exercise is in the style of Part 3 of the Reading paper.

> **ANSWERS**
> 1 E   2 D   3 G   4 B   5 F   6 A   (Sentence C is not used.)

C As suggested in the Student's Book, do a complete practice test. To save time in class, this would be best done as homework.

20.2 Paper 2: Writing   EXAM TECHNIQUES

A **ANSWERS**

Careless mistakes and slips of the pen:

1 *The castle <u>contain</u> many <u>treasure</u> and <u>painting</u>.*	contains treasures paintings
2 *Spelling mistakes are not serious but they do <u>lost</u> you marks.*	lose
3 *My brother has brown eyes and so <u>do</u> my sister.*	does
4 *Could you tell me what time <u>does</u> the museum opens?*	~~does~~
5 *Which one of you <u>payed</u> for the tickets?*	paid

Mistakes that may be harder to notice:

6 *After visiting the museum he <u>had not</u> very much time left.*	did not have
7 *His hair is very long, it's time for him to have <u>cut it</u>.*	it cut
8 *I <u>am</u> waiting for you <u>since</u> four hours.*	have been for
9 *They <u>never visited</u> Rome before their first visit in 1987.*	had never visited
10 *She <u>never wrote</u> a letter by hand since she <u>has</u> bought a computer.*	has never written ~~has~~
11 *I <u>am</u> learning English <u>during</u> five years.*	have been for
12 *A <u>suspicious</u> is <u>questioning</u> by the police.*	suspect/suspicious person being questioned
13 *Before they <u>had gone</u> out they <u>had been watched</u> the news on TV.*	went had been watching/watched

B For the answers to these questions, see 17.8 in the Student's Book.

C The two parts are in the style of the exam.

MODEL COMPOSITION FOR PART 1

Dear Bob,

Thanks for your letter. Given a choice between York and Cambridge, I think I'd recommend Cambridge. The main reason is that the two-hour journey to York would take four hours out of your day. I know this will disappoint Richard, but never mind.

In Cambridge Helen would enjoy looking at the paintings in the Fitzwilliam Museum and Kettle's Yard. But because this wouldn't appeal to you, Bob, I think Helen and Mary should concentrate on the museums before lunch. Meanwhile, Richard and you could go for a walk beside the river and explore the old colleges. You could all meet for lunch, perhaps in a pub by the river – the money you'd save by not going to York could be spent on a really good lunch.

Then after lunch why don't you hire a boat on the river before going together to admire King's College Chapel. By that time you'll be ready to catch the train to London, and you'll be back there in an hour or so.

Hope you enjoy your day! Send me a postcard!

Best wishes,

New Progress to First Certificate – This document may be photocopied.
© Cambridge University Press, 1996.

D Follow the marking scale reproduced in 13.7 (page 111) when marking your students' work. See the UCLES *Specifications and Sample Papers for the Revised FCE Examination* or the Teacher's Book of *Cambridge Practice Tests for First Certificate* for more details on marking.

20.3 Paper 3: Use of English   EXAM TECHNIQUES

This is a complete exam-style test. However, all the texts concern the topic of this unit and all come from the same source. In the exam the texts will all concern **different** topics. If there are any vocabulary problems, encourage everyone to try to answer the questions without looking up any words – as they'll have to in the exam.

PART 1 ANSWERS

1 A   2 D   3 C   4 B   5 A   6 B   7 A   8 C   9 B   10 B   11 D
12 B   13 B   14 A   15 B

PART 2 SUGGESTED ANSWERS

16 experience   17 than   18 seats   19 hour   20 sell/rent   21 from
22 many/most/some   23 instance/example   24 century   25 sport/game
26 living/livelihood   27 paid   28 children/sons/daughters   29 rather
30 between

PART 3 ANSWERS

31 It's *ages since I last saw/met* my old school friend.
32 The questions *were (too) hard to* answer.
33 I *had never visited/been to* North America before.
34 The *Pyramids were built by* the ancient Egyptians.
35 She *will/'ll soon have to* give up her job.
36 We *found that the shop* was closed due to illness.
37 The hill *was easy to climb* despite the heat.
38 You *shouldn't have put so* much salt in the soup.
39 It *is/'s too salty to* eat.
40 We *ran out of time so* we didn't finish the exercise.

PART 4 ANSWERS

| 41 ✓ | 42 so | 43 as | 44 if | 45 it | 46 ✓ | 47 an | 48 end | 49 ✓ | 50 with |
| 51 ✓ | 52 so | 53 ✓ | 54 ✓ | 55 about | | | | | |

PART 5 ANSWERS

56 industrial   **57** production   **58** employees   **59** purchasers   **60** marketing
61 manufacturers   **62** advertisements   **63** descriptions   **64** satisfaction
65 enjoyment

Finish by making sure everyone knows what they'll have to do in each part of the Use of English paper. For more information, see the Student's Book 9.7, 11.7 and 12.4.

20.4 Paper 4: Listening   EXAM TECHNIQUES

A For the answers to these questions, see 15.3 in the Student's Book.

B  Maybe explain what a teddy is before playing the recording.

ANSWERS (Questions 1–10)

1 about three or four   **2** playground/park   **3** alone   **4** (her) teddy
5 bite/get her teddy   **6** ran away/off   **7** empty/deserted   **8** fetch help/their father
9 their father   **10** liked/trusted dogs

TRANSCRIPT *2 minutes*

LIZ: I remember when I was very little, about three or four, my brother used to take me to the local playground. He was a bit older than me. And he used to look after me while I went on the swings and, you know, the slide and things. Well, one afternoon I went out with him after tea and I was sitting on one of the swings with my teddy bear and I was swinging away and talking to Teddy, you see, when it gradually dawned on me that I was all alone and that my brother had left me by myself and there was no one else in the playground at all. And it was starting to get dark. Then – ooh, I can remember it, it sends shivers down my spine even now – I saw this big fierce dog sniffing around the swings a…and as I was going backwards and forwards it started to bark at me. Well, first I sort of, you know, tried to be terribly brave and I wanted to make it go away so I shouted at it and it took no notice and started, you know, jumping up at me and trying to bite, well not me, but I think it was my teddy bear. Well, I started to cry and scream and got in a terrible state sort of trying to climb up the swing and…and no one came and it was getting darker and darker. And…er…oh, I was in such a state. Well, eventually I saw my Dad running towards me waving a big stick and shouting at the dog and he chased the dog away and took me in his arms and I…I clung onto him and he held…held me and I cried and cried and cried until eventually I suppose I stopped. Well, I never saw the dog again but I always made sure that, you know, after that there were other people in the playground when I went. And well, of course, later I realised that my brother hadn't abandoned me to be eaten by this dog. I suppose he must have run back home to fetch my father and…and er…I suppose he must have been very frightened too. But he obviously felt very responsible for me and he ran home to get help. But since then…whew…I've always been so careful with dogs and I've never trusted them.

Ask the members of the class to tell each other about an experience from their childhood that they'll never forget.

ANSWERS (Questions 11–15)

11 D **12** C **13** E **14** F **15** A (Sentence B is not used.)

TRANSCRIPT *5 minutes*

SPEAKER 1: I'll...um...I'll never forget the time, it was when my kid was quite young, he must have been about two I think...um...and I was working in the sitting room and he was going up the stairs and then suddenly there was this enormous crash, the biggest...er...loudest bang you've ever heard and things falling down and then one single scream and I rushed out of the sitting room and...to see Joe, my child, lying face down on the floor. And I rushed over to him and...um...shake...shook him and said 'Are you all right? Are you OK?' and couldn't rouse him, he was...he had his eyes closed, absolutely nothing. So I rushed to the phone, picked up the phone, dialled 999 and said 'You've got to come round here immediately. You've got to come round, this is happening', manic, you know, mad panic and everything. And I was just at a pause in what I was saying to the person on the other end of the phone and there was this little giggle and laugh and he'd been having me on all the time.

SPEAKER 2: Well, I'll never forget the time that I flew over the Grand Canyon. I was staying in Las Vegas and decided to go over in...in a plane because they do these sort of little flights in these tiny little planes, about 20 people can go at a time, you get a little commentary in your ears with these headphones on and you've got these great big windows that come up. And I remember...er...thinking 'Oh, this is nice, this is nice' as we approached it, 'Oh this is really rather amazing'. And then we approached it again, and approached it from all sorts of different angles, and kept flying over it. It was the most awe-inspiring experience, and I remember bursting into tears, quite unexpectedly at the...um..astou...just incredible vastness and beauty of the whole thing.

SPEAKER 3: . . . I'd been at work all day and I got off the train, went to the road where I'd actually parked my car and in its place was another red car, and I walked around this car, which was a Mini and was much smaller than my car and I don't know what I expected it to do, whether I expected it to change back into my car, but I was completely flabberghasted because there was no glass on the floor, there was no sign that anybody had forced entry into my car, and then of course it dawned on me that my car had gone, and was nowhere to be seen, so I had to then go and phone the police and...um...it...it was the most frustrating experience because I was actually about to move house.

SPEAKER 4: . . . it was last year, we'd been away on holiday and...er...we'd just arrived back from the airport. And...um...I went to open the front door and couldn't get in, it was locked and I...I kept thinking 'This is very strange' but my mind wouldn't really accept the fact that I couldn't open the door and so I kept thinking 'Well, perhaps somebody's in there who we'd sort of let stay in there while we were away and they've locked the door and they're asleep and they can't hear us' even though I knew that there wasn't anybody and that we hadn't let anybody sleep in the house. Anyway so we went round the back...um...and sure enough there was a window open, so I had to be brave and climb through the window. I sort of went around the house stomping loudly and shouting to see if anybody was there but there wasn't, and of course all the hi-fi and things and televisions and whatever had been stolen.

SPEAKER 5: I'll never forget the time I was inside my house and I heard bang-bang-bang from outside. And I thought. 'My gosh, that's either somebody making a hell of a noise or that's a gunshot'. So I opened my front door and looked outside and saw two men rush past me in rather a hurry...ha...so I rushed to phone the police, I didn't really know what had happened but I assumed that they had shot somebody. Phoned the police, came back outside, went along the corridor – we live along a corridor of flats – um...saw some people making a lot of commotion, saying 'He's been shot, he's been shot'. Anyway, what had happened was somebody had shot somebody else through the shoulder, narrowly missing the child that was standing behind him. And...um...er...it turned out that had I opened my front door just a second earlier, I would have been shot too because there were three shots and two of them went into that house and one went down the corridor right next to our front door and there's still a mark on the wall to this day the police have marked up and that would have been me, gone.

NARRATOR: That's the end of 20.4 and now you've come to the end of the listening exercises in New Progress to First Certificate. We hope you've enjoyed them and found them useful. Good luck with your exam!

C Parts 1 and 4 have not been practised. (Make sure that you do a complete practice test with the class before the actual exam.)

20.5 Paper 5: Speaking EXAM TECHNIQUES

A For the answers to these questions, see 14.2 in the Student's Book.

B Perhaps appoint a third student to be an 'Observer' looking at the guidelines at the top of Activity *25*. Student A looks at Activity *2* while Student B looks at *30*. Allow time for feedback from the 'Observer' (if there is one) before starting each step.

If your students need more practice in doing the Speaking paper, organise a series of mock exams with the help of another teacher.

20.6 Good luck!

Now's the time to make sure everyone in the class knows what their weaknesses are. Recommend (or do in class) relevant exercises from *Cambridge Practice Tests for First Certificate*. Students should concentrate on improving the areas they are weakest in, and not spend time on exercises that practise things they know well.

The lesson before the exam, give everyone a last-minute pep talk and remind them **not** to . . .
• spend too long on any one question
• get flustered if time seems to be short

And remind them to . . .
• make notes
• write legibly
• leave room to put in further ideas or make corrections later

CAMBRIDGE
EXAMINATIONS, CERTIFICATES AND DIPLOMAS
ENGLISH AS A FOREIGN LANGUAGE

University of Cambridge
Local Examinations Syndicate
International   Examinations

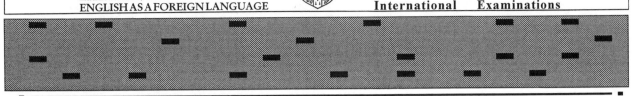

For Supervisor's use only

Shade here if the candidate is
ABSENT or has WITHDRAWN

→   —   ←

Examination Details	9999/01 99/D99
Examination Title	First Certificate in English
Centre/Candidate No.	AA999/9999
Candidate Name	A.N. EXAMPLE

• Sign here if the details above are correct

X

• Tell the Supervisor now if the details above
  are not correct

Candidate Answer Sheet: FCE Paper 1 Reading

Use a pencil

Mark ONE letter for each
question.

For example, if you think **B** is
the right answer to the
question, mark your answer
sheet like this:

0	A B C D

Change your answer like
this:

0	A C D

	A B C D E F G H I
1	A B C D F G H I
2	A B C F G H I
3	A B C D G H I
4	A B C D E F G H I
5	A B C D E F G H I

	A B C D E F G H I
6	A B C D E F G H I
7	A B C D E F G H I
8	A B C D E F G H I
9	A B C D E F I
10	A B C D E F G H I
11	A B C E G H I
12	E F G H I
13	A B E F G H I
14	A B C D E F G H I
15	A B C D E F G H I
16	A B C D E F G H I
17	A B C D E F G H I
18	A B C D E F G H I
19	A B C D E F G H I
20	A B C D E F G H I

	A B C D E F G H I
21	A B C D E F G H I
22	B C E F G H I
23	A C D E F G H I
24	A B C D E F G H I
25	A B C D E F G H I
26	A B C D E F G H I
27	A B C D E F G H I
28	A B C D E F G H I
29	A B C D E F G H I
30	A B C D E F G H I
31	A B C D E F G H I
32	A B C D E F G H I
33	A B C D E F G H I
34	A B C D E F G H I
35	A B C D E F G H I

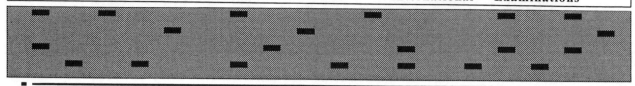

CAMBRIDGE
EXAMINATIONS, CERTIFICATES AND DIPLOMAS
ENGLISH AS A FOREIGN LANGUAGE

University of Cambridge
Local Examinations Syndicate
International Examinations

Examination Details 9999/03   99/D99

Examination Title First Certificate in English

Centre/Candidate No. AA999/9999

Candidate Name A.N. EXAMPLE

• Sign here if the details above are correct

X

- -

• Tell the Supervisor now if the details above
  are not correct

Candidate Answer Sheet: FCE Paper 3 Use of English

Use a pencil

For **Part 1**: Mark ONE letter for each question.

For example, if you think **C** is the
right answer to the question,
mark your answer sheet like this:

| 0 | A B C D |

For **Parts 2, 3, 4** and complete your
answers in the spaces for the
numbers like this:

| 0 | example |

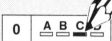

Part 1				
1	A	B	C	D
2	A	B	C	D
3	A	B	C	D
4	A	B	C	D
5	A	B	C	D
6	A	B	C	D
7	A	B	C	D
8	A	B	C	D
9	A	B	C	D
10	A	B	C	
11	A	B		
12	A	B	C	D
13	A	B	C	D
14	A	B	C	D
15	A	B	C	D

Part 2	Do not write here
16	16
17	17
18	18
19	19
20	20
21	21
22	22
23	23
24	24
25	25
26	26
27	27
28	28
29	29
30	30

Turn over for Parts 3 - 5 ➡

Part 3		Do not write here		
31		31 0	1	2
32		32 0	1	2
33		33 0	1	2
34		34 0	1	2
35		35 0	1	2
36		0	1	2
37		37	1	2
38		38 0	1	2
39		39 0	1	2
40		40 0	1	2

Part 4		Do not write here	
41			
42		42	
43		43	
44			
45		45	
46		46	
47		47	
48		48	
49		49	
50		50	
51		51	
52		52	
53		53	
54		54	
55		55	

Part		Do not write here	
56		56	
57		57	
58		58	
59		59	
60		60	
61		61	
62		62	
63		63	
64		64	
65		65	

CAMBRIDGE
EXAMINATIONS, CERTIFICATES AND DIPLOMAS
ENGLISH AS A FOREIGN LANGUAGE

University of Cambridge
Local Examinations Syndicate
International Examinations

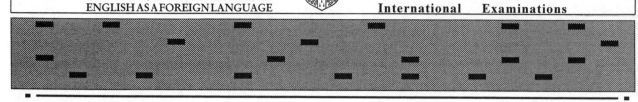

For Supervisor's use only

Shade here if the candidate is
ABSENT or has WITHDRAWN

➡ ▬ ⬅

Examination Details	9999/04	99/D99
Examination Title	First Certificate in English	
Centre/Candidate No.	AA999/9999	
Candidate Name	A.N. EXAMPLE	

• Sign here if the details above are correct

☒

• Tell the Supervisor now if the details above
  are not correct

Candidate Answer Sheet: FCE Paper 4 Listening

Mark test version below

A	B	C	D	E
▭	▭	▭	▭	▭

Use a pencil

For **Parts 1** and **3**:
Mark ONE letter for
each question.

For example, if you
think **B** is the right
answer to the
question, mark your
answer sheet like this:

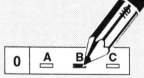

0	A	B	C
	▭	▬	▭

For **Parts** ~~2~~ nd ~~4~~
Write your ~~answers~~ ~~i~~
the spaces next to t~~he~~
numbers like th~~is:~~

0	*example*

Part 1

1	A ▭	B ▭	C ▭
2	A ▭	B ▭	C ▭
3	A ▭	B ▭	C ▭
4	A ▭	B ▭	C ▭
5	A ▭	B ▭	C ▭
6	A ▭	B ▭	C ▭
7	A ▭	B ▭	C
8	A ▭	B ▭	C

Part 2

		Do not write here
9		▭ 9 ▭
10		▭ 10 ▭
11		▭ 11 ▭
12		▭ 12 ▭
		▭ 13 ▭
14		▭ 14 ▭
15		▭ 15 ▭
		▭ 16 ▭
17		▭ 17 ▭
18		▭ 18 ▭

Part 3

	A	B	C	D	E	F
	▭	▭	▭	▭	▭	▭
20	A ▭	B ▭	C ▭	D ▭	E ▭	F ▭
21	A ▭	B ▭	C ▭	D ▭	E ▭	F ▭
22	A ▭	B ▭	C ▭	D ▭	E ▭	F ▭
23	A ▭	B ▭	C ▭	D ▭	E ▭	F ▭

Part 4

		Do not write here
24		▭ 24 ▭
25		▭ 25 ▭
26		▭ 26 ▭
27		▭ 27 ▭
28		▭ 28 ▭
29		▭ 29 ▭
30		▭ 30 ▭